T0293178

LEADING
THROUGH

Kim B. Clark

Jonathan R. Clark

Erin E. Clark

LEADING

THROUGH

Activating the Soul,
Heart, and Mind
of Leadership

HARVARD BUSINESS REVIEW PRESS
BOSTON, MASSACHUSETTS

Printed and bound in Great Britain by TJ Books Limited, Padstow, Cornwall

10 9 8 7 6 5 4 3

The web addresses referenced in this book were live and correct at the time of the book's publication but may be subject to change.

Library of Congress Cataloging-in-Publication Data

Names: Clark, Kim B., author. | Clark, Jonathan R., author. | Clark, Erin E., author.
Title: Leading through : activating the soul, heart, and mind of leadership /
    Kim B. Clark, Jonathan R. Clark, and Erin E. Clark.
Description: Boston, Massachusetts : Harvard Business Review Press, [2024] |
    Includes index.
Identifiers: LCCN 2024005388 (print) | LCCN 2024005389 (ebook) |
    ISBN 9781647827618 (hardcover) | ISBN 9781647827625 (epub)
Subjects: LCSH: Leadership—Social aspects. | Organizational change.
Classification: LCC HD57.7 .C5374 2024 (print) | LCC HD57.7 (ebook) |
    DDC 658.4/092—dc23/eng/20240505
LC record available at https://lccn.loc.gov/2024005388
LC ebook record available at https://lccn.loc.gov/2024005389

ISBN: 978-1-64782-761-8
eISBN: 978-1-64782-762-5

The paper used in this publication meets the requirements of the American National Standard for Permanence of Paper for Publications and Documents in Libraries and Archives Z39.48-1992.

Contents

PART FOUR

Leading Through Change
Making the New Paradigm a Reality

Preface

Are we not all leaders? Should we not all do the work of leadership?

Your answers to these questions depend on what—or who—you think a leader is and what you think a leader does. You'll find in reading this book that our response is an emphatic, "yes"—we are all leaders, and the world desperately needs us to do the work of leadership. We are not talking about a heroic CEO, or even a capable team of executives, but instead leadership that permeates entire organizations and serves as the currency of effective work and innovation.

We find ourselves in a profound moment of opportunity, one unlike any other in human history. The unprecedented power of technological advances has created impressive value, and yet it is clear that our organizations often fall short of harnessing that power to help people and communities thrive. The culprit is old ways of thinking, working, and leading—a paradigm that focuses on using power over people to control them, restricting personal agency, and enforcing compliance in a coercive, bureaucratic hierarchy—that are still with us, a deeply embedded and powerful legacy.

The leadership we need requires a new way of thinking, behaving, and organizing: a living paradigm that is flexible and adaptable. This book is our proposal for that new paradigm. One wherein we are all leaders—or can be. One that consciously seeks to do good and to make things better for the long term; that cares for people, helping them to thrive; and that mobilizes people to solve tough problems. This is the soul, heart, and mind of leadership. The new paradigm is designed to activate them throughout the organization.

This is what we call Leading Through.

We live in a remarkable time. Truly exceptional value, with thriving people and communities, is possible when we learn how to combine the productive power of technology and organization with the power of our humanity and a deep sense of purpose. We believe that realizing that potential more fully requires rethinking our organizations in a way that is truly different from what we've known. We've seen glimpses of this promise in recent years. And yet we've also seen what happens when legacy patterns and tendencies prevail, allowing power over people and short-term cost reduction to predominate over long-term viability and vitality through people.

During the early months of Covid-19 we saw remarkable demonstrations of the power of the human spirit, in concert with technology and purpose, to drive unprecedented innovation and even growth. This in spite of a crisis impacting every facet of our lives; one in which no one was unaffected—one in which we all lost something. It was the best of our humanity on display. In contrast, we have also seen the chasms that divide us widen and deepen—and not just on a global or geopolitical scale. Within organizations the chasm of broad discontent among the workforce has quickly overtaken that spirit of unity and innovation.

Many of us experienced an increase in our personal agency to manage our work lives to meet the complexity of our unique circumstances. Yet, for many that was short lived with the return of rigid controls and monitored expectations. Compassion and genuine care may continue to be the talk-track of many organizations, but in action and felt experience, compliance and control have returned to take away the newfound agency we had come to know.

The Great Resignation was our warning shot, and the widely reported, unprecedented levels of dissatisfaction and distrust in organizations must be our burning platform. We cannot afford to succumb to the familiar pressure to double-down on power and control, giving priority to quickly reducing costs at the expense of people, purpose, and genuine gains in productivity. The real costs are too great. We see them in the growing prevalence of burnout and the incidence of workplace bullying and harassment. We see it in the surge of adults reporting significant symptoms of anxiety or depression. We see it in the general discontent as reported through annual engagement surveys of workers across organizations and industries. And, more than likely, we all feel it—to some extent—ourselves. We are technologically more advanced than we have ever been. And we are miserable. But the glimmer of promise we saw in the earliest days of the Covid-19 crisis should give us hope. When we loosen our grip on consolidated power and control and expand our myopic focus on short-term costs (to prioritize people, purpose, and real productivity) something great—even miraculous—can happen.

This is the lesson of the last few years—and it isn't a new one. But still—almost universally—we revert to power and control in the name of the need of the times for quick fixes. In doing so, we continue to embrace a legacy paradigm that is driven by the pursuit and maintenance of power over people. And the story we tell ourselves—and the one we reward—is that this is good leadership. But the truth is that this paradigm—what we call the *Power Over* paradigm—is the very reason executives find themselves frustrated that they aren't getting as much out of their people and organizations as they believe they could be.

This is the paradox of the Power Over paradigm: we have a tendency to default to its ways of thinking, behaving, and organizing, even as it serves to limit our capacity to make things better. We need a new paradigm of leadership—the Leading Through paradigm—that helps to break through this tendency. The aim of *Leading Through* is to activate the power of our humanity—soul, heart, and mind—to create thriving organizations: power to create amazing value for organizations; power to improve the lives of people; and power to heal the divides and bridge the chasms that exist between us. It is this power that we hope to activate, power that is realized *through* others. What we hope to diminish—or leave behind—is the power we too often equate with leadership but that in our view works against it: power *over* others.

This shift in the concept of power—from power *over* to power *through*—is at the core of the Leading Through paradigm. It represents a comprehensive change in thinking, behaving, and organizing that truly recasts the concept and promise of leadership, broadly. Thus, we offer a definition of leadership in the new paradigm, including what a leader is—who they are, what they do, how they think. Importantly, we also address the far-reaching implications of our definition for what is needed from organizations and executives to activate this kind of leadership. We aim to go beyond simply sharing some new ideas and ways of thinking, to present a paradigm that is both meaningful (it resonates, makes sense and really does facilitate the reframing of our collective thinking) and actionable (it goes beyond the conceptual to also illuminate clear and specific actions to be taken). To do this, we've organized the book in four parts, as follows:

Part one ("A New Paradigm of Leadership: From Power Over to Leading Through") serves as an introduction to the new paradigm as an antidote to the legacy paradigm. The legacy paradigm—Power Over—falls short on what most of us want from our organizations: (1) it breeds organizational "darkness" (blurring vision, sapping meaning, and nurturing moral failure), (2) it wastes human talent and organizational potential, and (3) it stifles creativity, ingenuity, and innovation. In contrast, the new paradigm—Leading Through—overcomes and reverses these shortcomings by sharpening our understanding and practice of leadership and by enabling leadership to permeate everyone and everything in the organization. We articulate how it does so through careful attention to both the personal, human dimensions of the work of leadership and to the organizational dimensions that enable or impede that work.

In part two ("Leading Through People: The Soul, Heart, and Mind of Leadership") we take a deeper dive into the personal dimensions of leadership, building on three metaphors—soul, heart, and mind—to illustrate what leadership looks like when it permeates an organization more deeply: (1) it increases organizational "light" (it provides clarity of vision and deeper meaning and supports moral discipline) (the soul of leadership), (2) it harnesses the power within people, engaging them and helping them to thrive (the heart of leadership), and (3) it drives action, learning, and change, boosting creativity, ingenuity, and innovation (the mind of leadership). In doing so, we outline a set of frameworks for putting each of these personal dimensions of leadership into action.

In part three ("Leading Through the Organization: Activating Leadership through the Power of Modularity") we argue that realizing the full power of Leading Through requires a rethinking and redesigning of the organization. We outline how the organization must be built (or rebuilt) to enable the soul, heart, and mind of leadership to permeate everything the organization does. In doing so, we complete our portrait of the new paradigm with four chapters on the key conditions that help to make that happen. We draw heavily on Kim's research on modularity—complemented by Jonathan's research on effective management systems and Erin's experience advising organizations to implement new strategies—to present a series of flexible and adaptable frameworks and principles aimed at helping organizations operationalize the new paradigm and bring Leading Through to life.

Part four ("Leading Through Change: Making the New Paradigm a Reality") focuses on the practical implications of navigating the journey to Leading Through. Putting the new paradigm into practice in a way that overcomes legacy tendencies requires commitment, patience and, most of all, leadership. To support this effort, we outline a series of touchpoints—key outcomes that are reference points in the journey—that enable organizations to pursue the new paradigm in a modular fashion, evaluating and assessing progress on important dimensions, without requiring the whole paradigm to be implemented all at once. Executives and the boards to whom they are accountable play a critical role in this journey—a process that may involve deep self-reflection and a critical reassessment of values to facilitate letting go of legacy tendencies and building new ones. In this spirit, we conclude the book with a series of recommendations for implementing Leading Through and activating the soul, heart, and mind of leadership in the organization.

This book is a family project, and it has been a deeply personal experience for each of us. We have come to this work from many experiences—individual and shared—in our family, our church, and our communities; at school; in government; and from our professional work. That work includes research, writing, teaching, consulting, and leading organizations of different kinds. These experiences have had a profound influence on how we think about leadership, how we feel about it, what we do when we have opportunities to lead, and what we are becoming ourselves as leaders.

But just as importantly, leadership is part of our heritage. The seeds of this book were planted in each of us decades ago, the effect of a legacy of leaders and examples of powerful leadership within our own family. We have ancestor-leaders who have helped organize pioneering expeditions, established towns and organized communities, served in the military, held political office, built and sustained businesses, and in many more ways did the work of leadership to make the world a better place for others.

That heritage has been important for us. For example, Kim is an introvert by inclination, but he learned very quickly that exercising leadership in large organizations like the Harvard Business School, Brigham Young University-Idaho, and the educational system of the Church of Jesus Christ of Latter-day Saints required speaking to large groups and interacting with lots and lots of people all the time. These kinds of interactions only intensified as opportunities to consult with and serve on the boards of directors at major corporations materialized. He needed the example of our ancestor-leaders, who left a legacy of stepping outside what is comfortable and familiar, with a genuine concern for others, driven by a vision of a better world and a desire to innovate to make it happen. He has tried to live and reflect that legacy in all the leadership opportunities that have come to him.

He has also tried to pass that heritage on to his children. When he and his wife, Sue, began to take on responsibilities of leadership in their family, they said things like "remember who you are" to Erin and Jonathan (and their five siblings) more than a few times. And Sue often showed them what an effective leader looks like. We had a front row seat to watch her lead her family, and organizations at church and in the community with love, concern, and skill. We remember seeing her take on the school board about the bus routes they had prepared to bus the children all over the town when our neighborhood school was renovated. The routes were terrible, and Sue mobilized parents to draw up new routes that were much safer, and much more efficient, and lobbied the board to implement them.

Erin was paying attention. Starting with the night she burst into her parents' bedroom and announced that she was going to run for senior class president (which she did, successfully), Erin has continually embraced opportunities to lead. In her professional life these opportunities have included running executive education programs, working on human capital and strategy issues with Monitor and Deloitte clients (on just about every continent and from just about every industry), leading internal organizational development, and coaching colleagues and senior executives across the world. Erin has had many other opportunities to lead—including in her own family, with neighbors, and in her community. She has experienced many successes and built a beautiful family and thriving career. But she has also endured significant setbacks—personally and professionally. She has faced challenges, failures, and disappointments. She still has all the energy, focus, and concern for others of the young woman who burst into her parents' bedroom, but she too has needed the example and legacy of our ancestor-leaders to press forward. She now has much more empathy and a much deeper understanding of what it takes for people to thrive—in their work and in their lives. Like our ancestor-leaders, when she leads now, she builds the people around her because they know she cares, and they know she knows how to do hard things.

Jonathan was paying attention too, including watching and following the example of his older sister. When he was in junior high school, the principal and guidance counselor at his school marveled at Jonathan's ability to connect with everyone in the school. That ability to connect with people, to care for them and love them, explains in part why Jonathan has had many leadership opportunities in his personal and professional life. Throughout a career that began in consulting and has included pursuing entrepreneurial ventures and academic interests—organizing research teams and executing research projects, building and running academic programs, and initiating strategic change and renewal in departments and colleges at Pennsylvania State University and the University of Texas at San Antonio (UTSA)—Jonathan has also drawn on the example of our ancestor-leaders to step outside of his comfort zone and overcome serious challenges and obstacles and solve difficult problems, both personal and professional. When he takes on a leadership role now, he brings his capacity to connect and his ability to see opportunities for innovation, but also a sense of compassion—inspired, in part, by his sister—that allows him to lift and strengthen people around him more powerfully.

We share all of this so you will understand that we have been on personal journeys of leadership that have been an important part of writing this book. Our experience has been like a laboratory for developing *Leading Through*. We have first-hand, practical experience with the principles at the heart of the paradigm. But we also have sought insight about leadership in our studies. Some of that study has taken us into a deep probe of the academic and professional literatures on leadership, and into our own research. But we also have sought insight into leadership in our studies of history, religion, politics and biography, and the writings of leaders from all walks of life. We have reflected on the interplay between our experience and our studies, developed and taught courses to thousands of university students and executives, and helped many leaders and organizations to grasp and implement the ideas in the new paradigm.

We gratefully acknowledge the fact that we did not create *Leading Through* de novo. We have built on many important ideas from the academic and professional literatures developed over decades. We have benefited greatly from the practical experiences of many leaders and organizations we have known and studied. These all have been invaluable. We have added new ideas from our own research and experience and organized all of it into a rethinking of leadership and a new paradigm to make it more prevalent.

What we have learned about leadership is reflected in *Leading Through*. That learning has been deep, and we hope yours will be too. Through our experiences in leadership we have come to understand and feel in our hearts what the new paradigm means to us, to other people, and to organizations. We have a commitment to the principles, concepts, and frameworks we describe. That commitment is our personal answer to the questions Are we not all leaders? Should we not all do the work of leadership?

We have acted on that commitment to apply the ideas in the new paradigm in the organizations and teams we have led and lead now. We are trying to become better leaders ourselves and to help other people and their organizations increase substantially their capacity for leadership using the powerful paradigm we share in this book.

PART ONE

A NEW PARADIGM OF LEADERSHIP

From Power Over to Leading Through

CHAPTER I

The Legacy Paradigm

Power Over People and Organizations

It is the work of leadership that moves us to progress, succeed, and achieve together—sometimes in ways that are highly visible and even heroic. These are often held up as the hallmarks of what the work of leadership is all about. But more often the work of leadership is moving us in ways that are less celebrated yet nonetheless meaningful and important. In *every* setting and circumstance, the work of leadership is vital to the growth, development, and progress of people and organizations.

We have seen and lived the vital nature of leadership and know first-hand its power, but also its frustrations. Here are three examples from our experience:

- The head of marketing for an emerging product area at one of Erin's corporate clients struggled with the changes needed to reposition his team for an upcoming launch. Beyond the right strategy and plan, a successful lead-up and eventual launch would require a new level of collaboration and partnership across the organization. New to the area and to the company, he struggled with the siloed decision-making and hierarchical ways of working he inherited. His predecessor, a thirty-year veteran of the organization, had not only established a high degree of control but also a highly competitive environment in which teams and even individuals and their ideas were often pitted against each other. The result was a survival mentality that diminished collaboration within teams and made partnering across teams extremely difficult. Erin worked with her client to build and strengthen the relationships within the team of his direct reports; both one-on-one and in group settings, he focused on establishing meaningful connections, a shared sense of purpose, cultivating renewed energy and more intentional recognition of individual contributions. Just over eighteen months later, the area experienced its most successful launch and positioned the ways of working they established for the area as a model to be replicated by others across the company.

- When Jonathan joined the department of management at the University of Texas at San Antonio (UTSA), he discovered that the department was plagued by a history of divisiveness, factions, fear, power plays, and callous behavior. With the support of a core group of like-minded colleagues, Jonathan set out to change this. But the group faced opposition, some of it passive-aggressive in nature and some of it much more overt, including deliberate attempts to undermine collective efforts. There were even a few instances of bullying and harassment and isolated efforts to undermine the reputations of individuals. But the core group pressed ahead, striving to nurture a context of collegiality, kindness, diminished status differences, and shared purpose. There were collective efforts aimed at establishing clear standards and shared vision, and individual, one-on-one efforts aimed at engaging previously marginalized individuals, helping them to feel valued and appreciated, and giving them a voice. Over time, people grew to be more understanding, caring, kind, and supportive of each other. It was many months and years of work, but the result was a department full of engaged and committed colleagues and none of the divisiveness that prevailed previously.

- During Kim's time as president, BYU-Idaho created a new program called Pathway to make education more accessible to those all across the world unable to attend a traditional university campus. Pathway provided foundational academic preparation and a clear avenue for students to pursue online certificates, associate degrees, and bachelor's degrees from BYU-Idaho at significantly reduced cost. After several semesters, the leaders of Pathway discovered a troubling and tragic fact: many qualified Pathway students tried to enroll at BYU-Idaho but gave up and dropped out. The problem was a confusing, complex, and frustrating information system. (Pathway students in Mexico or Ghana, for example, would get messages like "Please visit the registrar's office.") BYU-Idaho's system was like a maze of bureaucratic rules and procedures embedded in a hierarchy of approvals, denials, and petitions, all designed to control what administrators and students could do. Kim and his colleagues initiated a major effort over many years to create a new information system for Pathway students and to make student services much less bureaucratic, much simpler, and easier to use. As of 2024, Pathway served more than 60,000 students worldwide, including more than 30,000 in certificate and degree programs.

These examples illustrate two aspects of the vital work of leadership we have encountered all throughout our years studying and doing that work:

- Mobilizing people to make things better helps people and organizations thrive. That is the work of leadership, and it is great work.

- The work of leadership is often very frustrating. The apparent absence of moral values, a priority on rules instead of people, and the waste of potential and barriers to innovation caused by a bureaucratic hierarchy focused on control are not impossible to overcome, but they seem to pop up almost everywhere in one form or another.

These frustrations are not caused by some random quirks in the organization, nor are they isolated incidents. Rather, they are manifestations of a whole paradigm of power—a reinforcing set of beliefs, attitudes, concepts, practices, methods, and structures that shape decision-making and action in the organizations where it holds sway. It is in effect a prevailing worldview that serves as an overarching guide for the work of the organization.[1] It is this paradigm of power that makes the work of leadership frustrating and difficult, if not impossible, to accomplish.

We call this dominant way of thinking the *Power Over* paradigm— shorthand for power over people and power over the organizations they steward. It affects everything in the organizations where it has influence. It consolidates power in the hands of a few, creating a hierarchy of authority supporting close supervision and often reinforced by a bureaucratic web of rules, procedures, and approvals. An important focus of this power and authority is to achieve control over people and their work, pushing for compliance through enforced discipline that ensures detailed execution. Yet its influence encompasses so much more than the "command and control" methods of those in authority. Power Over treats power, position, and status as ends in and of themselves, nurturing socially destructive tendencies and behaviors, including exploitation of others, corruption, and in the extreme, even physical and psychological abuse.

Power Over is subversive and deeply embedded. Understanding it helps provide some explanation for why executives who need to mobilize people to solve tough problems or seize promising opportunities are often disappointed in the results of their efforts. They need to do the work of leadership—and enable leadership in the organization more broadly—but that is not what they do. They exercise power over people using legacy methods, which almost guarantees they will achieve something less than what they seek. The deeply embedded Power Over way of thinking does not allow the people in the organization—including executives—to do the work of leadership. And yet, they think that is exactly what they are doing—the work of leadership. The Power Over paradigm is so deeply embedded that the executive actions that are its effect are often confused as "leadership" actions. They are not. It is that simple.

And the solution is likewise simple: we need a better paradigm, a new way of thinking, one designed for the true work of leadership. We need a paradigm that enables leadership to permeate the entire organization. It must be a paradigm so strong it can stand as a bulwark against Power

Over. We have been searching for that paradigm—a new way of thinking about leadership—for many years. This book is the result.

Our search began decades ago in 1979 on a beautiful spring day in Detroit, Michigan.

The Beginning

On that day a team of people from the US National Academy of Engineering visited an automobile company and one of its assembly plants just outside of Detroit, Michigan. The focus of the team's study was the competitive status of the US auto industry. The leader of the team, Bill Abernathy, was a professor at the Harvard Business School (HBS) and one of the world's leading experts on the auto industry. He had with him one of us, Kim, a new assistant professor at HBS who was in an automobile assembly plant for the first time.

What happened that day has rippled through the decades, influencing our research on the legacy paradigm of Power Over, our study of leadership, our work with organizations, the way we do the work of leadership ourselves, and ultimately, this book. It was, in every sense of the word, a seminal event. Here is what happened.

The plant was large, noisy, dynamic, and very interesting. But there also was a palpable sense of tension in the plant. Our visit and later studies taught us that it was tension born of a distant, adversarial relationship between the people working on the floor of the plant and the hierarchy of supervisors, managers, and executives who controlled everything done on the front line. The feeling of powerlessness of the people on the final assembly line, for example, was unmistakable. The moving line paced their work, and every action they took was highly choreographed.

The cycle time (the time to complete a set of tasks in one of the stations along the line) was about one minute, and the work in that minute was repeated over and over again with precision and minimal variation and direct and close supervision. Any changes in the actions of the work to solve problems, improve quality, reduce the risk of injury, or improve efficiency were made by the company's industrial engineering department, which had representatives in the plant. The workers were there to execute the one-minute tasks as choreographed by the industrial engineering group.

When we had a chance to meet and talk with front-line people and union leaders, we discovered something remarkable. Outside of work, the people on the assembly line engaged in a wide range of creative and leadership activities. They built boats, restored old cars, coached the local baseball team, ran local civic organizations, played significant leadership roles in their churches, presided over the PTA at the local high school, served in local government, and a host of other things.

We had seen talented and capable people in that plant doing highly repetitive work that used none of their true talents and skills. Even the opportunity to improve on the very actions of their work was the responsibility of others. People with proven talent for leadership walked into a workplace every day that did not engage that talent and, in fact, actively suppressed it. The people were like cogs in a machine. The loss of leadership and human potential was staggering.

What we saw in that assembly plant, we also saw all throughout the parent organization. It did not matter whether we were in the engineering department or in marketing or in finance or human resources or operations or product development, we saw the same reliance on power over people to achieve control and compliance through a web of bureaucratic rules administered through a coercive hierarchy and the same loss of human and technical potential.

Understanding the Power Over Paradigm and Its Effects

That day in 1979 we saw the reality of the Power Over paradigm. Although its elements have been widely studied, criticized, and even condemned in the many decades since, this way of thinking remains embedded in the organizational ethos of our time and continues to be widely influential. Over the last forty years we have seen the influence of that paradigm in many, many organizations.[2] Its effects have been damaging and even tragic.

We recognize that the influence of Power Over ranges across a spectrum from relatively little in some organizations to dominant in many others. We have seen that spectrum in our research and experience. But we have also seen that the paradigm is everywhere. It is in primary and secondary schools, in colleges and universities, in health clinics and large academic medical centers, in the newest high-tech startup and large, multinational corporations, in nonprofits, in local and federal agencies, and in families.

A few insights from our research and experience stand out:

- Many senior executives reject the idea that Power Over describes them or their organizations. They make strong declarations and commitments in clear contrast to Power Over. Yet, when we observe how they and their organizations actually work, it is the Power Over paradigm in action.

- Many people who work in organizations where Power Over has influence simply take it for granted. The role of power, the hierarchy, the bureaucracy, the emphasis on control and compliance are just how things are and have been in every organization they have ever been in from kindergarten to professional life.

- Power Over seems to be the human default option. It can seep into and grow in organizations almost imperceptibly until it becomes very influential. This seems to happen more easily as organizations get bigger.

- Power Over paradigm practices—coercive hierarchies, mandates, rules, procedures, controls—can pop up almost instantly in times of stress and intense pressure on executives, even when those executives have made commitments not to do that.

The Power Over paradigm is a serious problem. It is not a relic of the past that no longer has influence. It is a relic to be sure—some of its roots are ancient and some stem from the nineteenth century—but it is still with us. Power Over is like a legacy computer system—pervasive, deeply embedded, very influential, and almost invisible. Its effects are to weaken moral responsibility, damage human and organizational potential, and obstruct initiative and innovation in organizations of all kinds. We'll explore these effects further later in the chapter. But first, we want to describe what it really looks like at work in an organization.

As we explored its many elements, we found there are three primary dimensions that shape the influence it has in an organization: (1) Action: What is the dominant framework for action in the organization? (2) Integration: How are efforts across the organization aligned to a unified whole? (3) Power: What are the underlying power dynamics that facilitate work getting done?

Table 1-1 summarizes the paradigm using these three dimensions that our research showed were the key to its character and influence in an organization.

The Framework for Action

We emphasize four elements in the framework for action[3]—the governing design principle, the attitudes toward personal agency, the way the work is organized (structure), and where responsibility for innovation and improvement lies.

GOVERNING DESIGN PRINCIPLE

Control through compliance has long been the overarching principle governing the design of legacy paradigm organizations. Standardization and consistency were deemed crucial in classic industries like railroads, steel, and automobiles where the legacy paradigm took root. Executives in those industries decisively chose control over commitment as the means for achieving these outcomes. In the resulting paradigm, an important measure of executive effectiveness is how well executives and managers keep people in line and foster compliance with mandates, rules, and pro-

TABLE 1-1

The dimensions of the legacy paradigm

DIMENSIONS OF THE ORGANIZATION		THE POWER OVER PARADIGM
FRAMEWORK FOR ACTION	Governing design principle	Control through *compliance*
	Personal agency	Autonomy is a source of variability that needs to be *carefully managed*
	Structure	*Direct supervision* and standardization through a tall, coercive, bureaucratic hierarchy
		Centralized decision-making along hierarchical lines
		Action governed by *rules* and rigid operating procedures
	Responsibility for improvement	*Those in authority* or centralized technical staff groups assess and revise standards and procedures and pursue innovation and improvements
APPROACH TO INTEGRATION		Achieved through *executive action and hierarchical supervision*
POWER DYNAMICS		*Power Over*: power is expressed primarily as a means of coercing and controlling individuals and groups

cedures within the process.[4] The work is engineered so that those on the front lines operate like high-precision machinery.[5]

PERSONAL AGENCY

The choice of control over commitment is grounded in a decidedly elitist view of human dynamics. It isn't just that people are assumed to be inherently lazy and untrustworthy; it's that they assume most people aren't capable of making meaningful contributions without the controlling influence of executive authority. From this perspective, people are dependent on the wisdom and intelligence of those in authority, and autonomy is a potential source of variability (and deviation from executive direction) that needs to be carefully managed. Thus, in Power Over, personal agency is reserved for a select few, a variable to be minimized for those working on the front lines.

STRUCTURE

In the context of its governing design principle and approach to personal agency, it isn't surprising that in the Power Over paradigm, executives work through direct supervision within a hierarchical organization that is tall (many levels), impersonal, and thoroughly bureaucratic. Decisions are made at the top and flow down through the hierarchy, supported by a web of rules, procedures, and approvals that govern activity. Supervision is intrusive, and the hierarchy, with its many rules and procedures, is a powerful, coercive, centralized tool in the hands of senior executives for achieving the order, discipline, control, and compliance they seek.[6]

RESPONSIBILITY FOR IMPROVEMENT

Specialized staff groups have responsibility for improvement in Power Over organizations. There may be great merit in having specialized groups, but Power Over turns them into instruments of control, restricting innovation and improvement to a select few who engage in a sort of top-down, punctuated improvement overseen by executives, rather than continuous improvement driven by the information and experience of the front lines. Even within the specialized groups, the work of innovation and improvement is governed by rules, standards, and procedures that are designed to ensure control and compliance.

The Approach to Integration

Since the governing design principle is control through compliance, Power Over creates mechanisms of integration in that spirit. These mechanisms—centralized planning, budgeting, and resource allocation—have their own rules, processes, and approvals. Further, the hierarchy of supervision provides direct oversight of the implementation of these plans, budgets, and resources. All of this integration activity is wonderfully bureaucratic. In the modern form, there are templates, guidelines, rules, procedures, large binders, many PowerPoint slides, and many levels of approval. The whole integration effort is overseen by administrators who are the guardians and even owners of the rules, the procedures, and the approvals. They seek precision, discipline, and consistency. They often have their own agenda, turning the bureaucracy into a thing unto itself. It is all in keeping with the thrust of the Power Over paradigm to achieve control through compliance.

Power Dynamics

In the Power Over paradigm, the nature of power is power *over* people. Power is consolidated in the hands of very few who wield it to assert their prerogative and keep people in compliance. It becomes an end in and of itself, unleashing a competitive scramble for the sources of power and encouraging socially destructive behaviors. Power is used to create an unmistakable degree of separation and distinction between the powerful and the powerless, a separation that is often maintained by the visible symbols of status and the perks that come with it. All of this is fueled by a very limited (and distorted) view of power as a means of control over resources that give the possessor dominion over other people. That is why Power Over is characterized by lots of direct orders and assertiveness, with plenty of fear and coercion to go with it.

Beyond understanding the paradigm in action, we turn now to a review of its effects—the impact it has on people and organizations: its moral failure, its waste and loss of human potential, and its obstruction of innovation.

MORAL FAILURE—ORGANIZATIONAL DARKNESS

Leadership is always a moral work.[7] Leaders of teams and organizations hold the lives of people in their hands. Leadership is inherently aspirational—working toward something better. Its very essence is to lift and strengthen people and the organizations in which they work to create the better outcomes they seek. Leaders help people learn and grow and find meaning in their work. They seek to make things better, to do good, to improve the viability of the organization, to create value by making the organization stronger, more productive, and more effective in realizing its purpose. Power Over fails this moral imperative.

In the Power Over paradigm power is concentrated in the hands of people who are skilled in wielding power over people, in using the bureaucracy as an instrument of power, who thrive on being "in charge" and use their power and position to deliver results. These results are often rewarded, reinforcing an increasing scope of power and authority and the license of position to use it. This is why we see a high degree of correlation between those in executive positions and narcissism, Machiavellianism, and sometimes psychopathy (the "dark triad").[8]

Individuals living in the dark triad tend to self-promote and display a high degree of charisma, authority, self-confidence, dominance, and self-esteem.[9] They also have a heightened sense of entitlement and a lack of empathy and are preoccupied with power. We know that giving such people significant power—as the Power Over paradigm does—is a license to exploit others, to serve their appetites and inclinations for control and dominance, and to confuse their own interests with the interests of the organization.[10]

While many of the hallmarks of Power Over are often rationalized as "good management practice" or disciplined execution, at the same time, they also nurture and maintain these socially destructive tendencies and behaviors. When the people who have power yield to self-indulgence and a sense of entitlement, the results have the effect of creating something like the "dark triad" but more diffuse and at an organizational level—something we call organizational darkness.[11]

What do we mean by "organizational darkness"? While it exists on a spectrum and with varying degrees of "intensity," at its "darkest," what we have seen is the creation of an environment that lacks meaning (but for a few), is inconsistent, often unfair, confusing, capricious, and even cruel. It is a context that saps vision, understanding, and commitment. This is not just a theoretical argument. Instances of corruption, fraud, inappropriate sexual behavior, sexual assault, and harassment by senior executives of prominent (and less prominent) organizations in business, nonprofits, and government are legion.[12] This selfish indulgence can act as a catalyst for behaviors and attitudes in others that breed darkness all through the organization; lead to wasted talent and capital; create disillusionment, confusion, and discouragement; and destroy motivation, confidence, and even hope.[13] Darkness damages people, destroys value, and if not checked, can ruin reputations, brands, assets, and the organization itself. Over time, organizational darkness acts like a punitive tax on the organization, limiting its potential.

WASTE AND LOSS OF HUMAN POTENTIAL

The Power Over paradigm both wastes and damages the potential in the people, the technologies, and the organizations in which it prevails. But it is the waste and damage of human potential that matters most and is most damaging. We saw that waste in the automobile plant in 1979, and the more recent evidence of declining employee engagement shows that waste is still with us in great numbers. Only 20–25 percent of the people in recent worldwide surveys report significant engagement at work, while more than 60 percent report that they work in organizations that do little to develop them, do not value them, and give them little opportunity to use their talents, learn, and grow.[14]

This is the world of work in the Power Over paradigm, and it is the situation faced by millions of people every day. That does not mean that Power Over organizations have not and do not use the talents of their people. It simply means that when they do, what they achieve is far below their potential, and that potential diminishes over time. Power Over puts organizations on a lower trajectory of improvement in performance.

OBSTRUCTION OF INNOVATION

The Power Over paradigm stifles innovation. Its centralization of power and impersonal, bureaucratic hierarchy focused on control tend to accumulate rules, procedures, and approvals that become rigid and entrenched. It becomes infested with what Peter Drucker called "bureaucratic dry rot" that makes leaders and the organization inflexible, slow, and resistant to change.[15]

That effect is compounded by something we saw in the automobile company in 1979; the Power Over paradigm removes responsibility for improvement from front-line workers everywhere in the organization, including R&D and engineering. The effect is to make innovation much more difficult. For example, in our research on innovation in new products in the world auto industry, we estimated that Toyota could develop a comparable new vehicle with half the engineering hours and get it to market a year faster than their western competitors, all of whom were Power Over organizations.[16]

Part of the secret to Toyota's success was that the company learned how to vest responsibility for improvement of the work in their people all across the organization, including R&D and engineering.[17] The source of this enormous innovation advantage was in the underlying strategy to seek continuous improvement everywhere and to engage the whole person—body, mind, and heart—in the work. Toyota simply developed a very different approach to power, and ultimately, to leadership. Many have tried to replicate Toyota's approach, with varying results. What we see getting in the way of these attempts, nearly every time, are Power Over ways of thinking.

This is the Power Over paradigm and its effects. Although its modern roots are in the late nineteenth and early twentieth centuries, we are witnesses to the fact that this paradigm, with some adaptations to the modern world, is still influential in some of the most prominent organizations of our time.[18] Take, for example, Amazon.

Amazon and the Power Over Paradigm

Jeff Bezos founded Amazon in 1994 as an online retailer of books. From the time Amazon was a startup until he left the company in 2021, Bezos's approach to executive action and power and his strategy for innovation have had a deep and lasting influence on everything Amazon does.[19] Initially, the principles and practices established at Amazon were deeply rooted in the Power Over paradigm—and one might consider them to have been a success, given Amazon's growth. Yet just before he stepped down as CEO, Bezos made two important changes in the leadership principles he had established; changes that reflect an important shift and recognition of the costs that the Power Over paradigm had over time.

Leadership Principles at Amazon

Bezos articulated a set of principles and practices to govern the work of the organization (these are called leadership principles in the company). They laid the foundation for an extraordinary cascade of disruptive innovations. As the company became a retailer of everything, Amazon introduced numerous innovations in the online retail experience for customers, in delivery services, in web services, hardware, video streaming, and much else. Those innovations in products and services created a large, global organization, and one of the largest employers in the world.

From its earliest days, warehouse and fulfillment center operations have been critical to Amazon's success. Recognizing the importance of operations in delivering products to customers rapidly and accurately, Bezos also started early to lay down a set of principles to guide executive power and organization in the fulfillment centers.

Bezos focused on achieving high volume, precision, consistency, and low cost, and the ability to rapidly and efficiently build many fulfillment centers across the world. He focused on close monitoring of people's work in the centers through sensors, video, and software, coupled with rules and metrics of performance built into the software that managed people in real time at work. One metric, "time-on-task," gave supervisors and managers information about the minute-by-minute behavior of the workers. Improvement and innovation would come through the machinery, the sensors, and software.

While Amazon offered generous pay and benefits, the HR department worked with the people through an automated system designed to operate with minimal human interaction. The rules, standards, and policies were all embedded in software, and people accessed information and service by interacting with the code. For Bezos, automating HR was critical to allowing Amazon to add new fulfillment centers without having to hire an army of HR people. The effect of an automated HR system was literally to turn a person with a name and an identity into a number. Thus, people on the front line in the fulfillment centers became expendable "human resources" identified by a number in the system; they were appendages to the machines controlled by algorithms.

These policies and principles illustrate the longevity of the Power Over paradigm. In effect, what Amazon created in its fulfillment operations was a digital-era version of the industrial enterprises created in the Second Industrial Revolution. It was power over people in a flow-line, high-volume operation coupled with detailed supervision that could achieve rapid, accurate delivery at low cost. Amazon's next-day delivery program, for example, capitalized on the extensive automation, robust software, and integration of people as cogs in the fulfillment machine.

Bezos created another machine in the part of Amazon where ideas for such innovations were created and implemented by executives, senior managers, engineers, designers, marketers, product managers, and software engineers. The nature of that machine was rooted in the principles of executive action and power—called "leadership principles."[20]

Clearly, some of the principles extolled virtues that fostered innovation (e.g., customer obsession, simplification, learning, thinking big, and a bias for action). Amazon calls the principles of executive action "leadership," but the actual words that describe the use of executive power include *expect, require, relentlessly raise standards, drive, ensure, audit, skeptical, deliver,* and *never settle.* The organization developed practices and processes, metrics, and lots of data to make those words a reality in the lives of people in marketing, sales, software engineering, design, and management. Just reading those words and imagining those practices evokes images of the Power Over paradigm in the early twentieth century. They would fit very nicely in organizations like Ford, US Steel, Standard Oil, and Union Pacific in the 1920s. The difference is that in the corporate part of Amazon the focus was on innovation. People who survived became talented cogs in an ambitious innovation machine.

As noted earlier, just before he stepped down from his role as CEO in July of 2021, Bezos introduced two new leadership principles—strive to be the earth's best employer and success and scale bring broad responsibility. In the wake of attempts to unionize fulfillment centers, high turnover rates among the technical staff, increased losses of people the company did not want to lose, and significant changes in the nature of work, Bezos changed his tune.[21] This is "leadership" principle number 15:

Strive to be Earth's Best Employer

Leaders work every day to create a safer, more productive, higher performing, more diverse, and more just work environment. They lead with empathy, have fun at work, and make it easy for others to have fun. Leaders ask themselves: Are my fellow employees growing? Are they empowered? Are they ready for what's next? Leaders have a vision for and commitment to their employees' personal success, whether that be at Amazon or elsewhere.

These words (e.g., *just*, *empathy*, *fun*, *growing*, *empowered*, *personal success*) describe a very different approach to power and executive action; they *are* principles of leadership. Implicitly, Bezos acknowledged that whether looking back or looking forward, a new paradigm of leadership, especially of people, would produce a more effective, more viable, more vital organization.

Why Has the Power Over Paradigm Lasted So Long?

The Amazon story illustrates the persistence of the Power Over paradigm and its deeply embedded character. If an organization founded in 1994, with a commitment to disruptive innovation with sophisticated technology uses Power Over concepts in its core operations, that paradigm has to be deeply ingrained in the ethos of organizations in the twenty-first century. Why has the influence of Power Over lasted so long?

We believe three factors lie at the heart of the explanation:

- *Power and human tendencies.* Decades of research in psychology have shown that many people who achieve power and authority in a group use that power to exercise control and dominion over other people.[22] The Power Over paradigm not only gives license to that tendency, but it also reinforces it, feeds it, makes it legitimate, and uses it to achieve competitive objectives.

- *Co-opting the critics.* The Power Over paradigm attracted a significant array of powerful critics. The criticisms that began with Mary Parker Follett in the 1920s continued and increased as students of organizations, journalists, and novelists created a steady stream of writing and popular discussion that identified serious problems with the paradigm.[23] In response to legal and regulatory action by governments, Power Over paradigm organizations created specialized departments (e.g., health and safety departments to comply with workplace health and safety regulations and human resources departments to give more attention to the needs and concerns of people at work). These adjustments made Power Over organizations less dangerous and less draconian in their treatment of people, but they did not change their fundamental character. What happened illustrates the ability of the practitioners of the paradigm to co-opt their critics. In form and in effect, organizations simply created new administrative bureaucracies to address the demands of critics and governments.

- *The Power Over communities.* The Power Over paradigm has been reinforced by two communities in which it is embedded. First, the shared perspectives, experiences, and power of the executive community that developed around the paradigm has played an important role in its resilience. In an important sense, Power Over became a critical part of the social and professional DNA of leaders in organizations large and small. From 2000 to 2020, for example, most members of boards of directors had been born between 1937 and 1957. Their whole professional lives had been spent in a largely Power Over paradigm world.

Second, almost all children are educated from kindergarten through high school in Power Over paradigm organizations. Many who go on to colleges or universities find themselves immersed in the very same thing: power over people, a hierarchy of authority and power, and bureaucratic rules and processes. The saving grace is often the dedication of faculty and staff who help students navigate the Power Over system. But all of this means that generations of young people enter the workforce with the Power Over paradigm as their primary model of how organizations work.

For all of these reasons, the Power Over paradigm continues to be influential even though it is a moral failure, wastes human potential, and stifles innovation. Power Over is so common and so ingrained that its use has become like breathing for many organizations and executives. It has become the human default option for executive action and power. And yet there is also a recognized need for a different approach. And, like Amazon, many organizations are trying.

Our own quest has taught us that this new paradigm is emergent. We did not find it fully developed in the academic or professional literatures on leadership. Nor did we find it fully formed in an organization waiting to be described. What the academic literature and the world of practice offered were important ideas and valuable practical experience with approaches to leadership very different from Power Over. Our shorthand name for that paradigm is *Leading Through*, and we sketch it out in chapter 2, beginning with our definition of leadership.

Chapter Summary

- The work of leadership is vital in every setting and circumstance, but that work is limited and constrained by the dominant paradigm—the Power Over paradigm—guiding organizations today.

- Power Over is a serious problem, and its effects have been damaging to people and organizations through (1) moral failure, (2) the waste of human potential, and (3) the obstruction of innovation.

- We need a new paradigm—one designed for the work of leadership—that stands as a bulwark against Power Over and enables leadership to permeate the entire organization.

CHAPTER 2

Leading Through

A Paradigm of the Soul, Heart, and Mind

Bob Chapman is the CEO of Barry-Wehmiller (BW), a growing, very profitable organization with 2023 revenues over $3 billion and twelve thousand people operating in many countries around the world.[1] BW is Bob Chapman's pride and joy, not primarily because of the great financial success they have enjoyed, but because of the positive impact the company has on the lives of people. As Chapman has said:

> We are going to measure success by the way we touch the lives of people. *All* the people: our team members, our customers, our vendors, our bankers.[2]

That impact is rooted in a view of people as human beings with needs and great potential. For Chapman, "touch" means to lift, strengthen, inspire, engage, and empower. BW seeks that touch through "truly human leadership" (THL)—an approach to leadership based on real care for people, trust and stewardship that brings out and celebrates the best in people, personal growth through meaningful roles and the freedom to take initiative, treating people superbly, and positive communication to empower them.[3]

Chapman has backed up his commitment to THL with action over and over again. For example, in one of his many visits to BW's manufacturing facilities, he walked on the floor with the business leader and noticed that inventories of parts and supplies were kept in a locked cage on the production floor, a practice that did not square with BW's emphasis on trust and responsibility. Chapman made sure that the cages were eliminated in all BW manufacturing facilities.[4] There are many other examples.

In addition to rooting out practices that did not match THL, Chapman and his leadership team have developed practices and policies that support and reinforce the principles of THL in the daily lives of the people. They found ways to give people real voice, to recognize and celebrate success in living the principles, to give people more opportunity through cross-training, to develop games and incentives to make work fun, and to give people access to free well-being and health screenings. These were all ways to value people, celebrate them, and help them see their potential.[5]

Two interrelated programs—L3 and BW University—have had a particularly powerful effect.[6] L3 is a program in which teams of people in operations work on projects to improve and innovate using the leadership principles and problem-solving tools. BW University is a set of educational courses on the principles of THL and the tools and methods people need to put them to work. By combining education and practical application, BW has developed widespread understanding of the principles and deep experience in applying them among a very large fraction of their people. That includes people in all of their acquisitions who are introduced to the principles of THL the moment BW takes ownership.

All of this would have surprised the people who knew Bob Chapman and BW after he joined the company just a few years following graduation from business school. He got more and more responsibility[7] as a quintessential Power Over executive in a classic Power Over company. Chapman was a hard-driving, rigorous financial manager of cash, laser focused on control and compliance, a strategic acquirer, an executive who sought profits, wealth, and power. People were functions and objects to him, useful to achieve his goals, like cogs in the gears of BW machines. That approach was highly valued in a company steeped in the Power Over paradigm.

What changed? It was not the BW strategy or anything in the competitive environment. It began with Bob Chapman. Divorce and remarriage made him much more aware of the way he saw and treated people, and much more aware of how they felt about him and about working for BW. The people were not happy. They put in their time, but there was little energy or enthusiasm at BW. He realized that what he was trying to do at home—treat his wife and children well—was not how he treated the people at work.[8]

Two experiences gave Chapman ideas and hope. At a wedding he watched the bride walk down the aisle with her father and realized she was just like all the people at BW (someone's precious child) and BW could— and should—have a significant impact on their lives. After all, BW had them at work for forty hours every week. Second, a few small experiments with daily and weekly team-based competitions and recognition taught him that work could be fun. Moreover, people were happier and would work together to find ways to improve the performance of their team if they had some incentive and license to do things differently.[9]

Chapman realized he could create a new BW in which everyone went home each day tired but healthy, feeling good, and feeling fulfilled. That was the beginning of THL. What Chapman and his senior team have created over several years has had a significant effect on the people at BW and their families, and on BW's customers and everyone else that interacts with them. That has been true in turbulent times like the Great Recession, or the Covid-19 pandemic, and it has been true in new environments like its entry into bioprocessing centrifuge equipment and strategic operations in India and China. BW has created an approach to leadership in which people thrive and the organization flourishes.

A Definition of Leadership

Bob Chapman and BW are on a leadership journey. It is a transition from an old, dysfunctional paradigm to a paradigm that is new and different and much better for Chapman, for BW, and for everyone BW touches. That transition underscores the importance of a systematic approach to leadership focused on helping people thrive. We believe a key to that approach is clarity around what leadership is and what it means to the organization and its people. The starting point for the development of the Leading Through paradigm of leadership, therefore, is a close look at our definition of leadership and its implications.

While Leading Through responds to a real need in today's world, our definition builds on the work of Richard Hackman and Ronald Heifetz and, importantly, emphasizes both the individual and organizational dimensions of leadership—both of which are fundamentally human:[10,11]

> Leadership is the work that mobilizes people in a process of action, learning, and change to improve the long-term viability and vitality of organizations in three ways:
>
> - People experience increased personal growth and meaning in their work and lives.
>
> - Purpose is realized more effectively.
>
> - Productivity is strengthened.

Our definition of leadership focuses attention on what leaders do—on the work of leadership. Three words in the very first line capture that focus: *work, mobilize, process*. Each of them plays a crucial role in the Leading Through paradigm:

- *Leadership is work.* It is a particular kind of work, but it is work. Indeed, it can be hard work. Leadership requires sustained physical, mental, and emotional effort. Leadership requires energy, a lot of it. It requires attention that remains focused in the face of many potential distractions. Leadership is intentional; there is a desired, valuable result of the work. Getting that result is creative work, but it is work.

- *Leadership mobilizes people. Mobilize* is an energetic word.[12] It conveys a sense of joining, gathering, and moving with energy and enthusiasm to do the work. In the context of Leading Through, people mobilize to take action and change to accomplish the objectives and to learn from their experience. Learning is critical to the work of leadership, and mobilizing people must comprehend that essential outcome. Mobilize may apply to an individual, a small team, or a much larger group. An individual can mobilize to take action, as can an entire organization.

- *Leadership is a process.* The work of leadership is a series of activities with a sequence and phases focused on a desired result. The process is not a rigid set of rules, but a collection of principles to guide the activities necessary to initiate, mobilize, and empower the work of leadership. It is not just the capacity to act or even the action itself. Nor is it simply the influence necessary to mobilize people. All of those dimensions—the capacity, the action, the influence—are part of the work of leadership.[13] But in the Leading Through paradigm, the focus is on the process itself and what specific activities are essential to mobilizing and empowering people to act, to learn, and to change in ways that strengthen the organization. Those activities, therefore, are taken not only by the person who initiates the work of leadership, but by many others who are critical to the leadership process.

The work of leadership seeks three objectives—people, purpose, productivity—that are crucial to the long-term viability and vitality of any organization. These are the objectives of the Leading Through paradigm. They address the well-being of its people, the ultimate ends of the organization, and the productive use of all the resources that are critical to viability and vitality.

Viability means that the organization is capable of continued growth, development, and success. It means that the organization has sufficient financial and operational resources to continue to function effectively. Adding vitality means that the organization is healthy and strong, moving forward with energy and vigor. It implies that there is in the organization an animating spirit of inspiring purpose.

The leadership objectives have an interactive relationship as they improve viability and vitality. Purpose drives the work of the organization, including everything its people and its productive resources do. In turn, it is the work of those people and the productivity of those resources that creates the long-term viability and vitality that allow the organization to achieve its purpose.

We feel strongly about this definition. It reflects what we have learned from our study and experience, but it also captures how we feel about leadership. Leadership is work, but it is great work. The very words of the definition make that clear—*mobilize, action, learn, change, improve, meaning, growth*. We saw this in the BW example. What Bob Chapman and many, many other leaders and team members in BW accomplished truly qualifies as great work. Greatness is in the effect of leadership on the lives of thousands and thousands of people BW touches and in its tremendous economic and financial impact on the organization.

Of course, there are challenges in leadership. We know leadership can be hard. Mobilizing people is not easy, and the path to solving difficult problems may be uphill and rocky. Making people, purpose, and productivity joint objectives requires more depth of perspective and deeper understanding by leaders and their teams. Yet that is precisely why leadership is great work. It is meaningful and fulfilling because it takes initiative and creativity and stretches both leaders and team members. It is a process of action, learning, and change for individuals and organizations.

But we also know there is joy in this work. Joy comes from working together to make things better, seeing people grow and learn, and changing the organization so that it is more productive and more purposeful. Leadership opens up opportunities, gives people meaning, and strengthens the health, energy, and vigor of the organization.

It is the promise of making things better that is the focus of the Leading Through paradigm, and the work of Leading Through is both *personal* and *organizational*.

Leading Through Is Personal

Leadership is a deeply human, deeply personal work. Three metaphors that draw on our nature as human beings animate the definition of leadership and clarify its nature and influence on people and organizations. They also have significant implications for anyone who does the work of leadership. These metaphors are central to Leading Through.

- First, because the work of leadership is distinctly human and always seeks to improve long-term viability and vitality, leadership is a moral work—leadership seeks to do good and to make things better for the long-term.

This is the *soul* of the work of leadership—seeking to do good.

The moral responsibility of leadership is inherent in the work. By definition, leaders always seek to make things better—more viable and more vital. But they do that in ways that also are good. They seek to realize a higher purpose—the ultimate ends of the organization, centered on meeting human needs that are deep and meaningful. In pursuing those ends, the soul of leadership demands that leaders (and those they lead) strive to do what is right, because it is right, even when it is hard.

In that spirit, the work of leadership must overcome the organizational darkness we described in chapter 1. And, borrowing from the words of Dr. Martin Luther King Jr., "Darkness cannot drive out darkness: only light can do that."[14] Thus, the most important work in the soul of leadership is to generate light in the organization. Organizational darkness makes doing what is right more difficult. It damages people and destroys value. It is generated by arrogance, infighting, abuse, bullying, backstabbing, exploitation, harassment, discrimination, corruption, fraud, and the waste of talent and capital. There are many more. As Kim Cameron and his colleagues at the University of Michigan have argued, light, in contrast, makes doing what is right easier. It lifts people and increases value through attitudes, behaviors, and practices like kindness, generosity, respect, love, personal meaning and growth, shared purpose, a vibrant community, honesty, transparency, high standards of excellence, and the productive use of talent and capital.[15] There are many more. We pursue a deeper discussion of the soul of leadership in chapter 3.

- Second, people are the way leadership work gets done (mobilize people to act, learn, and change); they also are its first-order objective (increased personal growth and meaning). Therefore, creating an environment where people thrive is crucial. This means that care and concern for people above and beyond the functional tasks or outcomes of the work must be characteristic of the work of leadership.

This is the *heart* of the work of leadership—promoting human thriving.[16]

Relationships are central to the heart of leadership. In order to effectively communicate, motivate, mentor, teach, direct, counsel, learn from, inspire, and energize the people they lead, leaders need to build relationships of mutual commitment and care. It is through relationships of care, trust, high standards, and accountability that leaders help people thrive.

We capture the heart of leadership with a framework we call LIVE. The acronym stands for four drivers that help people engage and thrive—love, inspiration, vitality, and expression. It gives leaders a way to connect the work people do every day to their deeper needs. Thus, it helps people thrive in the work. And it really is about the heart—about caring for people and getting to know them; about inspiring them with a vision of their potential; about establishing energy-creating balance in their lives; about giving people voice and room to create. LIVE makes the heart of leadership real. We take a deeper dive on LIVE and the heart of leadership in chapter 4.

- Third, the work of leadership mobilizes people in a process of action, learning, and change. That process—the leadership process—is common across all settings and circumstances, even if the timing, details, and specifics within it may differ.[17] That means it is flexible, teachable, learnable, and repeatable.

   This is the *mind* of the work of leadership—advancing action, learning, and change.

The leadership process reflects specific patterns that are common, useful, and effective in every situation where improving long-term viability and vitality calls for action, learning, and change. That process is the domain of sizing up opportunities, creating a vision of the work, and setting direction. This is where leaders build teams and establish plans and engage people in the work. It is through this process that leaders activate the potential energy in people and teams and help them maintain disciplined attention and focus. This is the process of Leading Through.

The leadership process is a powerful but flexible framework for initiating projects and mobilizing and empowering people. It can be used with a single individual, a small team, a major project, an acquisition, or any other situation where action, learning, and change need to happen. It requires leaders and their teams to think clearly, creatively, and strategically. It requires the mind of leadership. We lay out the mind of leadership in more detail in chapter 5.

In Leading Through, the soul, heart, and mind of leadership are three dimensions in one. Without the mind, the soul and heart may produce commitment but struggle to mobilize it in the right direction. And without the soul and heart, the mind has a tendency to gravitate toward Power Over. These metaphors—the soul, the heart, the mind—are inseparable characteristics of effective leadership. And they have clear, direct, and practical implications for its personal dimension. Anyone who undertakes the work of leadership must attend to, and learn to lead with, their own soul, heart, and mind. They need to focus on doing good, on caring for people, and on thinking creatively to mobilize people in a process of action, learning, and change.

Leading Through Is Organizational

Our definition of leadership has significant implications for the organization. The three leadership objectives—people, purpose, productivity—and the strategy that supports them comprehend everything the organization does. A strong, vital, thriving organization cannot thrive in just one area of its work. Seeking an organization's full potential must encompass all of its people and all of its assets and resources. Thus, the soul, heart, and mind of leadership must permeate the entire organization.

The Leading Through paradigm *activates* the power of leadership all throughout the organization. And it must be activated. In Leading Through, everyone has the work of leadership to do in their sphere of responsibility and influence. But that also means that the work of leadership in a thriving organization will generate action and change in many different projects and initiatives.[18] Those many initiatives and projects could lead to chaos if they are not coordinated and integrated.

Thus, Leading Through comes face-to-face with the age-old conflict between freedom and unity. Leaders and teams thrive on autonomy and freedom of action. But the organization also needs consistency in action and purpose, it needs continuity and coherence in its work, and it needs a coordinated focus on its strategic goals and objectives. In short, to achieve its full potential, the organization needs both freedom and unity.

The Power Over paradigm treats freedom and unity as conflicting choices and decisively seeks unity through control and compliance, limiting freedom of action. In contrast, the Leading Through paradigm seeks to break the perceived tradeoff between freedom and unity, treating them as complementary features of a thriving organization. It does so by activating the kind of leadership that flourishes with freedom while also generating unity. We believe the key is found in the principle of modularity; a systematic approach to activating the work of leadership.

We discuss the power of modularity in more detail in chapter 6 but note here that it provides a means for organizing work into modules that function well together but can be designed, developed, operated, and improved independently. In Leading Through, modularity is achieved by making teams the fundamental unit of the organization and empowering them to work independently in a system that contains the critical information and supporting structure they need to work effectively with other teams and with the system as a whole. All of this is achieved through a *modular leadership system* that stands in sharp contrast to the operating system of the Power Over paradigm.

Table 2-1 compares the Power Over paradigm with the key organizational dimensions of the Leading Through paradigm and its modular leadership system.

TABLE 2-1

A comparison of two paradigms: Power Over and Leading Through

Dimensions of the organization		The Power Over paradigm	The Leading Through paradigm
FRAMEWORK FOR ACTION	**Governing design principle**	Control through *compliance*	Innovation through commitment and *initiative*
	Personal agency	Autonomy is a source of variability that needs to be *carefully managed*	Autonomy is a source of engagement and ingenuity that needs to be *empowered and preserved*
	Structure	*Direct supervision* and standardization through a tall, bureaucratic, coercive hierarchy	*Teams (modules)* supported by a flat, enabling hierarchy
		Centralized decision-making along hierarchical lines	*Decentralized decision-making* pushed to teams on front lines
		Action governed by *rules* and rigid operating procedures	Action governed by *principles* and clear guidelines
	Responsibility for improvement	*Those in authority* or centralized technical staff groups assess and revise standards and procedures and pursue improvements	*Everyone* is expected to initiate work on observed problems or opportunities
APPROACH TO INTEGRATION		Achieved through *executive action and hierarchical supervision*	Achieved through *visible information*, including leadership objectives, standards, strategy, and context
POWER DYNAMICS		*Power Over*: power is expressed primarily as a means of coercing and controlling individuals and groups	*Power Through*: power is expressed primarily as a means of unleashing the potential energy of individuals and groups

As the table illustrates, in the Leading Through paradigm, modularity (with its freedom and unity) is achieved by attending to the key dimensions of the organization in ways that differ sharply from Power Over: (1) a *framework for action* centered on teams that have the freedom—and responsibility—to not only do their best work but also take initiative to make things better; (2) an *approach to integration* that enables tacit coordination, mutual adjustment, and lateral relations across teams through "visible information"; and (3) a set of *power dynamics* that bring people together—rather than pull them apart—engendering feelings of trust and respect across the organization.

The Framework for Action

Leading Through represents a very different approach to organizing work than the legacy approaches of Power Over. We discuss these differences in more detail in chapter 7 but provide here a brief summary of how the dimensions of the framework for action create the organizational space in which people have the freedom to take initiative in a context of ownership and responsibility.

GOVERNING DESIGN PRINCIPLE

In Leading Through, executives choose commitment—to the organization, to meaningful purpose, to each other—over control as the means for engaging people in the work. The objective is not compliance with narrowly defined tasks, rules, and procedures, but the kind of initiative that results in continuous improvement and ongoing innovation. The work is designed to engage people on the front lines, enabling them to use their talents and energies to make things better.

PERSONAL AGENCY

Leading Through is motivated by a fundamentally different set of assumptions about people—that they aren't necessarily lazy and untrustworthy and that they are capable of extraordinary performance motivated by an internal drive to belong, to learn, and to create. In a Leading Through context of meaningful purpose and the promise of personal mastery, autonomy isn't a source of variability, but a source of energy and motivation to make things better.[19] Thus, in Leading Through, personal agency is honored, preserved, and extended as much as possible.

STRUCTURE

Instead of a tall, bureaucratic hierarchy and direct, intrusive supervision, the focal point of the organization in Leading Through is the team. These teams are interdisciplinary, formed to include all of the resources, knowledge, and functional expertise necessary to pursue the team's compelling purpose. There may be teams of different kinds, but each is supported by decentralized decision-making and a relatively flat, supportive hierarchy. Whether the team is responsible for ongoing operations and improvement or an ad hoc project, the work of the team is to take initiative based on principles and clear guidelines rather than rigid rules and operating procedures. In Leading Through, these features of the organization turn teams into modules, making the freedom and unity of modularity a real possibility.

RESPONSIBILITY FOR IMPROVEMENT

This structure reflects the paradigm's overarching principle of innovation through commitment and initiative. But it also recognizes that there is tremendous potential energy and capability in people. Leading Through seeks to formally unleash that potential by making innovation and improvement everyone's responsibility. Rather than leave improvement to executives and specialized staff groups, Leading Through embeds the agency and freedom of individuals and teams within a framework of accountability, creating a set of expectations that confer both ownership and responsibility to make things better.

The Approach to Integration

If the leaders and teams working in this system have what we call "visible information," they can coordinate and integrate their work with relatively little need for hierarchical or bureaucratic intervention. "Visible" means that teams know, understand, value, and use critical information about the organization's objectives, standards, strategy, and context in making decisions and taking action. When this kind of information is visible, it supports and preserves freedom by enabling unity without the need to default to authoritative control mechanisms. We discuss the magic of visible information in more detail in chapter 8.

Power Dynamics

In Leading Through, the potential for modularity to break the freedom-unity tradeoff rests on a critical foundation of supportive power dynamics. Power is essential in leadership, but in the Leading Through paradigm power is used to enable individual initiative and activate the potential energy that is in people and teams. In other words, in Leading Through, power works primarily in and through people and groups, not as a controlling influence over them. This distinction is fundamental to the differences between the Power Over and Leading Through paradigms. We discuss this dynamic in more detail in chapter 9.

The Leading Through paradigm is designed to achieve both freedom of action and unity of purpose and outcome. It creates the organizational context in which the soul, heart, and mind of leadership can permeate the entire organization. Achieving these outcomes requires carefully attending to both the personal and organizational dimensions of the paradigm. Part two of the book delves more deeply into the personal side—the soul, heart, and mind of leadership—and what *Leading Through people* looks like. In part three we focus on the organization and lay out in more detail how *Leading Through the organization* is crucial to activating the soul, heart, and mind of Leadership.

Chapter Summary

- The Leading Through paradigm is the answer to Power Over and is designed to facilitate the work of leadership, helping people to thrive, enabling organizations to realize purpose more effectively, and strengthening productivity.

- *Leading Through* is both personal and organizational:

  - The work of leadership is *personal* and is done person to person and person to teams by leaders who seek to do good (the soul of leadership), promote human thriving (the heart of leadership), and advance action, learning, and change in the process (the mind of leadership).

  - That kind of leadership is facilitated by an *organizational* context that is designed for both freedom of action and unity, enabling the soul, heart, and mind of leadership to permeate the entire organization.

PART TWO

LEADING THROUGH PEOPLE

The Soul, Heart, and Mind of Leadership

CHAPTER 3

The Soul of Leadership

Babcom is an Israeli company that delivers consumer call center services for Israeli companies in banking, insurance, and telecommunications, as well as business process outsourcing services for customers around the world.[1] It is a place where people from every ethnic and religious background in the region work together in peace and pursue shared objectives with respect for and trust in each other. In the context of a region torn by ethnic, religious, and political conflict, what Babcom has achieved is startling, particularly in the context of the kind of violence that has plagued the region for decades and erupted again in late 2023.

Imad Telhami, an Arab Israeli entrepreneur, started Babcom—Arabic for "your door"—in 2008. He sought to create a company that would employ men and women who lived in the social and geographic periphery of Israel from every religious and ethnic group in the country—Muslims, Christians, Druze, Arabs, and secular, religious, and ultra-religious Jews.

Telhami believed strongly that there were many talented people in these areas and groups who wanted to work but found few opportunities (the unemployment rate among Arab women, for example was 80 percent). He believed Babcom could attract them and create unity in its teams of people from diverse backgrounds and could make the teams effective and productive while lifting and strengthening the people. He believed he could create a growing, profitable company while helping people from marginalized groups find real success by working together to overcome barriers rooted in deep-seated cultural, religious, and historical differences.

At the heart of Telhami's strategy was a set of values and beliefs that became the core of Babcom's approach to leadership. Some of Babcom's most important beliefs included the following:

- We believe that people have the ability to grow, learn, and progress.

- We believe that high-quality service is delivered by high-quality people treated well.

- We believe that to serve at a high level, people need tools and skills, motivation, and freedom of action.

- We believe people of all backgrounds, religions, races, and ethnicities can work together well if we provide the right environment of trust and respect.

- We believe diversity is a strength; it helps deliver outstanding service.

Four values—Telhami called them Babcom's Keys—were taught to new recruits and displayed prominently throughout Babcom's operating sites. They were translated into specific leadership practices in hiring, training, coaching, and mentoring people at Babcom:

- Love to serve

- Commitment to excellence

- See the good in everything

- Improving together as a team

Telhami learned that making these beliefs and values come to life required sustained effort to create practices that reinforced them. For example, in order to make diversity a strength, to be inclusive, and to create belonging for everyone Telhami and his senior team had to validate religious and ethnic differences. It was not enough to respect those differences; Babcom had to value them. For example, in some of its sites Babcom deployed a shuttle bus that picked up workers on the night shift whose families did not want them traveling alone at night. Further, Babcom often changed the routes to accommodate the cultural concerns and desires of the workers' families. There were many other small and large actions that Babcom took to validate what their people valued.

The evidence over many years proved Telhami correct; Babcom grew profitably in an industry where it had no pricing power and faced stiff competition. It became an organization in which people of diverse backgrounds worked well together, had higher quality and lower costs than competitors, and provided jobs for thousands of people who grew and progressed beyond their expectations. And all of this while working in a social environment where the darkness of anger, resentment, and conflict was prevalent and dangerous. Indeed, from the perspective of 2024, Babcom had experienced five wars since its founding. Babcom's resilient culture was captured by one employee who said, "Babcom is the safe place."

What Imad Telhami did at Babcom was moral work; he sought to do good. Telhami himself had experienced the marginalization and barriers he sought to overcome. He felt them deeply. When he was hired early in his career to lead the engineering department at a leather clothing company, he was the only Arab in the organization. On his first day of work, the employees went on strike to protest the hiring of an Arab. When he left the company a few years later, the workers all went on strike to protest his leaving.

Telhami had experienced the darkness of discrimination and marginalization first-hand, and he had a burning desire to overcome those barriers and help people of all backgrounds grow and progress. All through his career he tried to help people see each other as human beings and to cultivate respect. Whenever he had opportunities to lead, he felt deeply the moral responsibility that rested on him. Babcom was his opportunity to put those values to work in a very diverse organization.

Thus, we see that the moral work of leadership is deeply personal. It is rooted in the soul of the leader, and it has an important spiritual dimension. We use the word *spiritual* intentionally to capture the human need for meaning, purpose, and connection that transcends the material facts of daily life. While some people, like the three of us, find spiritual meaning and connection in religious faith, others find it in humanistic values or moral philosophy or in nature, art, music, poetry, and literature. Practices like meditation, prayer, engaging with nature, service to others, reading, seeing and listening to inspiring works all feed the human spirit.

The connections, meaning, and purpose that come from attending to spiritual needs is an essential source of strength, motivation, and commitment for the moral work of leadership. Leaders with spiritual strength can inspire and motivate others (often with stories of their own moral and spiritual journeys) and help the soul of leadership permeate the organization. The challenge Telhami faced, and the challenge he met, was to live the values and beliefs he knew could break down barriers and bring people together, and to help everyone in the organization to live them as well.

The Soul of Leadership: From Darkness to Light

The moral responsibility Telhami felt is inherent in our definition of leadership. In the Leading Through paradigm, the work of leadership is to make things better, to improve the long-term viability and vitality of the organization. Moreover, it is to do good. That is evident in the three leadership objectives, each of which has an essential moral dimension:

- People experience increased personal growth and meaning in their work and lives.

- Purpose is realized more effectively.

- Productivity is strengthened.

It is good for people to grow personally, to increase their knowledge, skill, understanding, and capacity, to grow in qualities of character and virtue they value. It is good for people to do work that is meaningful to them with associates they value. Meaningful work increases their sense of personal value and purpose, and it is good to help people have those experiences.

It is good to seek a purpose—the organization's reason for being, its ultimate ends—that meets deep human needs. It is good to find ways to realize that purpose more effectively, both for the sake of the human beings whose needs are better met and for the sake of the human beings who value the purpose and do the work.

It is good to strengthen the growth of productivity of all the resources in the organization. The organization, its executives and its many leaders have a stewardship over those resources. Strengthening the growth of productivity increases the value of those resources, the value of the organization, and the returns—financial and otherwise—that accrue to those who have made the resources available. It is good to create a flourishing organization that is becoming more effective and more productive.

These are wonderful, even noble, objectives. And they should be; the soul of leadership is aspirational. As inspiring and aspirational as they are, pursuing these objectives must be grounded in the work—the day-to-day activities, tasks, meetings, discussions, technologies, interactions, decisions, communications, products, services, customers, clients, and vendors that are the stuff and substance of life at work.

It will not do to help people grow personally as a separate project divorced from their daily work. The same is true of purpose; it is the organization's activities, its products and services that meet those deep human needs. And there is no way to strengthen productivity outside of the work.

This fact, that leadership objectives have to be pursued *in the work*, has profound implications for the soul of leadership. Keep in mind that the Leading Through paradigm is aimed at enabling leadership that permeates the entire organization. Even in small organizations, making things better and doing good happens in the work: the countless decisions, actions, and interactions all across the organization every day.

It is true that the many people in the organization who make those decisions and take those actions come to work with a moral sense of right and wrong. They have a moral conscience that helps them judge what actions are good and what actions are not. They are drawn to the good—to those actions that lift and strengthen people and add value to the organization.

We believe that, in general, people want to do good and experience the personal growth and meaning, the personal connections and value that come from living according to their moral sense of right and wrong.

That value is real, but the preference for doing good is "in general" because those people, like all human beings, also have appetites, desires, passions, a threat response in their brains, anxieties and fears that if not checked and channeled can lead to behavior that damages other people. Moreover, people can get mired in wrongdoing, lured by satisfying their appetites (e.g., sexual assault) or by material rewards (e.g., backstabbing a rival to get a promotion) or by honors and recognition (e.g., earning an award by taking credit for someone else's work).

The Moral Context

The soul of leadership is precisely to do moral work with real human beings in whom there is an ongoing struggle between the lure of wrongdoing and the value of doing good. This means that the work itself and the people who do it need a moral context—a shared framework of moral values and beliefs. In the Leading Through paradigm, the foundation for that context is the set of moral values that are universally considered good, transcending social, cultural, national, and even religious differences. These universal values include things like care and respect for others, kindness, gratitude, honesty, integrity, fairness, loyalty, and trust, among others. Each of these are universally held to be moral imperatives because of a recognition of their value in encouraging and sustaining cooperation, an overarching behavior that is also universally valued.[2]

A moral context sustains behaviors and practices that together are a source of moral strength, encouragement, guidance and protection. This is what Telhami and his colleagues helped to develop at Babcom; it is what we have called organizational *light*. Of course, the reason a moral context is important is because organizational *darkness*—an amoral or even immoral context—can creep into the organization very easily and damage people and destroy value.

One of the most important, and most powerful, things that leaders do in Leading Through is to generate light in the organization. The physical light we experience every day is a plentiful source of symbols, metaphors, and analogies. Physical light, especially the light that comes from the sun, is essential to all life on earth. It provides heat and energy and initiates the essential processes for growth in plants and animals. That role alone has made light a shared symbol of life, goodness, energy, power, and hope throughout human history.

Human beings with sight also experience physical light as a wonderful source of vision. Light radiates, reflects, and illuminates. It makes vision possible and is, therefore, an important influence on communication, knowledge, guidance, and perspective. These effects of light are so good and so welcome that human beings use light as a symbol of enlightenment, wisdom, understanding, truth, hope, joy and happiness in religion, literature, drama, art, philosophy, and daily life. And, of course, in work.

Light also provides a rich source of symbol and analogy in the organizational world of relationships, personal development, and the work itself.[3] In that sense, organizational light comes from a supporting base of moral beliefs, values, and attitudes that support actions, behaviors, and practices that lift people, enhance vision, increase value, and create conditions for growth and increased strength in lives, reputations, assets, and the organization itself. Table 3-1 presents examples of actions that generate light and those that generate darkness.

The values, principles, and actions in the Light column define a moral context. They are recurring actions, supported by shared values and principles. Although we use light as a metaphor, the effects of the actions in the Light column are real. Love and care, for example, are action words. Demonstrated love and care for people have real effects on them. The actions in the Light column have effects that are not unlike the effects of physical light; they illuminate, they clarify, they create perspective, they give people encouragement and hope. In short, they energize.[4] These actions of Light are good; they lift people, enhance value, and strengthen the organization. They create a moral context in which the soul of leadership flourishes.

TABLE 3-1

The moral context of leadership: Actions, behaviors, practices

AREAS OF MORAL ACTION	LIGHT		DARKNESS	
	Underlying values/ principles of light	Actions of light	Underlying values/ principles of darkness	Actions of darkness
RELATIONSHIPS	People thrive when they are loved, valued, and respected	Love, care Kindness and generosity Trust Empathy Integrity Respect for the dignity of others Candor, honesty Connection with others Shared purpose Vibrant community	People with power can write their own rules	Contempt Arrogance Bullying Distrust Revenge Abuse Assault Harassment Exploitation
PERSONAL DEVELOPMENT	People learn and grow best when they are engaged in real, meaningful work with real responsibility	Opportunities to grow Energy Inspiration Real work with meaning Learning Investment in development	People conquer according to their strength Survival of the fittest; if you can't stand the fire, get out of the kitchen	Unjust criticism Favoritism Discrimination Alienation Exclusion Isolation, marginalization
THE WORK	People do their best work when they have freedom of action and are accountable to leaders who care for them and set high standards of excellence for them	High standards of excellence Freedom of action Accountability Productive use of talents and abilities Productive use of capital Transparency of information	Everyone is out for themselves; people have to be controlled Whatever is good for the people who have or seek power is right	Subtle sabotage Shirk responsibility Corruption Coercive control Waste of talent Waste of capital Opaque information Dishonesty, deceit, deception Infighting, backstabbing

In contrast, organizational darkness comes from actions that damage people, destroy value, and weaken the organization. The actions of darkness can range from petty theft to large-scale corruption, from contempt of a coworker to abuse and assault. A glance down the Darkness columns makes clear that where darkness prevails, people see terrible things happen around them and sometimes to them. Though we use darkness metaphorically, the actions are bad, even evil. And they have real effects. They damage people and breed distrust and cynicism, fear and discouragement.

People who work where darkness prevails face a context that is unfair, confusing, capricious, and cruel. Darkness is like a giant, punitive tax on the organization. It drains the organization of energy and its sense of meaning and purpose. It is an immoral context in which the soul of leadership simply does not and cannot operate.[5]

We have intentionally painted a bright picture of light, and a very bleak picture of darkness to sharpen the differences between them. We want to make clear that the actions in the Light column are universally good, and the actions in the Darkness column are universally bad. There are those who might argue that some darkness is inevitable since, as we noted above, human beings do dark things. Some may even believe that a strong organization can tolerate some darkness, since the organization cannot get rid of it all. Moreover, some may argue that darkness—like lying to get a better deal in negotiations—might be beneficial.

These arguments are all based on thinking born of the Power Over paradigm. In fact, as we noted in chapter 1, the histories of organizations steeped in Power Over are littered with the actions, behaviors, and practices listed in the Darkness column. What these arguments fail to recognize is that darkness does not strike all at once. It is not easy to recognize, nor is it self-contained, leaving most of the organization untouched. Darkness seeps into an organization like a mist, or a fog, in actions that deviate from light in small ways. Those small amounts of darkness cause real, even if initially small, damage. If the darkness is allowed to persist because leaders think it is inevitable or simply choose to ignore it, it eventually will weaken the moral context and lead to more and more darkness, and much more damage.

In Leading Through, a little darkness is too much darkness and must be driven out by generating light. That is part of the soul of leadership, but only part. Darkness is not just the absence of light. Darkness is a force that disrupts and destroys. Leaders at Babcom have to be constantly vigilant, constantly putting energy into the moral context and constantly seeking to drive out darkness. This is not just the work of the CEO and other executives, but rather of all the people who seek to do the work of leadership. Ehab Hussein, vice president of customer service at Babcom, explained: "The hardest part of my job is paying attention to the differences between all the cultures and heading off issues. Where there's trust, even if a mistake is made you can explain there was no intention to hurt. We treat with prevention. . . . But where there's a problem I speak with people from a place of respect. . . . At Babcom any topic is on the table."[6]

That approach—hiring for fit with the culture, educating people in the moral context, training them to act quickly to address issues or behaviors or attitudes that generate darkness—had to penetrate into every site and team at Babcom. Everyone had to know and understand the moral context, including the underlying beliefs, values, and principles, and that context had to live in the people. Further, leaders had to recognize that they had to drive out darkness in a way that generated light. Otherwise, they might drive out one kind of darkness only to create another kind themselves.

The commitment to generating light and driving out darkness creates a dilemma the resolution of which is at the heart of the soul of leadership. Leadership seeks to make things better, both for the organization and its people and for the people it serves and influences. Yet, no matter how big or small, the work of leadership is about change, and that change may be hard for the very people the work of leadership is supposed to lift and strengthen.

Leadership involves hard decisions about tough problems. It sometimes requires actions that may cause stress, discouragement, and difficult adjustments for people in the organization. Change, even change that means good things for people in the long run, may still be hard. Change that eliminates jobs, disrupts valued relationships, or reduces personal opportunities can be very hard and painful.

Moreover, the work of leadership must deal with real human beings who have lives outside of work that may create terrible stress for them. Real human beings have bad days or weeks. They make mistakes, and cause conflicts. They and the people they love experience mental and physical illness, and sometimes those challenges get in the way of the work they committed to do.

These very real personal situations require the work of leadership to be focused on individuals. How the leader addresses personal problems will have significant consequences for the people and for the leader's relationships with others. For example, when a leader does not take action to deal with a person who fails to perform, the people who are performing at a high level get discouraged.[7] Not only does the lack of action by the leader make their work harder, but they feel that the leader does not really care about them.

A leader who really cares, who builds relationships, one-by-one, must do hard things to strengthen the team and the organization. A leader who does that will earn the trust and commitment of the people. Because of that trust, that leader will be able to help people find meaning and purpose in their work and lives.

Thus, the work of leadership is not just about making hard decisions, like dealing with the person who does not perform. It is about finding the best way to address that situation, for the person who does not perform and for all the other people that are. In the new paradigm, leaders do their very best to find ways to address very difficult situations (e.g., helping people change, firing someone, coping with a recession, selling a division, eliminating a product line, closing a site, dealing with difficult personal issues) in ways that generate light and drive out darkness, something that is possible, even in the most difficult times and challenging circumstances.

An example comes from an experience Kim had while serving as dean at HBS. A staff member in one of the departments was angry, disruptive, and performed far below expectations. There were many efforts over many months to help the staff member improve, but to no avail. All of this had been documented in detail. However, the human resources group would not permit the department to remove the staff member, for fear of union retaliation. Knowing that the staff member had been given ample opportunities to improve and had damaged morale and productivity in the department, Kim intervened. After a discussion with the head of HR, the staff member was let go. The response of the head of the union? "What took you so long?"

In hard times and facing difficult issues, there may be hard tradeoffs to make, and there may be wrenching decisions, but it is the work—and the challenge—of leadership to mobilize people through a process of action, learning, and change to address those dilemmas. It is in that process that people will find creative solutions to the short-term issues that strengthen the organization and improve its long-term viability and vitality. It is one of the great purposes of the Leading Through paradigm to encourage, facilitate, and support that work.

The Cycle of Virtue

We hope it is clear that generating light and driving out darkness is not ancillary, optional, soft, or easy. It is the very essence of the work of leadership and what it means to be a leader. It is hard work, but it is good work. It is light, power, and vitality instead of darkness, impotence, and apathy. It is done by people—leaders—who choose to make light a central part of their lives and their identity. What does that look like? What does that mean?

In the first place, it means they must embrace the moral context—its underlying beliefs, values, and principles—and the light-generating actions it sustains. They cannot give them lip service. The people on their teams and the other people in the organization can spot hypocrisy in an instant. Words like *candor, love, trust, empathy,* and *accountability* have to become descriptors of what leaders do day in and day out. The integrity of leaders must be rock-solid.

Second, leaders who do moral work effectively must stand against the actions of darkness. That stand has to be clear and unmistakable. They must be people who despise corruption and fraud, harassment and abuse, marginalization and bullying. They must be people who likewise deplore discrimination and the waste of talent and capital and who seek to live by, and hold themselves and others accountable for, high standards of excellence. The moral courage of leaders must be exemplary.

It is precisely because of these responsibilities that the soul of leadership is rooted so directly in the souls of leaders themselves. This is where the strength of the human spirit is so needed. Leaders are much better equipped to do the moral work of leadership with integrity and courage if they can look inside of themselves and find spiritual strength in the meaning and purpose of the work and their connection to the people they lead and influence.

We recognize that doing the moral work of leadership is a demanding responsibility. However, we also know from our own experience that a person does not have to be perfect to do that work. None of us is perfect. All of us have weaknesses. All of us make mistakes. All of us, even those with experience, need to continue to grow and learn. We stand by our description of ideal moral leaders, but we hasten to add that such leaders develop over time through experience, learning, and growth.

We have found the following framework—the cycle of virtue—to be a useful way to think about cultivating leaders who develop the character and moral strength to do the work of leadership well.[8] We use the word *virtue* to capture the idea of strength and power through moral excellence.[9] The cycle of virtue works in leaders but is sustained by, and in turn strengthens, the moral context of the organization. The soul of leadership is, therefore, most powerful and effective when everyone doing the work of leadership seeks to live the cycle of virtue depicted in figure 3-1.

The cycle of virtue begins with:

- *Moral discernment*, a keen sense of what is morally right and just, of what generates light and what generates darkness, based on the universal values the leader and the organization embrace. Of course, an established moral context helps define what is light and what is darkness. But even a strong moral context does not prescribe how to deal with all the myriad issues leaders must face. Thus, moral discernment isn't just about knowing what is right or

FIGURE 3-1

The cycle of virtue

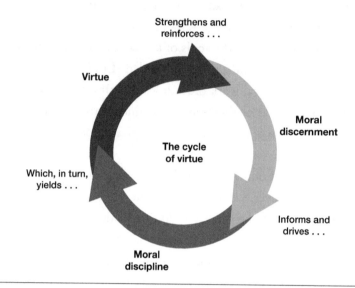

wrong; it's also about understanding how to apply that knowledge in a variety of circumstances. With the context as guide, with experience, and with open communication and learning, leaders develop discernment of what is right and just. Jonathan has had to face this dynamic with faculty members who have trouble discerning that asking students for (uncompensated) help with administrative tasks or for (uncompensated) research assistance can be exploitative, especially when the student is enrolled in the faculty member's course. Similarly, in the context of consulting projects, Erin and her colleagues often find themselves in the position of needing to remind themselves and their clients of the appropriate parameters and range of flexibility in the things they are asking of the teams they are working with—in terms of the volume, timing, and overall scope of work being asked of individual consultants.

Moral discernment informs and drives:

- *Moral discipline*, the ability to generate light and drive out darkness by developing the commitment and discipline to *do what is right*, *because it is right, even when it is hard.* This is where the soul of leadership really happens. This is where leaders take action in specific situations that generates light and drives out darkness. Sometimes those actions are difficult. Here is an example: the director of a new mental health initiative at a large academic medical center received an offer of an unrestricted eight-figure gift with the implied, unstated condition that the donor's son be awarded a faculty position. Despite the fact that the gift would have had an incredible impact, the director turned it down. As he saw it, violating the integrity of the process to hire new doctors would have done severe damage to the hospital. In short, it would have meant darkness, not light.

Moral discipline, in turn, yields:

- *Virtue*, the strength and power of moral excellence. The exercise of moral discipline that leads to moral excellence, or virtue, addresses all sources of light—in the small and in the large. Moral excellence is as much at stake when a leader decides how to talk to a team member who needs correction, as it is when a leader confronts a real moral dilemma like the following: A junior corporate officer discovered a major violation of accounting rules for recognizing revenue just before a critical filing with the SEC. With pressure building to approve the filing, the officer knew that restating the revenues would have a serious negative effect on the corporation's stock and would likely lead to layoffs (including the officer) and significant financial losses for the people in the organization.

Of course, people do not arrive at a life of moral excellence in a day or a week or a year. It is a lifelong quest. People make mistakes and also may struggle with difficult issues. Where is that in the cycle of virtue? It is inherent in the cycle itself. It is why the cycle does not end. If the quest for moral excellence is focused on learning from experience and developing the capacity to exercise moral discipline more effectively, it will yield increased strength of character and moral excellence in a leader's life. That increase will strengthen discernment, and the cycle will continue.

Further, that personal learning and growth in virtue will influence others and strengthen the moral context of the organization.

Animating the Soul of Leadership through Purpose

People who live the cycle of virtue are prepared for, and engaged in, the moral work of leadership. That work is always about making things better, about doing good, especially through the three leadership objectives—people, purpose, productivity. Of these three, purpose has a distinctive connection to the soul of leadership. Purpose defines the ultimate ends of the organization, its fundamental aims, its reason for being. Purpose is fundamentally rooted in the work of the organization, in its moral consequences for, and the deep, human needs of the people the organization serves and influences.

Purpose, therefore, cannot be vague or generic, nor can it be a catalog of all the specific good things the organization might do. It certainly has to be about real needs the organization seeks to meet and real consequences the organization seeks to address. But it also has to be so aspirational, so ennobling, that it inspires the people in the organization and drives everything the organization does. An organization that defines and pursues that kind of purpose will meet deep human needs, and it will create a special community of people, centered on specific values and beliefs that support its purpose, sustained by the unique resources of the organization.

Defined and pursued in this way, an organization's purpose becomes an animating feature of the moral context. It gives life and meaning to the values and beliefs championed by the organization. It frames the work of the organization in moral terms. To find that kind of animating purpose, leaders need to carefully consider the impact of their work on two groups: the organization's *customers* and the organization's *neighbors*.

Customers

The work of the organization has a direct effect on the lives of its customers. Their needs are both immediate and deep. Immediate needs are evident in the language marketers and customers use to talk about products and the way they use them. In the market for yogurt, for example, the customer's immediate needs may reflect concern with taste, texture, cost, and nutrition. Words like *protein level, smooth, tart, sweet,* and *probiotics* are the language of immediate needs in that market. Unmet immediate needs—better smoothness and higher protein at lower cost, for example—present competitive opportunity.

Deep needs spring from a more profound level of human concern and may not be expressed at all when the customer thinks of or speaks about the products of the organization. However, those needs are real and important. In the yogurt example, deep needs may be associated with the desire to provide a home where individuals and families can thrive in a busy world—a home where children are healthy and enjoy family meals. There may be even deeper needs at work here too, including the deep needs of parents to create a loving, healthy, trusting relationship with their children and to connect with other parents who have similar desires. Although yogurt is a relatively small item, its purchase and use spring from these deep concerns.

Chobani Yogurt provides a rich example of how an organization might seek to meet deep, human needs.

In 2005, Chobani did not exist. In that year its founder, Hamdi Ulukaya, who grew up on his Kurdish family's dairy farm in eastern Turkey, bought an old yogurt plant.[10] He decided to develop a thick, protein-rich yogurt he loved as a child. Chobani hit the market in 2007, and by 2023 was a $1-billion-plus organization with a wide range of yogurt-based products.

Clearly, Ulukaya had struck a consumer nerve. What did Chobani do?[11]

- Defined purpose: "make high quality, nutritious food accessible to more people, elevating communities and making the world a healthier place."[12]

- Developed a yogurt that was much thicker and higher in protein, with real fruit on the bottom. It was a Greek-style yogurt with no preservatives. The product tapped into growing concerns and unmet needs for health and wellness and was especially attractive to young people.

- Used social media to create a community of people who loved Chobani yogurt and what it stood for. They invited people with Chobani "love stories" to share them. The invitation and the stories went viral. Stories flooded in.

- Cultivated the community, receiving over a thousand tweets and 150 Facebook posts every day. When the company developed a new flavor, they sent sample products to hundreds of fans in their community. Further, they created recipes for high-quality food that used Chobani yogurt, thus supporting their community in creating "high quality, nutritious food."

It is clear that social media and other communication technologies create new opportunities to nurture a community of customers that interact with the organization and with each other. That community may become a two-way channel through which customers receive support and connection that helps to meet their immediate and deeper needs, and the organization receives important insights about ways to meet those needs more effectively.

Deep human needs, especially those not met well (or at all), are a competitive opportunity. Thus, pursuit of purpose is intimately connected to the strategy of the organization. It may unlock new sources of value for the organization and create a stronger relationship with customers. It also may affect the people who work in the organization, including their sense of identity, and the purpose and meaning they derive from their work.

Neighbors

The work of the organization touches the economic life and personal well-being of the organization's neighbors, and their communities. Neighbors have immediate and deep needs, and the organization's work will influence them, for good or for ill.

Clearly, the organization will seek to meet its legal and regulatory requirements.[13] But making neighbors part of purpose requires a deeper, more profound commitment. Purpose is a leadership objective, and in that spirit, the organization (with all of its leaders) seeks to use its work and its resources to generate light and drive out darkness in the lives of its neighbors and their communities. Depending on the nature of the organization's work and its scale, that commitment may involve the environment, health care, training, education, clean water, sustainable energy, or any number of issues related to its work and important to neighbors and communities both local and global.

As part of purpose, the needs of neighbors combine with needs of customers to define the ultimate ends of the organization. They become a central part of the organization's identity. Moreover, as we noted earlier with customers, there are opportunities for leaders to pursue purpose in ways that create value for the neighbors and the communities in which they live, but also for the organization. The key is innovation. Consider the example of DTE Energy.[14]

DTE is an energy company in the midwestern United States that developed its purpose closely aligned with its influence on customers and users, and cognizant of its influence on neighbors. The tag line read, "We serve with our energy, the lifeblood of communities and the engine of progress."

A video, designed to introduce DTE's purpose to its people, "showed DTE's truck drivers, plant operators, corporate leaders, and many others on the job and described the impact of their work on the well-being of the community—the factory workers, teachers, and doctors who needed the energy DTE generated. The first group of professional employees to see the video gave it a standing ovation. When union members viewed it, some were moved to tears. Never before had their work been framed as a meaningful contribution to the greater good. The video brought to life DTE's purpose: 'We serve with our energy, the lifeblood of communities and the engine of progress.'"[15]

DTE's purpose connects to customers and neighbors, is rooted in the work, and is aspirational. The reaction of DTE's people underscores two ways in which defining its purpose to include its neighbors could create value for the organization. First, DTE may be able to attract and retain talented people who identify with the purpose and want to be associated with DTE. Second, people in DTE may feel greater commitment to the organization and derive greater meaning from the work. These effects may lead to more motivated and more productive people in DTE. Thus, neighbors receive value through DTE's work, and DTE receives value by elevating the needs of its neighbors and their communities to its higher purpose.

Yet DTE could not truly be the "lifeblood of communities and the engine of progress" only by supplying customers with energy the way DTE always had done. Having defined its higher purpose, DTE needed to find new, innovative ways to work together with its neighbors and communities that would create value for them and for DTE.[16] Here are some examples of actions DTE took:[17]

- DTE made a major commitment to renewable energy (wind, solar) to reduce its carbon footprint. Customers could join a program that allowed them to choose the level of renewable energy in their personal electricity use.

- It invested in health, education, and social services in the local communities where it operates, both financially and, perhaps more importantly, through the voluntary work of its ten thousand employees.

- It created a pipeline into employment through training and internships for people in its communities.

- DTE also developed innovative programs to help its customers save energy, and it used social media and other technologies to support, educate, and listen to its customers.

DTE's search for shared value makes clear that the organization recognizes the moral consequences of its influence on its neighbors and their communities. The actions to phase out coal-fired power plants and to invest significantly in wind and solar are not public relations gimmicks. They represent a commitment to be a good steward of its environmental resources and, thus, to be "the lifeblood of communities and an engine of progress." The old DTE could make the lights come on, but the new DTE, animated by purpose, can do that in a way that is more sustainable and provides new value to its neighbors. Making neighbors part of its purpose establishes DTE's identity as a force for good in its work and makes a strong statement about what it stands for and what DTE means in the world.[18]

We recognize that an organization that adds the needs of neighbors to its purpose faces constraints on how it will pursue that leadership objective. The organization must match the needs of its neighbors and their communities to its scale, resources, and commitments. Those needs are very likely to be far greater than any one organization can address. But the organization can do something important; it can make a difference for good. Focus and priorities are crucial to that effort. And while it won't be able to solve every problem, the organization can help solve some and, in doing so, ensure that it doesn't create new ones. If this is done wisely and well, the organization can lift and strengthen its neighbors and its communities in ways that enhance its long-term viability and vitality.

Creating and realizing shared value over the long run is only achievable when purpose becomes a leadership objective and the soul of leadership permeates the organization. That means every leadership project in the organization should have some aspect of purpose—or a clearly aligned derivative—as one of its objectives. When this happens, purpose permeates the organization. It becomes real in the lives of people—employees, customers, and neighbors. It is transformed from a distant, lofty slogan into a living, animating objective connected in substantive ways to the daily work of the people.

It is in that connection between their everyday efforts and an inspiring purpose that people find meaning in their work. That kind of meaning frames work in moral terms, helping people to see the good they do every day and motivating them to live up to the lofty purposes, values, and beliefs of the organization. It is in the connection between everyday work and the good it accomplishes that teams find inspiration to search for new ways to create value. It is the soul of leadership that establishes that connection in a powerful way, motivating people to increase light (and dispel darkness) in the organization and enabling them to realize purpose more effectively.

Chapter Summary

- In Leading Through one of the most important things leaders do is to increase *organizational light* (a context that uplifts and illuminates the organization) and drive out organizational darkness (a context that is unfair, confusing, capricious, and cruel). This is the soul of leadership.

- There are at least three ways leaders generate and sustain organizational light (and keep out organizational darkness):

  - Build and maintain the *moral context*, a shared framework of moral beliefs, values, and attitudes that guide the work of the organization.

  - Cultivate and teach the cycle of virtue, which begins with *moral discernment*, informing and driving *moral discipline*, and in turn yielding *virtue*, or the strength and power of moral excellence.

  - Animate the moral context and cycle of virtue through purpose, vividly articulating the organization's ultimate ends—its reason for being—and generating deeper meaning for people.

CHAPTER 4

The Heart of Leadership

Best Buy is a highly regarded retailer of electronics and technology products and services with annual revenues in 2023 of more than $45 billion, ninety thousand employees, and more than a thousand stores.[1] However, in the years immediately following the Great Recession of 2008–2010, Best Buy was in desperate need of a turnaround. It was reeling from a public scandal involving the previous CEO and struggling in the face of new competitive threats. At that very moment, Hubert Joly, the CEO of the Carlson Companies, with businesses in travel and hospitality, became Best Buy's CEO. Many thought Joly was crazy for taking on the job. Joly had no experience in retail, the company's operating performance had been in sharp decline, and analysts and reporters were convinced the company's days were numbered.[2]

In the face of such turmoil, employee morale was at rock bottom and turnover was high. Before Joly was announced as CEO, he shopped in Best Buy stores to see the reality of the company's frontline people—referred to as "Blue Shirts" in the company—and their relationship with customers. What he found was troubling. When he walked into those Best Buy stores, he entered a Power Over paradigm world. It was a world of disengaged employees, many unhelpful rules, few caring people, and frustrating customer service. The Blue Shirts—Best Buy's in-store employees—seemed not to matter. And that translated to how they behaved toward customers.

Joly set out to change that and much more with an approach to leadership grounded in a belief that "work can be part of our search for meaning and our fulfillment as human beings. If we each shift the way we consider the nature of work, from a burden to an opportunity, then we can start transforming business."[3]

The key for Joly was to connect an individual's personal search for meaning to their work at Best Buy and the organization's purpose. Best Buy's purpose was to enrich customers' lives through technology.[4] Joly established three principles to guide the organization in achieving that purpose:

- The ideal Blue Shirt is an "inspiring friend" who engages and connects with customers.

- People are a source of creativity, initiative, ideas, and energy who can do great things.

- Treat people as individuals and help them flourish.

Joly believed that establishing genuine human connections was critical to unlocking the potential in people. That kind of connection meant that executives, managers, and supervisors all throughout the organization had to know people on a personal level, including knowing the challenges they faced, what they hoped to achieve in life, and how they felt about their work.

Joly related an example of a store manager who had taken this principle seriously:

"What is your dream?" Jason Luciano, manager at the Best Buy store in Dorchester, Massachusetts, asked every single person on his team this question. By figuring out what drove every person on his team, he truly connected with each one of them. But his real genius was then to find a way to link their dreams with the company's purpose.

He told me about a Blue Shirt whose dream was to be able to move into her own apartment. What fundamentally drove her was to find independence. If she remained on an hourly wage in the mobile-phone department it would be difficult to afford her own place. Together, they drew up a plan for her to become a supervisor or assistant manager. What would it take? What skills did she need to develop to get these promotions? And how could he help her get there? With the support of her manager and the team, the young woman grew in confidence, helped improve the performance of her unit, and became someone who inspired her colleagues. When a position to lead the computing department opened up, she got it. Eventually, she fulfilled her dream and got her own apartment.[5]

As this story suggests, Joly not only succeeded in getting his executive team, along with regional and district managers, to embrace these principles, but he ensured that these principles permeated the entire organization, all the way to store managers and frontline people. Of course, there were many other things that Best Buy did over the seven years that Joly served as CEO—strategic decisions to use stores as online distribution centers; forging partnerships with Apple, Microsoft, and Google; creating home-service teams, and so on. But at the core of the turnaround of Best Buy—the company went from "being on life support" to five consecutive years of sales growth and a 263 percent increase in shareholder return[6]—was the commitment to help people find meaning at work, see people as sources of initiative and creativity, treat people as individuals to help them flourish, and forge genuine human connections of respect, value and care.

Leadership Is Personal

The experience of Hubert Joly at Best Buy highlights the personal nature of leadership. In fact, the soul, heart, and mind of leadership are *always* personal. Leadership is fundamentally human. In our definition of leadership, human beings are both the primary objective and the means by which the work of leadership is accomplished. People are emotional learners, with hopes and dreams, a longing to belong, a desire for meaning and purpose, and tremendous potential.

From this perspective, a "leader" is not an abstraction, a distant figure, or an impersonal force. A leader is a person, with skills and abilities, attributes, characteristics, and feelings. The same is true of the people with whom the leader seeks to connect—those they seek to mobilize and empower. In Leading Through, leaders seek to lift and strengthen people, helping them grow and learn, make progress in achieving their potential, and find meaning in their work. It is an emotional relationship defined by mutual commitments—of care, respect, trust, value, candor, high standards, and support—that bind people together. This is the heart of leadership and the heart of the new paradigm.

Our purpose in this chapter is to present a framework for the heart of leadership that really works. We call it LIVE, which stands for love, inspiration, vitality, and expression. LIVE provides a structure for understanding the needs and interests of people and for helping them thrive. The framework can be used to assess where problems may lie in ourselves, in the people we work with, in teams, and in organizations. It also can be a guide for taking action to solve those problems and help people thrive.

LIVE: A Framework for the Heart of Leadership

We did not get this framework from a book or articles or cases. While research, case studies, and insights from practice have been helpful in developing, sharpening, and confirming the ideas, the framework has its origins in our personal experiences. The framework itself and our confidence in making it a central part of the Leading Through paradigm have been hard won. LIVE has been battle-tested on the front lines of our own leadership and our own lives. It works.

We have seen it in our research, in our experiences leading organizations, working for leaders as members of teams, and as board members, consultants, coaches, advisors, and partners. These experiences have come in many different kinds of organizations, including large, global corporations, entrepreneurial startups, our own families, hospitals, nonprofits, schools, and universities. Moreover, as much as we have seen and felt the principles working, we have also seen the contrast of their absence working with other leaders in the very same roles.

In our personal lives we have learned that LIVE is what we, ourselves, need to thrive. Like most of us, we have navigated across the full spectrum of human experiences ourselves and in our families—the death of loved ones, life-threatening illnesses, accidents, surgeries, addiction, divorce, learning disabilities, mental and emotional illness, and much else. And we have taken home with us the stress and frustration of a difficult environment at work. We also have experienced much of life's goodness— miraculous recoveries from addiction and from Covid-19, surgeries that went well, finding jobs, effectively managing our mental and emotional health, overcoming failure, healing from serious injury, flourishing after divorce and the loss of loved ones. We live in gratitude for many more good things. And we have taken home with us the meaning and hope of a great environment at work.

In all these experiences, in the adversity and the prosperity, we have learned that LIVE is powerful. We have led and been led with and without it. There have been times when we have lived with it and there have been times when we have lived without it. We have learned that no matter what happens to us and to our organizations, no matter what forces affect us, we and the people we lead and work with not only thrive personally, but are far more effective, more resilient, and more energetic and determined when we use the principles in the LIVE framework to guide both our personal lives and our leadership.

L Is for Love: *Connecting and Belonging*

Any time we talk about the first element of the framework—*love*—with business executives, even in one-on-one meetings, we often get a little snicker or a quizzical look. We use the word love broadly, but intentionally, to mean human connections of understanding, appreciation, compassion, and care.[7] It usually does not take long for executives to recognize that they and everyone around them flourish on these kinds of human connections. They need to love and to be loved. They need to feel love and to help others feel loved. In Leading Through, the personal work of leadership is sustained by creating human connections of love. Without it, people cannot thrive.

Establishing meaningful human connections—important both virtually and face-to-face—takes concerted effort. In the work of leadership it cannot be an afterthought. We need each other—in work and in life. Human connections of love are fundamental to human well-being and happiness.[8] It turns out, the Beatles weren't far off when they famously sang, "All you need is love, love is all you need." It may not be the only thing we need, but it is essential.

We need it, but we face increasing challenges. The US surgeon general recently declared an epidemic of loneliness in which the effect of the global Covid-19 pandemic has dramatically accelerated an already declining sense of connection and belonging.[9] And alongside that decline has come a sharp increase in the incidence of depression, anxiety, and suicidality. The report cites many factors that have contributed to this dramatic increase. A number of them can be connected to the deeply embedded effect of the Power Over paradigm across different spheres of our lives, but especially in large organizations.

While not intentional, a Power Over mindset amplified by the global pandemic and the rise of new technologies has caused organizations to drift further and further from the sense of connection and belonging people need. Even when they recognize it and advocate for policies and programs designed to address it, they fall short. Why? Because leadership is personal and the work of leadership—including the cultivation of connection and belonging, the love we all need—doesn't happen in the policies or programs; it happens in individual human to human interactions.

Love is expressed in many ways but generally involves some combination of attention, affection, appreciation, and acceptance.[10] When leaders love people, connect with them, care about them, listen to them, appreciate them, invite them to bring all their talents and abilities to their work, meet that action with positive experiences, and create that sense of belonging, what they get is like magic. When they don't, what they get is something different. Consider the case of Lucy, an employee at one of the organizations with which Erin worked.[11]

Lucy was a newly hired associate with academic credentials and work experience in scientific research. She was hired into an area she thought would utilize her experience and expertise but soon found herself feeling like a nameless cog in the gears of a machine that did not use her skills. Despite repeated inquiries and requests to be reassigned, her work that first year was in areas that were completely new or where she had little experience. Her performance suffered. Lucy was placed on a performance plan and given six months to show improvement, or she would be let go. It was an anxious time for Lucy. She had ongoing project work to attend to while she felt like a spotlight shined on her every move. This was when Erin first met Lucy and the team she was working with.

In this time of anxiety and worry for Lucy, Erin had the opportunity to get to know her. She and Lucy connected. Erin found her to be knowledgeable, articulate, and capable. It didn't fit with what she had heard or with the experience Lucy had described. It was clear that Lucy had been arbitrarily placed with the team she was part of rather than the one she had specifically applied to be part of (one where the work was a good fit for her capabilities and expertise). As a result, Lucy was undervalued, her skills underappreciated, and sadly, her voice ignored. It was as if Lucy's managers did not really see her, hear her, or know her at all. Erin felt that Lucy had great potential. So much so that she decided to take a risk and step outside of her normal role and advocate for Lucy.

As Lucy's advocate, Erin connected with the managers of Lucy's area to help them to see Lucy in a different light. She helped them to see the good things that could happen if they were to assign Lucy to the team that could directly use her experience, skills, and talents. As a result, Lucy was assigned to the team she had wanted to be part of from the very moment she was hired.

Part of Erin's work with this organization included working with team leaders to use the principles of LIVE, and she took special care to do so with Lucy, her new team lead, and the rest of the team. It turned out that Lucy's new team leader had not been aware that someone with Lucy's specific background had been hired and saw immediately the opportunity to leverage her experience. The team leader took genuine interest in Lucy, got to know her, valued her, and helped build a sense of belonging with the new team. Lucy began to thrive.

In subsequent performance reviews Lucy's star began to shine. All of what had been experienced before went away. Lucy was flourishing and so was her new team. The performance of the team and its interpersonal dynamics improved. Because of the leadership of her team leader and the love that came with it, Lucy's newfound sense of belonging to the team acted like a catalyst that sparked increased engagement for everyone. It was like magic. A thriving human being is a powerful force.

It would be easy to see Lucy's experience as a story about finding the right fit between a person's skills and talents and their work assignments. But there was something more fundamental that kindled these changes. Getting the match right was important (more on that later), but Lucy needed human connections of love and belonging to thrive. She needed people around her who took the time to get to know her, to listen to her, to value her, and to care about her. When she had that, and a good match, she really did thrive. But that's only part of the magic. The rest of the magic is that as LIVE principles were applied to Lucy, the team leader experienced a change and so did the rest of the team: they all thrived. And their performance—as a team and as individuals—improved across the board.

Lucy's story is also an important cautionary tale. Helping Lucy thrive required the concerted effort of Erin and eventually her new team leader to connect with her. That effort is a critical part of the work of leadership. Yet it did not happen in Lucy's first year with the organization. This woman of extraordinary talent and ability was not seen, was not heard (despite many attempts), and was not understood, and that led to the waste of Lucy's talents. Fortunately, applying the principles of LIVE filled the gap Lucy experienced, and *love* was the first ingredient.

I Is for Inspiration: *Learning, Growing, Becoming*

What would happen if you were consistently inspired at work? Imagine that you make new connections between your work and the organization's purpose, or your team leader helps you to see new connections between your work and your personal goals, or you hear new inspiring stories about coworkers or customers, giving you a new perspective on your work and life. Those connections, stories, examples, and new perspectives could just stay in your mind, filed away somewhere, but they don't. These ideas animate and enliven your mind and heart. They interact with the experiences, feelings, and emotions you already have, and that creates a cycle of growth wherein new ideas and new possibilities are discovered, explored, and shared. You are learning. You are growing. You are becoming more. And as you engage in the work of leadership to mobilize and empower those around you, so are they.

Inspiration is another word we use with intention. The word *inspire* comes from a Latin root that means to breathe into. Its earliest use in fourteenth century English used the Latin to create a powerful metaphor of a divine source acting "to influence, move, or guide by divine or supernatural influence or action." In common usage today the word *inspire* captures both the sense of an influence that is animating, enlivening, invigorating, and exalting and something that impels, motivates, and arouses to action.[12]

Inspiration is a process of learning that involves the reception of new ideas and insights that provide a glimpse of energizing possibilities. But it is not simply about being inspired *by* something; it also involves being inspired *to do* something, the kindling of a desire to make important things happen.[13] In this way, inspiration is a key aspect of helping people to thrive and is essential in the work of mobilizing and empowering others effectively. If love is about nurturing a context of connection and belonging, inspiration is about learning, growing, and becoming more.

When we are inspired, we are moved toward something greater than ourselves, the pursuit of which infuses our lives and work with meaning, growth, and fulfillment.[14] An important catalyst in this process is a purpose—the ultimate ends to which we aspire—that transcends daily routines and is meaningful. In organizations, if that purpose is expressed clearly, memorably, and vividly, and if it is centered on things that people value, it can both inspire people and help them find meaning in their work.[15] Two things are essential for an organization's purpose to be both inspirational and effective.

First, as noted in chapter 3, leaders need to help people see the connection between the work they do every day and the purpose of the organization. NASA did this effectively during its race to the moon in the 1960s. For example, when President Kennedy visited NASA, he asked an employee who was mopping floors, 'Why are you working so late?' The custodian responded, 'Because I'm not mopping the floors, I'm putting a man on the moon."[16]

Second, leaders need to make purpose even more personal, and thus more inspiring. When they do, they lift people by helping them develop an inspiring vision of their personal potential. They help people see avenues of personal progress and continued growth and learning that connects their personal vision to the organization's purpose. The message is, "You can grow and learn and do great things here that will help us realize our remarkable purpose." That means the leaders know enough about their people to help them make those individual visions real and develop a personal plan for pursuing it.

This dynamic was at play in Lucy's experience. Before being reassigned to a new team, Lucy had plenty of opportunity to learn and grow through new experiences and exposure to new challenges. The difference was that it was happening in an area completely unrelated to her personal sense of meaning and value. She couldn't see herself becoming more of who she wanted to be and found little drive or motivation.

In retrospect, Lucy admitted she could have put more energy and effort into learning about new areas. She had the learning skills and capabilities to "get up to speed" and "adapt." But added to the lack of connection already noted, Lucy felt that doing so would mean sacrificing her long-term goals of making an impact that matters in an area of importance for her personally. Lucy chose to pursue the role at this organization because of that personal passion and interest. Despite sharing that, in detail, in the hiring process, when she was ultimately assigned to a team, it was her generalizable skillset that was considered first.

After Lucy was reassigned, Lucy's new team leader asked her a set of questions similar in spirit to the one Jason Luciano, the Best Buy manager, asked his people, "What is your dream?" The intention was to understand how to connect Lucy's work to her personal goals. Both Jason Luciano and Lucy's team leader opened the door to new possibilities for their people. Lucy felt the enlivening power of inspiration, prompted by the actions of her team leader. She made connections between the work of the new team, the work of the organization, and their impact on society that, in turn, inspired not only Lucy but the team leader and other members of the team as well. Together, they also explored new avenues of opportunity for each of them individually and how they could each grow in their knowledge and expertise in the pursuit of their shared purpose.

The search for meaning and personal growth in the work changed the work. And it changed those doing the work.

V Is for Vitality: *Personal Energy That Energizes Others*

If inspiration is about the personal motivation to improve and innovate in work that is meaningful, *vitality* is about the personal energy to sustain the action, learning, and change necessary for that work. Vitality and inspiration are closely connected in the LIVE framework, and both are essential to helping people thrive at work.

We think of vitality as positive personal energy for meaningful action. Our focus on action is shared by the words dictionaries use to define vitality, including *force, power, vigor, animation, lively, energetic, activity,* and *strength*. In LIVE, that energy is positive, directed toward personal growth, the objectives of leadership, and the long-term vitality and viability of the organization.

The personal energy at the heart of vitality is driven by both physical and emotional sources. On the physical side, personal energy generally derives from the condition and care of our bodies, the extent to which our bodies function properly and are properly fueled. From this perspective, the significant investments organizations make in both employee health benefits (e.g., access to good health care and preventive services) and healthy living programs (e.g., for exercise, proper diet, sufficient sleep, etc.) are an important aspect of cultivating vitality in the workplace. Some organizations, like RC Willey, are taking employee health a step further by providing on-site clinics to make accessing preventive and other health care services easier for employees.[17]

On the emotional side, personal energy comes from the ability to cope with and manage emotions, including the regulation of stress and anxiety, and is tightly intertwined with good mental health and the ability to think clearly and make good decisions. Notably, emotional energy is generally amplified by a feeling that one is important and valued (a key aspect of *love*) and that one's actions have meaning and purpose (a key aspect of *inspiration*).

But patterns of thought and emotion are complex and often necessitate more deliberate and mindful care and attention. Many organizations worldwide have recognized the importance of mental health and have invested in a range of programs to address it. Despite all that effort, the percentage of employees experiencing poor emotional and mental health, including burnout, distress, depression, and anxiety, is stubbornly high.[18] In the United States, the surgeon general's report on loneliness and other recent studies suggest that like their counterparts across the world a large majority of employees in the United States have experienced poor mental health. Further, the evidence is clear—for a significant fraction of people all over the world, poor mental health directly affects their engagement and performance at work.[19]

The creation of programs for the well-being of employees, such as free mental health screening or access to mental wellness apps or even meditation rooms, may be of some help to people, but they do not address the underlying problems caused by the workplace itself. Here again, we see the influence of the Power Over paradigm. By far the most significant factor related to poor mental health at work is the organizational darkness that makes the work environment toxic—bullying, abusive language, and so forth.[20] The solution lies in focusing on vitality as an intentional outcome and generating light through the soul and heart of leadership. That kind of effort is fundamental to the work of leadership.

Take, for example, the serious problem of burnout—the extreme depletion of mental, physical, and emotional energy.[21] Burnout has become a hot topic in the wake of the pandemic. It is a major issue leaders and their teams face as they do the work of leadership.[22] So too are bullying, disrespect, sexual harassment, contention, lying, hypocrisy, and other forms of organizational darkness that damage people physically and emotionally. Even the work itself (e.g., workload, poor job design, lack of resources) can become a source of darkness, draining personal energy from otherwise very capable people.[23] This was part of Lucy's experience.

While not rising to the level of harassment or bullying, working in an area where she felt no sense of belonging, connection, purpose, or meaning drained Lucy. Add to that the mismatch of her skills and capabilities against the work being done, and Lucy's assigned work became a source of stress and anxiety rather than energy and joy.

When Lucy moved to her new team, Erin taught her and her team leader the LIVE principles as a means to improve her performance. As the team leader learned about Lucy's need for vitality, he decided he ought to consider similar questions about the whole team. He looked at the workload, patterns of interaction, and overall team norms characteristic of the work culture on their team and was disheartened by what he found. There was an underlying tone of competitive tension, a tendency for everything to be urgent, and a generally accepted and unspoken rule of being accessible on weekends and during nonworking hours. The team leader raised these issues with the team and asked an important question: "What would have to be true for our team to make our physical and emotional well-being our primary objective?"

After some initial skepticism (one team member asserted that this would mean ignoring work altogether!), the team identified two principles to focus on: (1) after-hours and weekend calls and emails are an exception rather than a standard way of working, and (2) there should be more open check-ins and transparent discussion about the timing and pace of work, in particular around certain milestones. Keeping these two principles at the forefront of the team's focus became an important part of the work of leadership for the team leader.

Helping people experience work in a way that is energy-increasing and contributes to effective balance in their lives is the key to vitality. It is not simply a problem for the human resources department, although most companies treat it that way. Real, sustainable vitality is an opportunity for leadership—*personal* leadership—and the Leading Through paradigm treats it that way. Under LIVE, effective leaders work with people personally, helping them to acquire and preserve positive personal energy, enabling them to work more effectively, act on opportunities to drive learning and change, and contribute to the viability and vitality of the organization.

E Is for Expression: *Voice and Creativity*

People who love and are loved, who are inspired and inspire others, who have vitality and spark vitality in others are well prepared to do meaningful work. People who thrive act on their inspiration and energy and give *expression* to their experience, knowledge, wisdom, and skill. In LIVE we focus on two forms of expression. First, people who thrive have voice—the opportunity to share their ideas and contribute to making meaningful decisions. Second, people who thrive have the chance to create—they contribute to developing and producing something new, through either improvement or innovation. With voice and creativity, people experience the joy of expression; they thrive by making meaningful contributions to work they value.

VOICE

Voice involves both ideas and decisions. Voice in ideas means there are channels through which people can share their ideas and perspectives with colleagues about issues or problems or opportunities facing the organization.[24] Voice in ideas requires that people have confidence that their ideas will be heard and understood. Voice in decisions means that people have influence in the decision-making process.[25] Influence covers a range of activities from having the responsibility to make decisions, to offering in-depth analysis, to commenting on different options, to simply casting a vote, and much in between. Of course, the degree of voice in decisions varies along that spectrum, but if people are not involved in that process in some way, they have no voice in decisions.

Having voice—in ideas and in decisions—played an important role in Lucy's case. Before meeting Erin, Lucy had limited voice in ideas and in decisions. In her new sphere of responsibility she was given agency and autonomy to work on identifying problems and solutions. She was engaged with colleagues on ideas, and she both informed and made decisions. Lucy had voice in her sphere of responsibility.

But outside of her specific area of work, Lucy's voice was limited. Even though Lucy had relevant knowledge and experience, and even though her team leader recognized her potential to contribute more broadly, it did not happen. The organization simply was not focused on giving people voice of either kind. Voice came with position and thus was an aspect of positional power and authority. As a result, Lucy had little voice outside of her new team.

Contrast Lucy's experience with the leadership of Hubert Joly at Best Buy, with its ninety thousand people and hundreds of stores. Joly went to great lengths to give people in the organization more voice. The people on the front lines—the Blue Shirts—made decisions all the time about how to solve customer problems and get customers what would be best for them. Leaders of the stores increased the engagement of their people in how to make the stores work better, so frontline people had voice in ideas. That same pattern was observed all the way up to Joly and his colleagues who had organization-wide responsibilities.

Voice and the actions that facilitate it resonate in the new paradigm. People thrive because they have voice in ideas and decisions in their sphere of responsibility and influence. But they also have a sphere of concern which is much wider, encompassing the whole organization. In the Leading Through paradigm, ideas may come from anywhere, and people may share those ideas and may act on them. Thus, people have broad scope for voice in ideas and opportunity for influence in decisions outside their immediate sphere of responsibility.[26]

CREATIVITY

Human beings need to create to thrive. In the LIVE framework leaders do three things to help people think creatively and do creative things:

- They give people work that matches their talents and skills but stretches them just enough to grow, learn, and create productively.

- They inspire people with a vision of their potential to do that work, stretch that way, and accomplish important work that the people value.

- They give people voice for creative ideas and creative work.[27]

When Lucy was assigned to her new team, there was a good match between her knowledge and expertise and the requirements of the job. The new situation also challenged Lucy to stretch her talents, skills, and abilities to learn, grow, and create. In that context, Lucy began to flourish. She was productive, she had influence in solving existing problems, and she had real responsibility to identify new opportunities and generate creative ideas that moved the work forward.

As with love, inspiration, and vitality, setting the stage for expression through voice and creativity requires personal relationships and personal understanding of the people involved. Leaders who build those relationships see and know the people as human beings with talent, skill, potential, and challenges—as we've seen with Lucy's experience. If leaders don't know the people personally, they will struggle to inspire people, to help them grow, to do any of the work that helps people find expression in voice and creativity. Unfortunately, the evidence suggests that is too often the case. The result is that "creativity gets killed much more often than it gets supported."[28] But where leaders build personal relationships and do the work to support voice and creativity, truly amazing things happen.

In 2017 Hurricane Maria struck Puerto Rico with devastating winds and rain. Davian Altamiranda, the Best Buy district manager based in Florida, soon learned that the 300 Blue Shirts in Puerto Rico were in desperate straits. Many had lost their homes and most were without food or water. Altamiranda knew these people; they were not just names or numbers to him. He was inspired and motivated to think creatively about what he could do to help them. An idea came to him: charter a cargo plane and take supplies and money to his people. He acted quickly, called Amber Cales, regional VP, who supported him and found a way to charter the plane (she also had to be creative to pull that off!).

A few days later Altamiranda and his team arrived with emergency supplies and distributed $200 in cash to each of the 300 employees on the island. That was the first of fourteen trips the cargo plane made to bring supplies and to take people to the mainland for medical treatment or to be reassigned to other Best Buy stores if they chose to transfer. Best Buy continued to pay its employees for four weeks and gave each of them a $1,000 advance to keep them afloat. Best Buy reopened its store in San Juan three months after the storm, and all three stores on the island experienced 10–15 percent annual sales growth that year.[29]

Amber Cales summed up what happened in Puerto Rico and in Best Buy in general: "If you wear this Blue Shirt, we are going to help you and it doesn't matter how." That is the power of expression, people animated by love, inspiration, and vitality contributing ideas and creativity to make things better.

aLIVE: Aligning to LIVE

Love creates a context of connection and belonging, fertile soil for inspiration, vitality, and expression. Both love and inspiration are directly tied to emotional well-being, a critical element of vitality. And the personal energy—both physical and emotional—of vitality are essential for action-oriented expression through voice and creativity. But these outcomes are not foregone conclusions. To realize the synergy, people need to experience the elements of LIVE together. For example, when voice is pursued with the connection and belonging of love and the insights and meaningfulness of inspiration, the fruit—both for the individual and for the organization—will be more abundant than if voice is pursued in the absence of love and inspiration.

The four elements of LIVE create experiences that help people thrive. That is especially true when the experiences under the framework are aligned with one another in the Leading Through paradigm. Alignment occurs because leaders are intentional about helping themselves and their people experience love, inspiration, vitality, and expression in integrated ways. When that happens, LIVE becomes aLIVE. Under alignment, the four principles are not independent; they are synergistic. They reinforce one another, thus expanding people's growth and learning, the energy and spirit they feel, and the meaning they derive from work.

But alignment between the elements of LIVE is only half the story. The other half depends on what you do as a leader with your personal experience. Let's imagine that you experience love and inspiration, have the personal energy of vitality, and exercise voice and creativity. Instead of just enjoying those benefits for yourself, you take action to love others on your team, to inspire them, strengthen personal energy and vitality, and facilitate expression through voice and creativity. What happens?

You align yourself with your team and the people around you. You build others up, energize them, and help them find meaning in the work. They, in turn, will align with you, inspire you, increase your personal energy, and amplify your voice and creativity. There will be more power in the work, you will grow and accomplish important things together. You will experience the gratitude and joy that accompany meaningful work. This dynamic is a sort of paradox: The only way you can personally experience the full impact of LIVE in your own life and leadership is to strive to give love, inspiration, vitality, and expression to others. When you do—as we see in the example of Lucy and her team—you and your team will come aLIVE and thrive together.

Chapter Summary

- In Leading Through, leaders seek to help people thrive—lifting, strengthening, and meaningfully connecting with those they lead. This is the heart of leadership.

- *LIVE* is our framework for leaders to understand the needs of people and help them thrive:

LOVE is about creating connection and belonging.

INSPIRATION is about learning, growing, and becoming.

VITALITY is about personal energy and energizing others.

EXPRESSION is about voice and creativity.

- The four elements of LIVE create experiences that help people thrive, especially when they are well *aligned* with one another in the context of Leading Through; when this happens LIVE becomes aLIVE.

CHAPTER 5

The Mind of Leadership

The Multiple Myeloma Research Foundation (MMRF) is, in its own words, "the largest nonprofit in the world focused on accelerating a cure for each and every multiple myeloma patient."[1] Multiple myeloma (MM) is a cancer of blood plasma cells that build up in the bone marrow, crowding out healthy blood cells. The damage in the bone marrow may lead to anemia, bone damage, decreased ability to fight infection, and damage to the kidneys and other internal organs. It is a deadly disease.

MMRF has made significant progress in fighting MM and finding a cure for this very complex disease. As of 2023, MMRF had raised over $500 million for research, helped fifteen new drugs through clinical trials to FDA approval, created a tissue bank for research with samples from hundreds of patients, and built a longitudinal database of clinical data on patients at different stages of the disease and linked that data to specific genetic information about the disease in each patient. Overall, the work of the foundation has helped to increase life-expectancy for MM patients by a factor of three.

MMRF is a nonprofit, but it likes to think of itself as a biotech startup that can move quickly to raise money to capitalize on new opportunities and speed the development of new ideas into approved therapies. However, its roots are not in labs or hospitals. MMRF got its start when Kathy Giusti, an executive at G.D. Searle, a pharmaceutical company, was diagnosed with MM. Although her doctor told her the disease was stage I and therefore in the "inactive" category, the outlook was not good. All the available evidence suggested she had three to four years to live.

Giusti began reading about the disease and spoke with physicians who treated MM patients. She found that MM received relatively little research funding, few scientists were doing research on the disease, and there was little communication among the scientists who were. Giusti and her identical twin sister, Karen Andrews, decided to build MMRF to fund research and create communication networks to accelerate the development of new therapies.

Success in fundraising helped Giusti, as the foundation's CEO, to build a network of donors, as well as physicians and scientists involved with the disease. She recruited a board for the foundation from her network of classmates at Harvard Business School and leveraged their relationships to find new donors and new advisors.

The fact that Giusti was a patient with the disease played a significant role in her ability to raise money and engage people in the work. Many were inspired by her personal story and her vision of what MMRF could become and what it could do—help patients live longer and ultimately be cured. However, patients had very little information about research on the disease, and doctors and scientists had limited ways to communicate with patients. As a result, many promising medicines were never tested because the scientists developing them could not find enough patients to run a clinical trial.

With an eye toward addressing this issue, the foundation moved aggressively to build a patient database. Giusti and her team were in a position to find patients and help them understand what was happening and how they could help move things forward. The key was to build a database of MM patients that could be shared with researchers doing work on the disease. Moreover, the foundation recruited experts in the design of clinical trials so Giusti and her team could advise on protocols and trial management. The upshot was that MMRF not only funded research, but it became a valued link between patients and scientists, and in getting drugs into and through clinical trials much faster than before.

From its beginning in 1998 until today, MMRF has had a remarkable impact on treatment of the disease. A three-fold increase in life expectancy means that compared to the time of Giusti's diagnosis when only 20 percent of MM patients lived for five years or more, today about 60 percent of MM patients will survive for five years or more, and 30 percent will survive for ten years or more. That progress continues. By 2023, MMRF was raising more than $45 million annually for research, investing in a promising pipeline of new concepts and new drugs, making significant progress in accelerating clinical trials, and had become a trusted source of information and community for thousands of MM patients. And Kathy Giusti? She has survived MM and breast cancer and continues to pursue her dream of curing MM and other cancers.

The Leadership Process

The work that Kathy Giusti initiated with MMRF reflects the soul and heart of leadership; she has done the work of leadership with virtue and empathy. But that work also reflects the mind of leadership—careful thinking, analysis of opportunities, setting priorities and direction, making decisions, and solving problems. The story of MMRF illustrates that the soul, heart, and mind of leadership working together have real power.

At the very beginning of MMRF, there were people and organizations in the MM world with strong commitments to do what was right for patients. Once Giusti was diagnosed, she certainly became one of them. And yet, it wasn't until Giusti took initiative to address the problems impeding the work on MM—connecting with others, bringing the right people and perspectives together, planning, organizing, and focusing attention on things that mattered—that real progress was made in finding a cure.

Kathy Giusti's story is inspiring, and it is instructive. Her work with the mind of leadership (and its heart and soul) illustrates what we call the leadership process—the work that propels people, groups, and organizations toward a more desirable future.[2] In the Leading Through paradigm the leadership process is not a long checklist of detailed rules with fixed steps and specifications. Rather, it is a series of activities enabled and governed by leadership principles. Importantly, everyone in the organization can learn to use the leadership process because its activities create patterns of action, learning, and change that are repeatable and teachable.

The Giusti story illustrates the three phases of the leadership process:[3]

- *Initiate.* Giusti identified problems and opportunities, sought deeper understanding of the underlying issues, gained perspective and relationships with key stakeholders, and connected her effort with other relevant work.

- *Mobilize.* She enlisted the support of influential partners and mobilized a core team with a compelling direction and a plan to find a cure for MM.

- *Empower.* Finally, Giusti worked hard to ensure that the core team had the motivation and resources—including not only money, but also expertise—necessary to engage in the action, learning, and change necessary to make progress on the vision while maintaining focused attention on the work over long periods of time.

As we've noted in our prior discussion, the work of leadership in Leading Through positions teams at the center. The work of leadership happens, primarily, in and through teams. The leadership process and its phases frame that work in a way that can be taught and applied generally.[4] It is a process that can be practiced by leaders of all kinds, in all settings and in every part of an organization.

Consider, as another example, the case of a dermatologist at a major hospital. During a surgical procedure, the doctor received the wrong medication from the pharmacy and administered it to the patient. The effects were not serious, and the right medicine was obtained quickly. However, she knew that other patients in the hospital had suffered serious adverse effects from inaccurate delivery of the wrong medicine or the wrong dose. She decided to take action. She began by talking to key decision-makers in the pharmacy, then to the key people in the hospital—the CEO, the chief of medicine, and the VPs of safety and compliance. She sought to understand the problem better and to enlist support for an effort to create a zero-error medicine delivery system.

This physician-leader mobilized a team of six people, each of whom touched the medicine delivery process and had the right expertise. The team shared the same vision of success—a system that made zero errors. She helped the team get the resources they needed and the authority to act, experiment, and change the process. The team did great work. They developed a new medicine delivery process that yielded virtually zero errors consistently.

In the sections that follow, we examine the leadership process in more detail by focusing on the activities that are essential to each phase. We identify the principles and patterns that facilitate the work of leadership, no matter the setting or what position an aspiring leader holds or what a team's responsibilities are. These principles and patterns apply to the work of an ongoing operating team, for example, where the leadership process can be effective in mobilizing the daily work of the team and in determining when the team needs to pursue improvement and innovation. The same is true for a project team initiated to pursue a particular innovation like a new product or a new process technology or an effort to remake and renew an entire organization.

No matter what kind of team it may be, the work of leadership is done by all the members of the team using the leadership process. In every setting and circumstance, the leadership process provides a powerful frame for mobilizing the necessary action, learning, and change.

Initiate: Identify and Connect

In the first phase of the process, a leader takes initiative to *identify* and assess a potential opportunity or problem and *connect* the issue to the perspectives and priorities of the relevant stakeholders. Collaboration is essential to the Initiate phase. The leader must communicate and work with others to share ideas and develop a deeper understanding of the issue. When carried out effectively, leaders avoid unilateral directives, instead producing a collective vision and path forward that is embraced by key stakeholders. In doing so, the leader gets to know potential team members and partners who might be mobilized to support the effort.

Identify: Assess Problems and Opportunities

Identifying and assessing problems and opportunities hinges on understanding the nature of the issues. Some issues concern a need to make something we already have work better, while others reflect a demand for something different altogether. For organizations, this distinction reflects the difference between the need for the work of leadership to improve everyday operations and the need to initiate innovation. That distinction is often obscured by the erroneous assumption that everyday operations should be routine; an assumption that can lead to complacency and missed opportunities for innovation. For leaders, the only thing that is routine is the ongoing need for action, learning, and change.

In that context the difference between issues that are purely technical in nature and those that involve people—especially those that have significant moral and/or behavioral implications—is critical. Heifetz and Linsky have given us a useful example:

> When your car has problems, you go to a mechanic. Most of the time, the mechanic can fix the car. But if your car troubles stem from the way a family member drives, the problems are likely to recur.[5]

The work of the mechanic is technical. Changing the way a family member drives—say, a spouse or teenager who thinks the family SUV is a race car—is a human problem, requiring changes in attitudes and behavior. It also may have implications for family culture and the family's moral context. This distinction between technical and human change is important. Pursuing technical change is a very different thing than pursuing changes in human behavior, attitudes, and culture.

Almost all problems and opportunities require changes that are in part technical and in part human and organizational. Changes that are technical generally require expertise, technologies, and other resources that require very little change on the part of the people involved. Changes that are human are very different.

Although Giusti had met her need for fundraising with technical support, she confronted the need for human change when she realized MMRF needed to establish effective and robust communication channels between the researchers themselves and with patients. Increased funding of research would have limited impact unless doctors and scientists would share their early-stage findings with colleagues doing related work and their sponsoring institutions would support them.

Change that is human may involve adjustments to behavior, attitudes, values, routines, roles, and practices, as well as the policies they work within. It also may have important implications for the moral context in which they work.

This leads to our first principle for identifying problems and opportunities: *assume at the outset that the work to address every problem or opportunity is going to require change that has moral and human dimensions.* Some issues may turn out to be purely technical and require only a little expertise or application of existing technologies to bear fruit. But many seemingly technical issues also have important moral and human dimensions, requiring significant action, learning, and change on the part of the people involved. That is exactly what the dermatologist discovered in her hospital. She clearly needed the expertise of her core team members, but her work to make clear the moral imperative of an error-free medicine delivery system helped to motivate significant changes in the attitudes, priorities, and behavior of the people involved in the system.

Unfortunately, all too often, leaders assume that the issues are technical, requiring only technical solutions. This may not be surprising given the pervasive influence of the Power Over paradigm, which treats people as technical elements and resources to be managed. Doing so generally doesn't resolve—and may even exacerbate—the underlying issues. A good practice that puts our first principle to work is to use the leadership process to address every problem or opportunity no matter what it looks like at the outset. When leaders view things through the lens of the soul and heart of leadership, they are more likely to avoid the pitfall of missing the hidden moral and human implications of an issue that may seem "technical" on the surface. And, if an issue turns out to be primarily technical in nature, initiating a leadership process will help to make that clear.

Our second principle is designed to support the first: *make watching for potential problems and opportunities an everyday activity.* Unfortunately, where Power Over prevails, aspiring leaders may feel like they don't have time to lead, in part, because they are constantly fighting fires. In Leading Through, a focus on potential problems and opportunities doesn't only happen in response to a burning platform. It happens every day. Leadership permeates the entire organization and serves as a protective force, a sort of preventive mechanism, ensuring that the conditions for platform combustion never materialize!

A simple way for aspiring leaders, and their organizations, to introduce this kind of everyday thinking into their daily activities is to ponder two sets of questions regularly:

- What are we doing that we should stop doing—or change how we do it? Of those things, which are the most important? Which offer the greatest impact on people, purpose, and productivity?

- What are we not doing that we should start doing? Of those things, which are the most important? Which offer the greatest impact on people, purpose, and productivity?

In the Leading Through paradigm, everyone in the organization has the work of leadership to do in their sphere of responsibility and influence. Thus, asking these questions regularly is everyone's responsibility (more on this in chapter 7). In this way, thinking about and acting on opportunities for innovation, improvement, and renewal is a continuous, ongoing activity.

Connect: People and Context

Making connections is a fundamental aspect of the work of leadership. Leaders simply cannot initiate and sustain a leadership process effectively unless they connect the opportunity to other people and to its relevant context. Talking with and listening to stakeholders, peers, and potential team members and partners will help the leader find people who may provide resources, support, credibility, and direct involvement to the effort. Moreover, discussing the opportunity with them may surface potential issues, generate new insights, and pinpoint gaps in the aspiring leaders' understanding of the opportunity.

The key is that all of these people will examine the opportunity from different vantage points and thus offer different perspectives about strategic and operating issues and related work in the organization. It is these differences and the connections among them that define the context in which the potential effort will operate. If done effectively, those discussions *enable the leader to develop a more vivid vision of both the work ahead and the improved future that will result if the work is successful.*

This is an important outcome, but what should a leader do to carry out those discussions effectively? In answering that question, we have found it helpful to think of the context as a human system—a set of people that interact and work together to serve a purpose. A good example is the hospital where the dermatologist worked. That is the context in which the new medicine delivery system had to operate. Thinking about the context of problems and opportunities as a human system suggests three objectives for leaders to keep in mind as they begin to gather information and involve others in the work:[6]

- *Broaden perspective.* Start by seeking out key stakeholders—those with an interest or "stake" in the system—and talking to them about the issue. Deliberately include people from different vantage points. Seek those you suspect will have a different perspective and help you see the issue from different angles.

- *Understand relationships.* Differences in perspectives are important, but so are the relationships between the people who hold them. Pay attention to who knows who and give special attention to people who seem to be especially close, for both personal and professional

reasons. It is especially important to identify strong interactions between people who have significant interests in the issue.

- *Clarify priorities.* Clarify the people and relationships that are most
  important to the work and to the vision of the work. Insight into
  the context shines a light on what the work ahead needs to succeed
  and what it might accomplish. Clarifying priorities creates focus.

When this work is done effectively, leaders connect with people and
gain an understanding of the context by listening. They listen to understand. They listen to gain new perspectives, to identify key relationships
and priorities. That information not only paints a more vivid picture of
the opportunity, but it also enables the leader to take responsibility for
assessing how the potential work fits with the organization's underlying
aspirations, values, principles, and norms, including the moral context.

As intuitive as the value of involving others sounds, many leaders make
the mistake of trying to go it alone. Consider the example of M. Douglas
Ivester, the one-time CEO of Coca-Cola who was abruptly pushed out
in December of 1999 after only two years on the job. *Fortune* magazine
described the situation as follows:

> It was hard to believe that . . . a man almost obsessed with doing
> things in an orderly, rational way would leave behind such a
> mess. . . . But Ivester [tried] to go it alone. At one point Don
> Keough [former President of the company] sent him a six-page let-
> ter with constructive suggestions on how he could improve his sit-
> uation. What did Ivester do? He sent Keough a one-line response,
> thanking him for his input. Ivester was never one to show signs of
> weakness. . . . He described himself as a wolf—highly independent,
> nomadic, territorial. . . . He would be different or be damned. Or,
> as it turned out, both.[7]

Not going it alone has another important consequence for subsequent
work in the leadership process: because it engages the leader with other
people—perhaps many of them—it provides an effective way for the leader
to identify potential partners and possible team members, whose support

will be crucial to the work ahead. From this perspective, efforts to connect the opportunity to its context lay the groundwork for the Mobilize phase of the leadership process.

Mobilize: Team and Partner

Leaders get things moving in the Mobilize phase of the leadership process. With a target effort in focus, the leader pursues two related activities in parallel. In one, the leader *builds a team*, invites and persuades others to make commitments, and forges the relationships that are essential to effective teamwork. In the other, the leader *builds a network of partners*, with people and resources to support work on the opportunity. It is the leader and the team members supported by the network that will drive the work forward and bring it to fruition.

Team: Organize and Lead the Work

How do leaders build effective teams? We approach that question in the spirit of this quote from Richard Hackman, one of the world's leading authorities on teams:

> The leader's main task . . . is to get a team established on a good trajectory and then to make small adjustments along the way to help members succeed, not to try to continuously manage team behavior in real time. No leader can make a team perform well. But all leaders can create conditions that increase the likelihood that it will.[8]

Effective teams are established on a good trajectory. What makes a trajectory good? A starting point is reality and clarity. The trajectory needs to be real. It has to connect to the objectives of the team's work, the organization's strategy, and its values. And the direction must be clear. It cannot be uncertain or ambiguous and be good. But as Kathy Giusti's experience illustrates, reality and clarity are not enough.

Kathy Giusti worked with her core team to build an organization to raise money to support more needed research and create communication channels that did not exist. But Giusti and her team also had something that made the trajectory come alive; they had vision. She and her team saw the day when a new drug or set of drugs would come to market that would cure multiple myeloma.

A vivid vision of the impact the work will have on the organization, its people, its customers, its purpose, and the productivity of its resources is therefore essential to a good trajectory. A compelling vision is a crucial element in generating the meaning and inspiration—both soul and heart—that energize a leader's efforts to establish the team on a good trajectory, anchoring the team members' commitment to the work and to each other.

Our research on creating a compelling vision—one that results in shared understanding and commitment—underscores the importance of the language leaders use to communicate the vision. A statement of the vision should be a "rhetorical portrait" of what the organization or the team aspires to achieve in the future. Word portraits that are long and vague are deadly, while those that are brief, tangible, and vivid bring the vision to life and make it memorable. A compelling vision contains concrete, image-based language chosen to create an emotional connection between what team members value and the purposes of the team's work.[9]

A good trajectory, therefore, is crucial in establishing the core team—the set of people who will lead various aspects of the work. So is helping the team to see themselves as a team—interdependent contributors who must work together and coordinate their efforts to bring the vision to life. That effort begins with clarity around who is on the core team and who is not. This may seem like a trivial matter to some, but getting that boundary right is a matter of balancing the need for a team that is "core" (and develops the familiarity and shared perspectives necessary to work well together) and the need for the team to interact well with people outside the core, sharing ideas and seeking resources and work of value to the team. The case of the thirty-three Chilean miners trapped in the San Jose gold and copper mine illustrates that balance. As described by

Faaiza Rashid, Amy Edmondson, and Herman Leonard in their analysis of the case:

> The rescue leader, Andre Souggaret, established a multi-
> disciplinary core team of 32 people to lead the rescue efforts. Lots
> of people wanted to be involved, but Souggaret created a "restricted
> access" perimeter at the rescue site. That was the boundary: the core
> team worked inside the line; everyone else was outside. At the same
> time, he and his team sought ideas, expertise and other resources
> outside the team that might help them find and rescue the trapped
> miners. The results were miraculous.[10]

In addition to clarity around who is on the team, helping people come together as a team also involves clarity around how the team is going to work. *How* that is determined is just as important as the details. We can all imagine a leader who simply tells everyone how things are going to work. That is a team headed toward a Power Over paradigm experience.

In Leading Through, teams collectively define roles and responsibilities—how they will coordinate their efforts, counsel together, and make decisions. The team leader's role is to facilitate that effort, keeping attention focused on the vision without prescribing how the work will proceed. That means each team member has significant responsibility to help shape the work, along with sufficient freedom of action in carrying out their day-to-day role (more on this in chapter 7).[11] In this sharing of responsibility, the leader and the core team come to a shared understanding of both the why and how of the team, thinking and working like a real team, establishing themselves on a trajectory toward the action, learning, and change necessary to bring the vision to life.

Partner: Develop a Network of Support

Developing a network of partners takes place in parallel with the building of the core team. In fact, the boundary between the core team and network of partners may only become clear as the efforts we describe here bear fruit.

Having listened and learned in the Initiate phase, leaders know the key people and understand their perspectives and relationships. They have identified potential partners and their connection to the central players in the relevant networks. The central people may not be in hierarchical positions of authority but are, nonetheless, influential.[12]

This kind of network effect played an important role in the creation of the MMRF. Giusti paid close attention to who the key scientists and researchers were and how they were connected to one another and other potential partners. At the same time she relied on her existing network of friends and classmates at Harvard Business School to find donors who could really make a difference.

Effective leaders engage with these central, respected people about the effort, sharing the value and emerging vision of what the work could accomplish. And, of course, they seek their perspectives. Even if they are not target partners, persuading them of the value of the work may be important in persuading people who are.

In this part of the work of leadership it is essential that the potential work of the team has solid content—a body of work with potential value, a vision of what it could mean, and relevance to the strategy and aspirations of the organization. The content is crucial. But communication with both central individuals and target partners always comes with two parts—the content and the wrapper. Thus, persuasion involves more than excellent content. Effective leaders "wrap" the content in ways that draw attention, spark interest, develop understanding, and secure support.[13]

The wrapper is not about obscuring the real nature of the issue, but rather, revealing it in a way that is meaningful. It is about the relationship the leader has or wants to develop with a potential partner. It conveys the meaning of the effort, its connection to the organization's purpose and values, and its potential impact on strategic objectives. The wrapper reflects a communication strategy in which the leader seeks to align the work of the team with existing aspirations, and perhaps with existing ideas or initiatives that already have currency in the organization.

Wrapping the content of a potential effort this way has a dual purpose: (1) it aligns the work of the team with the moral context and preexisting aspirations, and (2) it connects the work to other activities, ensuring that it does not unnecessarily fragment people or resources.[14]

Perhaps most importantly, an effective wrapper helps to further establish the *credibility* of the leader. Credibility rests on perceptions of the trustworthiness, competence, and dynamism of the leader.[15] Dynamism is closely related to the purpose of the wrapper—to help leaders really connect with people and communicate the value of the opportunity with positive energy.[16]

Credibility and trust are rooted in the soul and heart of leadership. That is not just a matter of perception. Leaders who embrace the cycle of virtue and the LIVE framework truly become more trustworthy and competent. That kind of credibility is like gold in building relationships and developing support for a new initiative. Leaders build on that credibility to define the content, wrap it in meaningful communication, and mobilize the core team and the network of partners to make things better.

Empower: Engage and Focus

The work of leadership in the Empower phase of the leadership process is to keep the creative work of the core team and network of partners moving forward with energy and focus. In that work the value of the soul and heart of leadership cannot be overstated. Both the cycle of virtue and the LIVE framework find deep application as leaders seek to *engage and enable* the core team and its members and keep their *attention focused* on realizing the opportunity before them.

Engage: Enable Action, Learning, and Change

Two sets of activities are crucial for strong engagement. The first includes activities that involve the whole team. We have already noted the work the leader and the core team do in the Mobilize phase to establish direction and how they will work together. When that work is done with virtue and empathy, it prepares the team to act like a team and collectively engage in the work. For example, at the beginning of the Empower phase, the team needs to develop a plan for the work, including a set of objectives, the anticipated resources it will need, and important checkpoints and milestones along the way. The plan is a living, dynamic guide for the team. It should be reviewed often and updated and adapted as needed. Effectively engaging the team in this kind of collective work is essential to the success of the work, and it strengthens the team.

The second set of activities focuses on the individuals on the core team. The very same principles used to build an effective team also apply at the individual level. In Leading Through, a core team is a microcosm of the organization, and each individual is a microcosm of the core team. The individuals on the team are leaders of significant elements of the work, and they need sufficient autonomy and freedom of action to design their work, set boundaries, and work with others to clarify tasks and responsibilities. They need love, inspiration, vitality, and expression. They need to see clearly that their work is linked to the vision of the effort. Giving them real responsibility for significant work that draws on their talents and skills does that; it confirms that they are valued, trusted, and accountable.[17]

These two kinds of activities occur all throughout a team's work together. Ensuring a supportive context for these activities is crucial for strong engagement of the team and its members. It also acts to protect the leader and the team from slipping into the control mode of the Power Over paradigm. Three strategies for leaders are essential to the work of engagement:

- *Focus primarily on ends rather than means.* Leaders need to understand the details of the work, but inserting themselves into every emerging issue to determine what to do is a serious mistake. It renders words about freedom of action and autonomy hollow, turns people off, and saps their energy. It creates disengagement and wastes human potential.[18] Focusing on ends helps leaders resist the urge to micromanage.

- *Make the team's learning and growth a personal objective.* Leaders help people on the team learn and grow by making that objective a personal commitment: (1) *create a culture of candor*—open and honest communication, coupled with psychological safety; (2) share ideas and perspectives and *engage in robust discussions* that are not dismissive; and (3) receive *ongoing, timely, and useful feedback* about progress in the work. The goal in aiming for this kind of team environment is to drive out fear and other elements that generate darkness and not light.[19]

- *Support making LIVE a reality for the team.* Teams need leaders willing to ensure that their members have love, inspiration, vitality, and expression. This involves ensuring that team members have the resources and organizational light they need to accomplish the work. This is a selfless work focused on doing what is right for both the people and the work—making LIVE a reality, letting go of selfish power (more on this in chapter 9), living and encouraging the cycle of virtue in the team, and driving out the darkness that drains the team of its energy. It also requires ongoing introspection. Leaders need to ask, What can I do better to support our team?

These strategies are critical to engaging the team in the work throughout the leadership process.

Focus: Maintain Disciplined Attention

Engagement activates energy in the core team that needs ongoing focus. The need for focus is inherent in work to innovate and improve where discovery of new things is the source of value. But those new things may distract scarce attention and resources from the main opportunity. We consider just two potential distractions—new problems and opportunities, and conflict—and discuss how a Leading Through approach helps leaders address distractions and keep attention focused on the needed action, learning, and change at the heart of the leadership process.

NEW PROBLEMS AND OPPORTUNITIES

When new problems and opportunities arise in the work, they create potential distractions by generating additional tasks that compete with the work already underway. When a significant new opportunity surfaces, it seems almost natural for core teams to simply layer new objectives and tasks on top of existing commitments. But that ignores important leadership work that needs to be done to avoid overload, distraction, lost productivity, delays, and poor quality. *The most important tool a team can use to help maintain disciplined attention is the leadership process itself.*

This is where the leadership of the core team members has real power. The team benefits when all team members have been taught and learned to practice the principles of the leadership process. Depending on the nature of the new opportunity, and where it falls in the responsibilities of the core team members, it may necessitate a reassessment of priorities. Is the new opportunity central? Does it mean we ought to realign priorities, refocusing time and energy? The effort to consider (or reconsider) priorities and workload is critical to staying focused. As Heifetz and Laurie have argued, "Too often, senior managers convey that everything is important. They start new initiatives without stopping other activities, or they start too many initiatives at the same time. They overwhelm and disorient the very people who need to take responsibility for the work."[20]

Kathy Giusti and her team faced this very issue when she discovered the potential power of her connections to multiple myeloma patients. She did not stop fundraising, nor did she stop trying to build new channels of communication. She did, however, adjust priorities and reallocate time, energy, and attention to the work of creating a patient database for clinical trials.

The power of the leadership process in addressing new opportunities also highlights the critical role of establishing the team in the Mobilize phase. That work is like a trial run for maintaining energy and focus. In the first place, team members discuss and determine how they are going to work together. In that process it is natural to consider how they are going to handle unexpected problems and opportunities, and the leader can teach the importance of using the leadership process to maintain focus. Second, in establishing direction in the Mobilize phase, the team and its leader will engage in precisely the kind of collaborative discussions and decision-making required to handle new opportunities that may develop.

CONFLICT

The leadership process, in general, and effectively establishing the team in the Mobilize phase also play a crucial role in dealing with conflict. Conflict—disagreements between members of the team—may have many sources. It may come from differences over a course of action or personal style or priorities or perceived neglect of duty or many, many other things. The core team members are human beings with emotions, passions, and opinions. They are on the team to lead a significant part of the work and may have strongly held views about what should be done.

No matter the sources of the conflict, the team and its leader can set the stage for productive conflict by embracing three principles that are taught, practiced, and ingrained in the establishment of the team:

- Conflict is an opportunity to learn, grow, create value, and move the work forward.

- Before we address a conflict, we always remember and affirm the common ground on which we stand. Our common values, vision, purpose, and commitments to one another are the basis for our unity as a team.[21]

- All members of the team wear two hats: (1) they lead their part of the work, and (2) they are a member of the core team. When they meet, they are not a representative of their special interest. They *are* the core team and seek to make decisions and take actions that are best for the overall effort.

Conflicts may be "resolved" in many different ways. Some of the most common, however—competition, infighting, power struggles, ignoring or avoiding the conflict, giving in, agreeing to disagree—do not lead to valuable learning and growth.[22] That only happens if the team members who disagree stand together on common ground and feel a sense of freedom and responsibility to resolve the issue themselves by digging deeper into the underlying issues. Because the team's learning and growth have become personal, team members with differences express their views to each other with candor and energy but engage in an integrative process in search of increased value. They do not see the conflict as a "fixed pie" situation, but rather, as an opportunity to create a bigger and better pie.[23] Such collaboration is the way to learning that opens up new ideas and better ways of working, creates value, and moves the work forward.[24] However, if they fail to resolve the conflict productively, they take it to the whole team.

Team members are human beings. Despite common ground and the best efforts of everyone, the intensity of feelings may become counterproductive. This is where a leader may need to be more deeply involved with the individuals whose feelings have gotten in the way of productive collaboration.[25] A leader who knows the people well, who loves them, who knows their hopes and dreams, is in a much better place to take direct action to reduce the stress and anxiety that sometimes come in resolving difficult conflicts. It may be hard, but it is important and valuable work. If it is done with the soul and heart of leadership, it not only moves the work forward, but it helps the people involved to learn, change, and grow in ways that put the team and its work in a better place.

The Mind of Leadership

The mind of leadership is the last of the three metaphors that we have used to characterize leadership in the new paradigm. The leadership process provides the framework in which the mind of leadership finds powerful application. In concert with the soul and heart, the mind of leadership becomes a powerful driver of the work of leadership. But its connection to the soul and heart cannot be overemphasized. Indeed, the soul and heart provide the context and tools that keep the mind of leadership from devolving into Power Over. Thus, the Leading Through paradigm depends on leaders learning to practice the soul, heart, and mind of leadership in concert together.

Our focus thus far has been on individual leaders, the people they lead, and core teams. All through our discussion we have highlighted the importance of and the need for a supportive context in which the soul, heart, and mind of leadership can flourish. We have argued, for example, that everyone has the work of leadership to do in their sphere of responsibility and influence. It is crucial, therefore, that the organization provide education, training, and personal development in leadership—soul, heart and mind—so that everyone who aspires to lead knows the principles and the process and has the opportunity to learn how to use them.

Organizational commitments and capabilities are a critical part of the Leading Through paradigm. In part three of the book, we turn our attention to the organization and its critical role in activating the power that is in the soul, heart, and mind of leadership.

Chapter Summary

- In Leading Through, the work of leadership is done primarily in and through teams in a repeatable process that can be understood, taught, and broadly applied. This is the leadership process—the mind of leadership.

- The leadership process has three phases—*Initiate*, *Mobilize*, and *Empower*:

  - Initiate: *Identify* problems and opportunities and *connect* them to the right people and context.

  - Mobilize: Build the *team* to organize and lead the work and *partner* to develop a network of support.

  - Empower: *Engage* to enable action, learning, and change and *focus* to maintain disciplined attention.

  - Realizing the promise of Leading Through requires that the mind of leadership be pursued in concert with the soul and heart.

PART THREE

LEADING THROUGH THE ORGANIZATION

*Activating Leadership through
the Power of Modularity*

CHAPTER 6

The Modular Leadership System

The Cleveland Clinic is one of the most highly respected hospital systems in the world. In 2023, the clinic operated 22 hospitals, with 76,711 caregivers, 3.4 million patients, $13 billion in operating revenue, and $400 million in research funding.[1] Throughout its history the clinic has focused on research-based innovation, improved clinical outcomes, and measurable quality. That focus has produced remarkable results. The Cleveland Clinic has been consistently ranked as one of the top five hospitals in the United States and in 2022 was ranked number two in the world.[2] It has outstanding clinical outcomes.[3] In cardiovascular surgery, for example, the clinic is ranked number one in the country and has achieved the best outcomes in the history of medicine.

But innovation and clinical outcomes only explain part of the clinic's growth and success. The other part has been a broad-based initiative to make empathy a defining characteristic of a patient's total experience at the clinic. The empathy initiative has led to significant change in every aspect of the clinic's work. That journey began in 2006 in a classroom at Harvard Business School when Toby Cosgrove, a nationally renowned heart surgeon and CEO of the clinic, attended a discussion of a case about the clinic.[4]

During the discussion, a student told Cosgrove of her father's decision to have heart surgery at the Mayo Clinic instead of Cleveland because the Mayo doctors had more empathy for patients. She then asked, "Dr. Cosgrove, what are you doing to teach your doctors empathy?" In his own words, Cosgrove was floored by her question. The idea that someone would choose a hospital based on empathy was jarring, all the more so when he learned the student's father was a cardiologist. Cosgrove wondered how anyone, given the choice, especially a physician, would not choose the hospital with the best outcomes. And yet, on reflection, he realized that in his own experiences as a heart surgeon, his focus had been on technique and procedure and the body system, but not on the patient as a whole person.

Like his predecessors, as CEO, Cosgrove had maintained a strong emphasis on excellence in clinical outcomes and innovative discovery. But he also had made it a point to focus employee attention on what the clinic called "Patient First care" and emphasized how improved quality and outcomes could result from thinking of the patient first.[5] However, that discussion and subsequent reflection convinced Cosgrove that success for the patient was about more than outcomes and more than thinking of the patient first; it was a matter of the total experience.[6] Just a few weeks after the classroom discussion, Cosgrove explained his new perspective in a letter to all the people of the clinic:

> Here at Cleveland Clinic, we've always positioned quality in terms of outcomes. But I have come to understand that there is more to quality healthcare than great outcomes. . . . The patient experience encompasses many aspects of care, from the physical environment to the emotional. . . . Sometimes we forget that patients feel cold in the operating room and could use a warm blanket. Or we forget that they might be hungry at a time when no food is being served. We can no longer do that. . . . Everything we do must communicate competence, compassion and caring. . . . In the end, patients who come to Cleveland Clinic will judge us on the experience they have. Whether it is a confident and healing experience is up to us.[7]

While the clinic had achieved technical excellence, technical excellence was not nearly enough if the Cleveland Clinic was to achieve its goals and truly put the patient first, not just as a way to better clinical outcomes, but as a way to a better overall experience for the patient.[8]

As jarring as the idea of empathy had been at first, Cosgrove embarked on a journey to make empathy a defining characteristic of the Cleveland Clinic and the experience of all its patients. Cosgrove and his colleagues set out to enable leadership along these lines across the organization in the spirit of the Leading Through paradigm. The patient experience needed to change so fundamentally that the empathy initiative would need to touch everything and engage everyone in the quest for improvement and innovation.

The Power of a Modular Organizing Framework in the Leading Through Paradigm

The Power Over paradigm is the antithesis of what Cosgrove and the Cleveland Clinic envisioned for their people and patients: a place where people take initiative to "imagine what another person is going through, work to alleviate suffering, and create joy whenever possible."[9] Indeed, the Power Over paradigm's moral shortcomings (it depersonalizes and damages people), waste of human potential (it ignores and wastes talent and creative energy), and stifling of innovation (it constrains ideas and initiative) can create an environment in which empathy is anathema to the established order. What Cosgrove discovered was a need to change the *soul*, *heart*, and *mind* of the organization, including its moral, interpersonal, and operational context. The clinic needed to reframe and remake how everyone experienced the organization so that empathy prevailed, propelling people all throughout the organization to "alleviate suffering and create joy whenever possible."

Power Over, with its focus on control through compliance, may be able to get certain types of work done—and many people accept and acquiesce to such systems—but the truth is that living and working in such a world can drain the meaning and purpose (and empathy) out of work and block personal learning and growth.[10] Compared to what is possible in Leading Through, the people and the organization are less capable and effective under the Power Over paradigm. Further, personal agency, or the freedom to choose and initiate action, is fundamental to creativity and innovation and, thus, to human thriving.[11] It follows that a greater degree of autonomy experienced at work will naturally result in more energized, engaged people and a more effective organization.

Such freedom is critical to activating the soul, heart, and mind of leadership. Yet many organizations find this kind of freedom elusive. Part of the issue may be that although freedom is critical to initiative, innovation, and progress, so too is structure. Without some degree of structure—an organizing framework—initiative could spiral out of control. As Ranjay Gulati has observed, the problem might be that most executives assume that the tension between "frameworks" (i.e., unity) and freedom represents a zero-sum competition: "The freedom of the outside world is banging at the corporate door, demanding to come inside. Yet most leaders are still afraid to open it because they continue to view freedom and frameworks as antagonists in an intense tug-of-war. And since a tug-of-war can have only one winner, they pour their resources into regulating employee behavior."[12]

From this perspective, what the Cleveland Clinic—and any other organization interested in helping their people thrive—needs is an organizing framework that allows the organization to drop the ropes, end the tug of war, and generate both freedom and unity. Increasing freedom is central to overcoming the moral shortcomings of the Power Over paradigm, stemming the waste of so much human potential and unleashing leadership and innovation; but there must also be integration that leads to unity. How does an organization get both freedom and unity? We believe the answer is found in the principle of modularity, a powerful approach to organizing in the new paradigm.[13]

A Modular Leadership System

The principle of modularity allows a system to be organized into components ("modules") that work well as a united whole but can be designed, developed, and improved independently. Modular systems are all around us. Consider, for example, smart phones, tablets, and computers. The modern processors that power digital devices have over 10 billion transistors. The only way the processor can be designed is to make it highly modular, with different design groups working independently on modules while relying on clearly specified interfaces to guide how the modules need to connect.

Once the designs are complete, modularity ensures that the devices will work well, but only if the modules have been produced according to the relevant interfaces. The software that runs the devices and provides different functions and applications is also modular. Not only is the operating system composed of modules, but a large fraction of the applications (or apps) arc designed and produced by completely different people, groups, or organizations. They function smoothly in the system because they and the system are modular.[14]

We also see modularity at work in clothing, in automobiles, and many other complex technological, biological, and human systems.[15] In all of these applications, modularity is valuable because it makes possible freedom of action—ingenuity, initiative, and innovation—within the groups working on modules, while clear specifications for modular integration ensure a cohesive unified whole across modules.[16] Thus, modularity is a principle of both *freedom* and *unity*.

The benefits of modularity in Leading Through depend on three aspects of the system design that can be applied to any organization. We've already presented them in our description of the factors that are most important in shaping the influence of Power Over in organizations (chapter 1) and how they compare, in contrast, in Leading Through (chapter 2). As we will see, when these aspects of the organization are carefully designed to touch everyone and everything the organization does, they form the backbone of what we call a "modular leadership system":[17]

- A modular framework for action

- Visible information

- The role of power

A Modular Framework for Action

In table 6-1 we replicate the comparison of the Power Over and the Leading Through paradigms first presented in chapters 1 and 2. Looking first at the framework for action, the contrast between the two paradigms is sharp. While the emphasis in Power Over is on *control through compliance* that is achieved by limiting personal agency, the governing design principle of Leading Through is *innovation through commitment and initiative* that is achieved by empowering and preserving agency. These overarching principles shape attitudes, practices, and the organization, and in Leading Through they evoke all three dimensions of leadership—soul (virtue), heart (empathy), and mind (initiative). The role of commitment—a key outcome of the soul and heart of leadership—in Leading Through is crucial. In Leading Through, we are not simply interested in initiative. We are interested in initiative that generates light (and drives out darkness), valuing and engaging people, helping them to thrive.

Generating that kind of initiative depends crucially on choices about the structure and use of authority in the organization. Modularity and the freedom that comes with it require, (1) making teams the fundamental unit of the organization, and the object of its supporting structures, (2) decentralizing decision-making and other resources to these teams, (3) relying on principles and guidelines rather than rigid rules and extensive operating procedures (i.e., coercive bureaucracy) to guide behavior, and (4) a system of accountability that supports this structure, pushing responsibility for improvement and innovation to the front lines of the organization.

In the modular structure of Leading Through, many teams will have responsibility for both ongoing operations and for periodic innovation. For example, a team responsible for a beauty product department in a department store will need to solve problems in its daily work with customers while also looking for opportunities to improve and innovate its offerings and processes. Both responsibilities require the work of leadership and benefit from the freedom to take initiative that a modular framework for action provides. Some of the resulting initiatives may require ad hoc project teams unencumbered by daily operations, but the model remains

TABLE 6-1

A comparison of the Power Over and the Leading Through paradigms

DIMENSIONS OF THE ORGANIZATION		The Power Over paradigm	The Leading Through paradigm
FRAMEWORK FOR ACTION	**Governing design principle**	Control through *compliance*	Innovation through commitment and *initiative*
	Personal agency	Autonomy is a source of variability that needs to be *carefully managed*	Autonomy is a source of engagement and ingenuity that needs to be *empowered and preserved*
	Structure	*Direct supervision* and standardization through a tall, bureaucratic, coercive hierarchy	*Teams (modules)* supported by a flat, enabling hierarchy
		Centralized decision-making along hierarchical lines	*Decentralized decision-making* pushed to teams on front lines
		Action governed by *rules* and rigid operating procedures	Action governed by *principles* and clear guidelines
	Responsibility for improvement	*Those in authority* or centralized technical staff groups assess and revise standards and procedures and pursue improvements	*Everyone* is expected to initiate work on observed problems or opportunities
APPROACH TO INTEGRATION		Achieved through *executive action and hierarchical supervision*	Achieved through *visible information*, including leadership objectives, standards, strategy, and context
POWER DYNAMICS		*Power Over*: power is expressed primarily as a means of coercing and controlling individuals and groups	*Power Through*: power is expressed primarily as a means of unleashing the potential energy of individuals and groups

the same: teams of interdependent people taking initiative and relying on the leadership process to address specific problems and opportunities in a modular fashion. Compared to the centralized, hierarchical system of the Power Over paradigm, many more people have the work of leadership to do in a modular leadership system.

Remarkably, the Leading Through framework for action is highly effective in both stable and dynamic situations. Here is an example. In Google's early years great emphasis was placed on what the founders called "moon shots"—bold, innovative initiatives to create new businesses or enter completely new markets using new technologies. After some years of great moon shot successes (and lesser-known failures), Luiz Barroso, one of Google's creative leaders realized there were opportunities in their existing businesses to improve quality and operations. Error rates in search could be improved, search could be faster, advertising notices to customers could be more relevant, and so forth.[18]

In response, Barroso advocated what he called "roof shots." Instead of trying to create a whole new business by shooting for the moon, these roof shot teams would seek significant improvement in an existing business and with existing technologies. For example, if error rates were running at 2 percent, a project might seek to achieve error rates of 1 percent. Google found that these improvements of one- to two-times baseline required lots of initiative and creativity, and lots of hard work. But sustained effort to create a cascade of these improvements over time yielded gains of an order of magnitude! It turned out that the very same values and principles and structure of leadership that supported moon shots were essential for roof shots too.

The point is that the framework for action with its mindset focused on initiative and personal agency, and a structure that supports teams through clear guidelines and broad responsibility for improvement, works well no matter the context or environment. This means that where dynamic and stable situations exist within the same organization, it is imperative that the very same mindset and principles prevail throughout the whole organization. That is why the fundamental unit of the organization in the new paradigm is the team—the right mix of people with the right resources using the leadership process to solve problems or pursue opportunities. In the new paradigm, teams are the modules.

We discuss these dynamics and the elements of the modular framework for action in more detail in chapter 7.

Visible Information

Table 6-1 also makes clear that in Leading Through, integration and unity depend on visible information (rather than executive action and hierarchical supervision). The framework for action pushes freedom of action out to individuals and teams and distributes authority and responsibility broadly throughout the system. It provides teams with clear guidelines and principles; they know the principles that guide how their work should be done, and they know what role the team is supposed to play in the system. But they need more specific information if their work is to be well integrated with other teams and other work in the organization. Without a mechanism for integration, all that freedom of action could become chaotic.

The answer is *visible information*. By making key information visible, teams can test how well they provide value in the system and ensure effective connection with other teams.[19] In the modular leadership system a team needs at least four kinds of information:

- *Objectives.* What the organization aims to accomplish with respect to people, purpose, and productivity (the leadership objectives) and the vision that brings them to life (the future it is trying to create).

- *Standards.* The organization's values (beliefs) and leadership principles (how it intends to operate).

- *Strategy.* This includes both strategic intent (where and how it will pursue its purpose) and strategic capabilities (the resource-based building blocks of competitive advantage).

- *Context.* The who (key people, knowledge, and expertise), what (resources, teams, and projects), where (the location of people, resources, and information), and how (key processes and principles to guide communication and the exchange of resources and information) of the organization.

This brings us to a crucial point: in many ways, making this information visible is also an effort to make the moral context of the organization visible. This is most clearly seen in standards, but the moral context should shine brightly in objectives, strategy, and context too. In this way, visible information is an important tool in the efforts of the organization to increase light and drive out darkness.

Making this information visible helps people to see things—including the moral and human elements of the organization—more clearly and provides the guidance and standards against which a team must gauge its work. Working within those boundaries, a team can solve problems and pursue opportunities with both freedom and unity.[20] It is precisely this kind of information that truly enables the promise of the modular leadership system: the soul, heart, and mind of leadership permeate the entire organization.

We know this is a prospect many executives and employees crave: the work of leadership done by people on the front lines, in departments, among senior leaders, in staff groups, everywhere. As shown in table 6-1, the Leading Through framework for action establishes the principle that everyone has the work of leadership to do. Visible information (including the visibility of the framework for action) makes that work possible.

Defining and specifying the four types of information are critical first steps in making information visible. At a minimum, visibility means the information cannot be hidden, obscure, or difficult to see. It must flow freely in the organization and be totally transparent and easily accessible. However, there is more to visibility than that. Visibility is determined by four aspects of communication and learning by leaders and their teams. As we outline in more detail in chapter 8, to be visible, information must be *known*, *understood*, *valued*, and *used*.

The Role of Power: Power Through, Not Power Over

Each of the elements we outline in table 6-1 play a critical role in the Leading Through paradigm and in the design of a modular leadership system that brings it to life and makes it a reality in organizations. They support teams and their leaders in the work of leadership all throughout the organization. But the role of power is especially critical. The work of leadership is energized and animated by power. Power is essential to leadership, but as we've seen, power can be expressed in very different ways. In the modular leadership system power is expressed primarily as a means of enabling and activating the potential energy in people and teams. The key concept, therefore, is *power through*, a concept central to the Leading Through paradigm. Power through recognizes that there is great potential in everyone, and the modular leadership system aims to harness the power of that potential wherever it can be found in the organization. It stands in contrast to the concept of *power over* that gives the Power Over paradigm its name.

Making power through a reality requires teams and their leaders to deliberately address how power is used with constant vigilance, and focused attention. Without that vigilance and attention, the darkness of Power Over can seep into an organization quite easily. With it, all the energy and vitality of Leading Through can invigorate the entire organization. Furthermore, making the framework for action and visible information in the modular leadership system stick requires this fundamental shift in how we think about power and power dynamics in organizations. We discuss these concepts and ideas in greater detail in chapter 9.

The Cleveland Clinic: A Modular Leadership System in Action

As the Cleveland Clinic embarked on its empathy initiative in 2007, it became clear that one of the big issues was the lack of timely and effective communication with patients. Patients were frustrated by delays in care with no explanations, with gaps in timely follow-up, with confusion about what was supposed to happen when, and with specialists appearing at the bedside without any understanding of the patient's concerns.

The clinic attacked those problems with a major redesign of the hospital around patient needs rather than physician expertise. Rather than organizing by clinical disciplines (e.g., surgery vs. medicine), the clinic was reorganized into patient-centered institutes. Each institute combined medical and surgical care for a specific disease or body system.[21] The idea was to put all the expertise needed to care for a patient across the full cycle of care for a specific condition in the same unit. This allowed the clinic to apply the principles of modularity using multidisciplinary teams. For example, patients receiving care at the George M. and Linda H. Kaufman Center for Heart Failure Treatment and Recovery (a component of the clinic's Heart, Vascular & Thoracic Institute) received care from teams that included experts in cardiology, cardiac surgery, infectious diseases, immunology, pathology, pharmacy, nutrition, bioethics, and social work.[22]

In traditional healthcare organizations, each of these areas is typically organized separately in functional silos where most physicians and/or physician groups operate very independently. This causes two problems:

- Specialists who need to work closely together do not work together as a team. Physicians from different specialties may not even be in the same location or organization.

- The necessary visible information is hard to find, let alone to see. It is not known, understood, valued, or used by the people who need it most.

The Cleveland Clinic sought to solve these problems by creating (1) a modular framework for action that put specialists together in the same unit, often practicing in the same location, sometimes even caring for patients together at the same time in the same room; (2) a physical and organizational context—with visible information—in which smooth co-ordination and integration could be achieved, including across institutes; and (3) a shift in the role of power to activate and enable these changes (decision-making authority and access and control of resources were all decentralized to institutes, centers, and the care teams within them).

The pursuit of greater empathy in patient care thus led to a radical new framework for action that addressed all four of the key sources of visible information and recast the role that power would play in caring for patients:

1. *Objectives.* The organization shifted the focus of its objectives from an exclusive productivity orientation (with special emphasis on the technical excellence and quality of care) to a set of objectives

that were also people- and purpose-oriented, with special emphasis on the primary importance of patient needs. Productivity and quality were not forgotten. Rather, productivity concerns became embedded in a larger purpose-oriented framework focused on people. These renewed objectives were eventually codified in the organization's "care priorities":[23]

- *Patients.* Care for the patient as if they are your own family.

- *Caregivers.* Treat fellow caregivers as if they were your own family.

- *Community.* We are committed to the communities we serve.

- *Organization.* Treat the organization as your home.

This framework was brought to life by an overarching vision:

- *Vision.* "Our vision for Cleveland Clinic is to be the best place for care anywhere and the best place to work in healthcare." (Note the importance given to both patients *and* employees.)

2. *Standards.* Inspired by its newfound objectives, the clinic sought to establish a set of specific values to direct attention and behavior toward people. These values (and clarifying principles) were:

- *Values and principles.*

    · *Quality and safety.* We ensure the highest standards and excellent outcomes through effective interactions, decision-making, and actions.

    · *Empathy.* We imagine what another person is going through, work to alleviate suffering, and create joy whenever possible.

    · *Inclusion.* We intentionally create an environment of compassionate belonging where all are valued and respected.

    · *Integrity.* We adhere to high moral principles and professional standards by a commitment to honesty, confidentiality, trust, respect, and transparency.

- *Teamwork.* We work together to ensure the best possible care, safety, and well-being of our patients and fellow caregivers.

- *Innovation.* We drive small and large changes to transform healthcare everywhere.

  – The organization vividly communicated these standards in a variety of ways, including through an internal video that went viral on YouTube ("Empathy: The Human Connection to Patient Care").[24]

3. *Strategy.* Far from being forgotten slogans on a wall or website, the organization's new objectives and standards became the aspirations guiding its strategy, including both strategic intent (where and how the organization will create value) and strategic capabilities (including the allocation of resources aimed at generating new capabilities that create value).[25] The clinic redefined its strategy to be more deliberately patient-centered, very clearly establishing that it planned to create value for patients by delivering care in a more collaborative way, with empathy as its guiding star. These intentions became the focus of resource allocation processes aimed at new capabilities, including investments in new people (for example, Cosgrove hired Dr. James Merlino as chief experience officer), new structures (for example, the institutes), and new projects (for example, the clinic launched an effort to orient, educate, and train every single one of the its employees on the empathy initiative and how to practice empathy and invited them to "take ownership" of the patient experience and its improvement).[26]

4. *Context.* Through its efforts to orient, train, and educate every one of its employees, information about context not only became well known, but people learned to value it and use it. Contextual information was essential, since the institutes, the care priorities, the new vision, and standards all created new ways of working in the clinic. All caregivers needed critical information about human connections, with guidance and direction for how the people

in the system should come together (e.g., through empathy, inclusion, integrity, and teamwork), including when communication and coordination were necessary across institutes.

The clinic's efforts make clear that the organization intended its newfound objectives, standards, strategy, and context to be vividly known, understood, valued, and used all throughout the organization. Our research suggests that when critical information is truly visible, it dramatically improves coordination.[27] That is because visible information facilitates a shared understanding of both what the organization is trying to accomplish and how it aims to accomplish it. It provides crucial interfaces and criteria for testing how work done all throughout the organization fits with the larger whole.

These efforts have had a significant influence on the patient experience and the satisfaction of employees at the Cleveland Clinic. In surveys of patients from 2007 through 2019 the percentage of patients who described themselves as "extremely happy with their experience"—this was the top box score—climbed from 60 percent to over 80 percent. The measured satisfaction of patients with their experience with nurses increased five times more than the national average, while experience with doctors increased eleven times the national average. Over this same period employee satisfaction increased from a top box score of 55 percent to 92 percent. At the same time, the clinic continued its record of medical innovation and outstanding patient medical outcomes. It is perhaps not surprising that the clinic also grew substantially during this period, generating record revenues.[28]

The Cleveland Clinic's empathy initiative and the changes it generated provide an excellent example of the power of a modular leadership system in the Leading Through paradigm. With teams working in a supportive structure all over the hospital system, with power given to those teams to take initiative, and with visible information that was known, understood, valued, and used, the Cleveland Clinic experienced the dynamic impact of increased innovation in all aspects of the patient experience.[29] In the next three chapters we delve into the modular leadership system in more detail, including additional examples of its power in practice.

Chapter Summary

- Activating the soul, heart, and mind of leadership requires a context characterized by both freedom and unity. Such freedom and unity can be achieved by implementing organizational systems grounded in the principles of modularity.

- A modular leadership system is established through careful attention to three aspects of system design:

  - A *framework for action* that prioritizes initiative and personal agency and positions teams as the fundamental unit of the organization.

  - Approaching integration through *visible information*, ensuring that the information necessary to unify the work of the organization is effectively known, understood, valued, and used by everyone.

  - *Power dynamics* built on the idea that there is great potential in everyone, and the goal of the system is to activate that potential power wherever it can be found.

CHAPTER 7

A Framework for (Freedom of) Action

The Morning Star Company is the largest tomato processor in the world.[1] With about 40 percent of the US market, Morning Star had estimated revenues in 2023 of $1.2 billion to $1.4 billion, and employed about three thousand people during its peak harvesting season. Located in the San Joaquin valley in California, the company is involved in greenhouse operations, as well as transplanting, growing, and harvesting tomatoes. It transports tomatoes to its processing plants, where most of the tomatoes are used to make tomato paste; the plants also produce diced tomatoes. The tomatoes are processed and packed into a variety of different packs and containers and shipped to large consumer products companies and supermarkets.[2]

Morning Star got its start in 1970 when Chris Rufer, a student at UCLA, started the Morning Star Trucking Company to haul tomatoes from the fields to the processing plants. Over time as Rufer gained experience and built the company he came to believe strongly that people needed freedom of action and autonomy to exercise leadership and to find meaning in their work. That required people to do what we have called the work of leadership—socialize their ideas, build relationships, develop a network of partners, and mobilize others to take action. Today Morning Star gives its employees significant freedom and responsibility to drive improvement throughout the organization. This is true not just for managers and other professional employees, but for everyone, even college interns.

As Paul Green, the colleague at Morning Star responsible for talent strategy and the development of people noted, "If an individual has an idea that is truly superior for the organization, then the individual should be able to persuade others as to its merits. [At Morning Star] your leadership skills are severely tested . . . as you constantly have to answer the question, 'what kind of leader are you when no one has to listen to you?'"

This kind of initiative—taking the lead without authority—is not limited to an employee's specialized area; everyone at Morning Star has the right to suggest changes in any area of the company. As one colleague described it, "Since we believe you have the right to get involved anywhere you think your skills can add value, people will often drive change outside their narrow area. . . . We have a lot of spontaneous innovation, and ideas for change come from unusual places."

A colleague who worked as an electrician at one of the processing plants made a comment that captured the attitude and practice Morning Star sought to achieve in all of its people: "I enjoy coming to work because I know I can make a difference. I don't have someone in management telling me what to do. If something goes wrong you make the decision, you get the parts, and you put it in working with others."

Just like the patterns of leadership we have noted at Barry-Wehmiller, Babcom, Best Buy, the Multiple Myeloma Research Foundation, and the Cleveland Clinic, the Morning Star experience highlights the power of leadership that permeates the entire organization. That is the promise of the Leading Through paradigm and its framework for action.

The Framework for Action in the Leading Through Paradigm

The idea that the work of leadership is valuable all throughout an organization only works if people everywhere in the organization have sufficient personal agency—the freedom to choose and to act.[3] In the Leading Through par-

TABLE 7-1

The modular framework for action

DIMENSIONS OF THE ORGANIZATION		The Power Over paradigm	The Leading Through paradigm
FRAMEWORK FOR ACTION	**Governing design principle**	Control through *compliance*	Innovation through commitment and *initiative*
	Personal agency	Autonomy is a source of variability that needs to be *carefully managed*	Autonomy is a source of engagement and ingenuity that needs to be *empowered and preserved*
	Structure	*Direct supervision* and standardization through a tall, bureaucratic, coercive hierarchy	*Teams (modules)* supported by a flat, enabling hierarchy
		Centralized decision-making along hierarchical lines	*Decentralized decision-making* pushed to teams on front lines
		Action governed by *rules* and rigid operating procedures	Action governed by *principles* and clear guidelines
	Responsibility for improvement	*Those in authority* or centralized technical staff groups assess and revise standards and procedures and pursue improvements	*Everyone* is expected to initiate work on observed problems or opportunities

adigm, they are the ones, after all, that initiate, mobilize, and empower the work of building and sustaining a thriving organization.[4] Making that happen is the focus of the framework for action in the design of a modular leadership system that brings the Leading Through paradigm to life.

In this chapter we delve more deeply into that framework beginning with table 7-1, which summarizes its key elements. That table also includes the framework for action in Power Over for comparison.

Governing Design Principle: Initiative, Not Compliance

A defining characteristic of the Leading Through paradigm is the prevalence of *initiative*—proactive work aimed at solving or preventing problems and seizing opportunities intended to make things better.[5] In Leading Through, people all throughout the organization feel a sense of freedom and responsibility to initiate—and, subsequently, mobilize and empower—change that improves the viability and vitality of the organization. Initiative is abundant in Leading Through, but not just any kind of initiative. The kind of initiative we have in mind reflects both virtue and empathy, bringing the soul, heart, and mind of true leadership together to make things better for the organization.

That kind of initiative is like the kindling of leadership. Although kindling is typically small, its effects are powerful. Consider this description of the role of kindling in releasing the energy of "a massive pile of wood" by Dr. Dale G. Renlund, a noted cardiologist and religious leader:

> Imagine at the center a small mound of kindling, topped by a layer of wood chips. Sticks come next, then small logs, and finally huge logs. This woodpile contains an enormous amount of fuel, capable of producing light and heat for days. Envision next to the woodpile a single match, the kind with a phosphorus tip. For the energy in the woodpile to be released, the match needs to be struck and the kindling lit. The kindling will quickly catch fire and cause the larger pieces of wood to burn. Once this combustion reaction starts, it continues until all the wood is burned or the fire is deprived of oxygen. Striking the match and lighting the kindling are small actions that enable the potential energy of the wood to be released. Until the match is struck, nothing happens, regardless of the size of the woodpile.[6]

Initiative kindles the potential energy of people and teams in the Leading Through organization. In contrast, Power Over explicitly pits the organization's framework for getting work done against the freedom of the people doing the work, stifling initiative. There are many practices that contribute to this state of affairs, but five stand out to us as particularly important:

- A perspective that casts autonomy as a source of variability that needs to be controlled

- A preference for direct supervision and hierarchical authority as the default means of ensuring the coordination of work across functions

- A preference for centralized decisions implemented through hierarchical supervision

- A preference for rules and rigid procedures that are designed to restrict behavior and dictate employee action

- A preference for relying on those in authority or centralized staff groups to drive innovation and improvement

The contrast with the Leading Through paradigm and its modular framework for action is sharp.

1. Empowering and Preserving—Not Killing— Personal Agency

Personal agency—the ability to organize and execute one's own courses of action—is crucial to the kind of initiative that is at the center of Leading Through. Barry-Wehmiller (BW) describes its approach along these lines as "lighting fires versus fighting fires." Bob Chapman, the company's CEO, has written, "In our organization, we celebrate those who light fires in others by caring, listening, recognizing, and inspiring. . . . Once we find that light, we can share it with others and encourage them to allow their fires to be lit and kindled and grown and shared with the organization."[7]

The kind of fire Bob Chapman and his colleagues have discovered at BW is motivating and engaging. Research and experience over many decades have made clear that this kind of engagement at work depends deeply on intrinsic motivation—the drive to act that emerges from inside of us, rather than from external sources.[8] Intuitively, the possibility of that kind of internal drive can be greatly diminished and even eliminated when our ability to influence the path forward is deliberately constrained. In other words, intrinsic motivation and engagement at work will always be limited in an environment where autonomy and personal agency are inhibited.

In a world where Power Over remains so influential, it is no wonder that relatively few people report feeling engaged at work. In Power Over, personal agency is carefully controlled, with power and bureaucracy constraining personal agency by enforcing adherence to established authorities, rules, and procedures; what they want is *compliance*. This is a very common experience. Indeed, compliance was thoroughly ingrained in most of us in grade school. Seth Godin offered some insight as to why this might be the case: "It's easier to teach *compliance* than *initiative*. Compliance is simple to measure, simple to test for and simple to teach. Punish non-compliance, reward obedience and repeat. . . . Schools like teaching compliance. They're pretty good at it. To top it off, until recently the customers of a school or training program (the companies that hire workers) were buying compliance by the bushel. Initiative was a red flag, not an asset."[9]

The Power Over paradigm is still buying—and creating—compliance by carefully controlling personal agency. Jonathan observed this dynamic at work when he was named chair of the department of management at the University of Texas at San Antonio (UTSA). He found that engagement and morale among staff in his department was very low. It didn't take him long to discover the reason: in addition to the crushing weight of the bureaucracy they dealt with every day, a sort of informal hierarchy of control had emerged (and been allowed to persist) in which college-level staff dictated many rules and expectations, including periodic checks on behavior. For example, college staff would check department staff cubicles just before 5 p.m. to ensure that staff weren't leaving early (it didn't matter if someone had come in early or worked extra hours the day before; there were consequences for staff who were not sitting where college staff thought they should be at the appointed time).

To counter these influences, Jonathan made it clear to college staff that their rules and checks were no longer necessary. And he tried to make the following messages clear to his department colleagues, not only in word but most especially in his own behavior over time:

- I don't care how you do your work (or even where). The value you bring to the table is entirely dependent on the contributions you make to a well-functioning department (and to helping the department improve) not on how you do it, or where you're sitting at a particular time.

- You know more about how this department, college, and university work than I do. The faculty and I need your knowledge, experience, and wisdom to ensure this department can be the best it can be. If you observe things that you think need to change, please help us to see what you see so we can work together to make it better.

- I appreciate you and the hard work you do on behalf of our faculty and students every day. I trust your judgement and your ability to act in the best interests of the department. Please feel free to do so based on your knowledge and experience.

There were many other things Jonathan did, but these messages (and corresponding actions) were aimed at improving staff engagement by increasing their sense of personal agency at work. Although these changes couldn't eliminate the university bureaucracy, they did improve engagement. Department staff became a recognized go-to resource for ideas, expertise, and wisdom for other departments in the college. Over the years, they became recognized leaders who regularly took initiative to make the department and college a better place to work and learn.

Notably, Jonathan's messages and actions were consistent with the three strategies we outlined in chapter 5 for increasing engagement as part of the leadership process: (1) focus primarily on ends rather than means, (2) make the team's learning and growth a personal objective (invite ideas, creativity, and feedback), and (3) support making LIVE a reality for the team. When aimed at increasing personal agency, these strategies help to increase and preserve sufficient autonomy, unleashing the human spirit and helping people to be more engaged at work.

2. Teams, Not Hierarchical Authority

In the modular framework for action, teams are the way work is organized. Instead of relying on highly specialized units in a hierarchy with many middle-managers, teams are the fundamental unit of the organization.[10] There is a structure, but it is designed to support teams.

Teams represent a powerful and liberating alternative to the direct supervision in a coercive hierarchy. Teams have long been recognized for their capacity for generating action, learning, and change in organizations. Jeffrey Pfeffer observed more than two decades ago that, "Organizing people into . . . teams is a critical component of virtually all high-performance management systems."[11] Similarly, Richard Hackman has argued that teams are advantageous because they "have more resources, and a greater diversity of resources. . . . Teams have great flexibility in how to deploy and use their resources. Teams provide a setting in which members can learn from one another and thereby build an ever-larger pool of knowledge and expertise. And there is always the possibility that a team will generate magic—producing something extraordinary, a collective creation of previously unimagined quality or beauty."[12]

Although the idea of teams is popular, and many organizations believe teaming is important (88 percent according to research by Deloitte), only a small subset report that teams with people from different disciplines or functions are a primary means of getting work done.[13] Our research suggests that most organizations have little trouble establishing teams that operate within the same disciplines, like market research or supply-chain management. These are either *functional teams* that work on projects within functional silos or *lightweight teams* that are largely functional but have a project manager who coordinates schedules and communications.[14]

It is much more difficult to implement teams that truly cut across functional areas. Many organizations struggle to break down the barriers between traditional silos and give teams responsibility and freedom of action.[15] However, that is exactly what happens in Leading Through, where two kinds of teams are especially important:

- *Heavyweight teams*, where authority and responsibility for the work reside not with functional units but with the core team. The core team has a leader and key team members who lead different aspects of the work. The team is the focal point of decision-making and project work.

FIGURE 7-1

The four types of teams and their characteristics

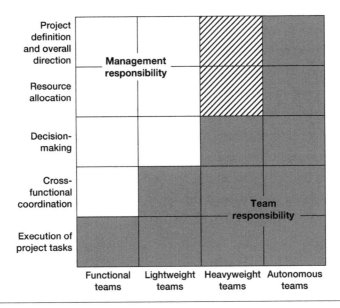

• *Autonomous teams* are like heavyweight teams except that all people working on the project—core team and subteams—are moved completely out of functional areas. The team takes overall responsibility for every aspect of the team's work.

Figure 7-1 provides a visual summary of the characteristics of each of the four types of teams we have mentioned.

In the case of both heavyweight and autonomous teams, the key innovation (and distinction from functional and lightweight teams) is that the team becomes a unit unto itself, a "real team" with authority, ownership, and accountability that truly cut across disciplinary boundaries.

The central role of teams working under the guiding principle of innovation through commitment and initiative raises an important question about efficiency. Since teams are the fundamental unit of the organization, they will have operating responsibilities. Would it not be better to use teams on major innovation projects and leave the operating responsibilities to the functions where they can focus on execution and efficiency?

Our simple answer is a resounding No! Defining operating responsibility as executing tasks defined by some specialized group is exactly the Power Over paradigm in action. That approach may create compliance, but it misses opportunities to learn and to make the process more effective. And we certainly won't get energized, engaged people.

In Leading Through, teams become the owners of their work. They may work under essential constraints (e.g., regulations, technical requirements), but as they work to make improvements, the process, the checklists, and the sequences become theirs. They may be supported by groups with technical expertise, but the team owns the process and its outcomes. They pay close attention to the way things are working and thus to the very things that drive efficient operations—discipline, detail, precision. And so, we get improvement, innovation, and an efficient operation. Moreover, we engage the whole person and thus get even more—energized teams and people who thrive. Professional service firms, including consulting firms like Deloitte, where Erin works, have moved closer and closer to this model where firms are organized around client service areas (heavyweight teams) and engagements (autonomous teams) to serve specific clients/needs.

ING Group, a multinational bank based in the Netherlands, provides another example of making such teams the foundation of the organization. In 2015, ING embarked on a transformation process aimed at redesigning the organization with inspiration from agile methodology. Principles like "We work in high-performing teams" and "We empower teams" guided the redesign.

The resulting structure, dubbed the "Way of Working" (WoW), broke the organization into roughly 350 relatively autonomous, interdisciplinary teams focused on clear objectives. (ING called these teams "squads.") A team might have members with expertise in channel management, marketing, IT, or business intelligence, among other areas.[16] The team would be located together and would have "end-to-end" responsibility for a specific product or objective.[17] The bank then organized the teams into business groups focused on an interconnected mission (e.g., retail banking, mortgages, mid-sized commercial clients—ING called these groups "tribes").

The only layer of structure on top of teams was the business group or tribe. Each group had about 15 teams working toward related objectives. What little hierarchy remained in ING's structure supported and empowered the work of the teams. The group ensured that objectives and priorities were clear, that teams had the resources they needed, and that the teams shared knowledge and insights. Group leaders provided coaching to help individuals and teams become high performing.[18]

Since making the change, the company has grown rapidly, from $18 billion in revenue in 2015 to more than $46 billion in 2022 (and from an operating margin of $6.6 billion in 2015 to a margin of more than $18 billion in 2022). Several other firms—for example, Spotify—have implemented a similar structure with excellent results.[19] As these cases illustrate, making teams the basis of the organization improves creativity and problem-solving and allows the organization to rely on team (peer) accountability rather than hierarchical supervision. As Jeff Pfeffer has observed, "Teams permit removal of layers of hierarchy and absorption of administrative tasks previously performed by specialists, avoiding the enormous costs of having people whose sole job it is to watch people watch people who watch other people do the work."[20]

But that is not to say there is no hierarchy in the Leading Through paradigm. As the ING case illustrates, hierarchy has a role to play even though the organization reduces its size and influence.[21] The objective in Leading Through is not to rid the organization of hierarchy. It is to get the hierarchy right. We want to avoid the "too much structure" problem we have seen so often where executives use hierarchy to bolster their power and cement their control in the spirit of the Power Over paradigm.[22] But we also want to avoid the "too little structure" problem where there are teams, but no principles or values, no support, no help, only confusion, conflict and failure.[23]

We believe that some hierarchy is a necessary, inevitable, even natural, characteristic of all well-functioning systems.[24] Both the natural and social worlds provide compelling evidence of that reality.[25] But it is important to keep in mind that the whole point of the right hierarchy—something lost in Power Over—is to help the people doing the work be effective and successful.

In that spirit, a hierarchy of managers and supervisors works best when they provide support and resources, watch out for the well-being of people and teams, and serve as a backstop to help resolve conflicts.[26] WL Gore pursues this approach to hierarchy by eliminating titles (everyone has the title of "associate") and by replacing the concept of direct supervision with the concept of sponsorship. Every employee has a sponsor whose role is to advocate for and ensure the well-being and success of those assigned to them.[27] Morning Star takes a similar approach, ensuring that there are well-defined support structures in place, particularly to help resolve conflict when it arises. Incredibly, the company estimates that only ten to twelve issues require hierarchical intervention each year.[28]

So, there is hierarchy in the Leading Through paradigm. But its nature is totally different. Instead of issuing orders to address problems or opportunities (coercing compliance), managers and supervisors in Leading Through support their people in taking initiative to drive action, learn, and change, thus enabling initiative and leadership. The limited hierarchy may provide some guidance and counsel, but it is the people in the teams that do the work of leadership—identifying problems and opportunities and either resolving them through mutual adjustment within and across teams or building a new team to address them.

Making teams the fundamental basis of the organization sets the stage for taking layers out of the hierarchy and repositioning it as a support to the teams rather than the primary means of getting work done.

3. Decentralized, Not Centralized, Decision-Making

The shift from control to agency and from hierarchical supervision to teams unlocks the door to decentralized decision-making. In the Leading Through paradigm senior executives walk through that door and do something that is very difficult for many executives (and aspiring executives) to do. They stop trying to consolidate their power and bolster their authority by centralizing decisions.[29] Of course, that also means they stop trying to establish tight control through bureaucratic rules and procedures, tall hierarchies, and a seemingly unending trail of approvals—all hallmarks of the Power Over paradigm.

Instead, the Leading Through executives must become senior leaders with responsibility to create the right structure so that decisions are made as close to the action as possible. That means making sure people doing the work on the front lines, and everywhere else, have the information, the perspective, and the skill needed to make decisions that affect their work. There are, of course, some decisions that senior leaders need to make, but their primary involvement in decision-making is to create a structure that pushes decisions to the front lines as much as possible. A consequence is that senior leaders and managers in the supportive hierarchy have to reframe their roles and let go of the tendency to control and micromanage.

Whole Foods has long carried out its work by relying heavily on this kind of decentralized structure. As described by Robert Bruce Shaw in his book *Extreme Teams*:

> The company is built around small, highly focused, and cohesive teams. Each new hire becomes a member of a team within a store—such as produce, meat, seafood, bakery, or prepared foods. These teams range in size from 10 to 50 people, depending on the work to be done and the size of the store. Each team operates in many respects as an independent business, making a range of decisions, including what products to offer and how they are promoted. Approximately 10 percent of a store's goods are ordered by headquarters staff in Austin, Texas, and another 30 percent come from the firm's 12 regional offices; all other product decisions are made by the in-store teams.[30]

Think of the implications: 60 percent of everything sold in a Whole Foods store is determined by teams with responsibility for a particular area of the store. Further, those same teams make the majority of hiring decisions in the organization. In other words, most of the organization's operational decisions have been pushed to the front lines.

As we saw in the Cleveland Clinic story in chapter 6, many healthcare organizations are moving in this direction, seeking to capitalize on the integration benefits associated with decentralized decision-making by interdisciplinary teams.[31] For example, the Women's Integrated Pelvic Health Program (IPHP) at Northwestern Medicine brings together various clinicians and physical therapists caring for patients with various pelvic disorders. The program's facilities are organized around a central core, where physical therapists work and can easily collaborate with physicians and other providers who work in offices and meeting rooms that are close by. The idea is to ensure that "specialists from different disciplines work jointly to develop innovative, integrated, patient-centered care plans that move beyond discipline-specific approaches to address common pelvic floor problems."[32] Consider this description of how things work at IPHP and think about your own experience receiving healthcare services:

> Physical proximity means that therapists are constantly interacting with surgeons and having informal interactions about patients. The frequency of interactions between surgeons and physical therapists in the Center leads to teamwork that is obvious to patients. One of the crucial benefits of actually working shoulder to shoulder is that communication between personnel is in conversations rather than relying on clinical notes or emails that must be written and read carefully and immediately. Patients draw comfort when two or more clinicians see them at the same time so that there is no chance of confusion about next steps for any of them, including the patient.[33]

This structure enables significant decentralization of decision-making and coordination. Care teams have the freedom to jointly determine the best plan and path forward for each patient. Such freedom and collaboration are no longer hindered by the barriers and constraints of traditional hierarchical silos.

This example underscores the critical role of the modular leadership system in making decentralized decision-making work coherently in the Leading Through paradigm. The leadership standards and other visible information support communication and alignment *within* and *between* teams and their units. The system also makes it possible for everyone to have a concrete, vivid understanding of the purpose and priorities of the organization.

Such visible information, coupled with clarity around purpose and priorities, enables teams and units to make critical decisions. If needed, they coordinate through a process of mutual adjustment, adapting work within teams to ensure alignment between them. Moreover, when leaders initiate new projects and mobilize teams, visible information makes it possible to connect and align the idea or project with existing work already underway. More on this in chapter 8.

4. Principles, Not Rules

An essential element in the modular framework for action is a reliance on principles rather than rules. This approach is an important part of creating the organizational space to sustain a decentralized structure centered on teams with personal agency. Rules tend to prescribe specific behaviors in advance of when action is needed, leaving people with very little room for agency. In contrast, principles tend to be less specific and more general and universal, preserving more freedom of action. As an example, "give customers a compliment during every interaction" might be considered a rule because it stipulates a specific behavior in advance, leaving little room for discretion, whereas "always treat customers with kindness" would be considered a principle because it provides general guidance without specifying a specific behavior in advance, leaving considerable room for discretion.

Barry-Wehmiller uses this approach. Efforts there to enable autonomy and freedom are referred to as "just enough structure." That is, "once we define the right process, we allow for maximum possible freedom within that process. We define 'winning' and then give people the freedom to execute. Just enough structure means that we have established some guardrails but not imposed so many rules that they stifle individuality, personal judgement, innovation, or creativity."[34] These very same ideas have been implemented in a very different business by Netflix, a producer of media content and a subscription streaming service. Netflix has sought to remove traditional policies and rules but provide enough structure and process with overarching principles and values to guide action.[35]

Where rules prevail, those in authority typically create "too much structure." They attempt to regulate behavior without sufficient consideration of the varied circumstances that are often best known by those doing the work. In the modular framework for action of Leading Through, principles prevail. Deciding what to do is left to the individual or group within a framework of principles that provide guardrails.

When Alaska Airlines set out to improve customer service in 2015, it devised a system of principles that pushed significant discretion to the front lines in terms of responding to and solving customer problems. The framework, dubbed "Beyond Service," was designed around four pillars of service: safety, caring, delivery, and presentation. Although the framework created clear and unambiguous expectations, it also explicitly avoided attempting to capture and specify all of the problems and decisions frontline employees might encounter. In doing so, it avoided hamstringing service providers with rigid rules they were expected to apply regardless of the circumstances.[36]

Professional basketball player and coach Derek Fisher described this same kind of dynamic in contrasting the coaching styles of Jerry Sloan, the longtime Hall of Fame coach of the Utah Jazz, and Phil Jackson, the eleven-time NBA champion coach of the Chicago Bulls and Los Angeles Lakers:

> Coach Sloan's approach . . . [is] old-school. . . . While I have great respect and appreciation for his approach to rules, I also realized that I couldn't take that same approach with my kids or as a coach. . . . Nuance and allowing for individual differences seems more like the ideal approach to take. In contrast to Coach Sloan, Phil has far fewer rules. . . . Phil simply makes the objectives clear, then lets his players decide on how to behave to produce those results. . . . He understands the need to find a balance between a rigid system and too little discipline that meets everybody's needs.[37]

Shifting from rules to principles represents an important mechanism for infusing the work with the kind of agency that is critical to initiative.

Principles preserve agency by creating the space for individuals and teams to decide how best to carry out their work within the boundaries proscribed by principles. Frameworks built on principle protect the freedoms people enjoy and allow them to use their talents, skills, and capabilities to take meaningful action.

Guiding principles are particularly meaningful and effective if they are grounded in the organization's purpose and priorities. The framework of principles "growing out of the organization's purpose and priorities" becomes like a conduit through which the light of purpose and priorities guides work on the front lines.[38] We discuss this critical source of light in more detail in chapter 8.

5. Everyone Owns Improvement and Innovation, Not Just Those in Authority

The framework for action in the new paradigm is designed to increase commitment and support initiative that leads to innovation. The framework applies to everyone. Everyone has the work of leadership to do. That means everyone is responsible and accountable for improvement and innovation.

Making everyone responsible for taking initiative to improve and innovate stands in contrast to organizations stuck in the Power Over paradigm. They do not delegate responsibility for improvement and innovation to the front lines, even if they use language that would seem to encourage it. Indeed, most do not even push it very far down the hierarchy. Instead, improvement and innovation are the primary responsibility of centralized staff groups (think "performance management" or "research and development").

A centralized group may be very valuable. If you are leading a medical technology organization, for example, you need an R&D group of skilled scientists and engineers to develop next-generation products. However, if Power Over governs the organization, including the R&D group, centralized control of all innovation and improvement processes will stifle initiative and creativity and sharply limit opportunities for innovation all through the organization.

Things are very different for organizations under Leading Through. First, they disconnect responsibility for innovation from hierarchical authority, removing another bureaucratic barrier to agency and initiative. Second, they encourage initiative by explicitly making action, learning, and change something that is expected of everyone, not just a few. In doing so, they shift expectations and significantly lower the perceived barriers to proactively challenging the status quo. The result is a shift from a reactive to a proactive mindset. In other words, in Leading Through people stop waiting around for feedback, direction, and permission and, instead, proactively seek to make things better.[39]

This is an organizational stewardship. It is not limited to improving the specific role people play or the jobs they do or the group in which they work, as important as that is. It is also about making improvement and innovation in the whole organization. Morning Star is a good example. They refer to this as "total responsibility"—"professionals initiating communications and the coordination of their activities with fellow colleagues, customers, suppliers and fellow industry participants, absent directives from others."[40] In other words, at Morning Star everyone is held accountable for initiative to solve observed problems, regardless of the nature and scope of the issue. As Chris Rufer, the founder of the company tells it, these kinds of expectations "underlie family and community relationships," so why not work relationships too? Most of us can imagine taking proactive initiative to solve problems and improve things in our families, neighborhoods, and communities. Consider the following thought experiment offered by Rufer: "Imagine I got back from a three-day trip and the kids were dirty and told me they had not eaten in three days. . . . What would I do? I would feed them and give them a bath. Now think about a similar situation in an average organization: you come to work and you hear about a problem. In most cases, you would not do anything about it, because it is not your problem. Somebody else in a different, well-defined role created it, so you do not need to fix it."[41]

The idea behind "total responsibility" is for everyone to feel a sense of responsibility to each other for taking initiative to make things better, regardless of whether the problem arises in their own work area or not.

The key phrase there is *to each other*: at Morning Star commitment and accountability derive more from collegial relationships than from traditional performance management systems.

A similar notion prevails at Barry-Wehmiller, where accountability shifts "from a mechanism for assigning blame to an opportunity to work with others to create an organization that's better for all. To do this, we have to recognize that we are each stewards of the lives next to us and around us every day in our organizations. We are all accountable to each other."[42]

The Leading Through paradigm incorporates a key to making this happen: a culture that values and rewards collective, team-oriented behavior, rather than self-centered conduct. The San Francisco 49ers of the late 1970s and 1980s put that idea into practice under then-coach Bill Walsh. Walsh described one poignant example of how this approach played out on the field, benefiting the team:

> At halftime during a midseason game with the New Orleans
> Saints, I told our offensive team that if we got near the Saints'
> thirty-yard line I was going to call a specific pass play that I'd been
> saving for the situation. Sure enough, early in the third quarter we
> got to the Saints' twenty-seven-yard line, but in the heat of the
> moment I forgot about the play I'd promised. . . . Steve Young,
> our backup quarterback, who was standing close by, immediately
> leaned over and reminded me of what I had said earlier. I listened;
> we scored. . . . Steve was selfless, team first, in bringing forth in-
> formation that his "rival" quarterback, Joe Montana, would use
> successfully. . . . Steve was like that—a team player. . . . Everyone
> understood the only welfare that mattered was the organization's. If
> our ship sank, we all drowned.[43]

Recognition and celebration of proactive, team-minded behavior is critical to Leading Through. Consider the experience of employees at Barry-Wehmiller, where they preach and practice the principle of "responsible freedom." As described by Bob Chapman, "Responsible freedom encapsulates two ideas: freedom, the opportunity to exercise personal choice, to have ownership of the work that you do and the decisions you make; and responsibility, ensuring that personal choice is exercised with care and concern for other people and the requirements of the organization. Whatever you call it—empowerment or responsible freedom—it is fundamental to driving fulfillment in any organization. . . . Most people are merely compliant at work; their potential remains buried under layers of apathy and cynicism."[44]

To ensure that freedom is exercised responsibly, "with care and concern for other people and the requirements of the organization," Barry-Wehmiller makes recognizing such behaviors a fundamental part of everyday life in the organization. As Chapman puts it, "We want our people to realize that small appreciations that are well expressed and genuine have a ripple effect that is more powerful than they might realize. We don't assume that this will happen by accident. Everything we do in our culture that we think is important, we support systematically. We teach people how to do it well, put programs in place to support it, and support the everyday practice of it."[45]

That is why Barry-Wehmiller runs a leadership program for all employees that includes a course on recognition and celebration. Employees learn how to reward and celebrate initiative in ways that are "personal, memorable, creative, sincere, timely, proportionate, significant and meaningful." At Barry-Wehmiller recognition spans the full spectrum of possibilities, from quiet personal conversations to loud, boisterous, and formal celebrations.

One final, critical note about making improvement the responsibility of everyone in the organization: even if organizations successfully create the conditions for personal agency, freedom of action, and a strong sense of responsibility and accountability, the work of leadership will not permeate the organization unless people have the resources they need to engage in improvement work. That includes *tools* and *time to do the work*. Without tools like the leadership process or frameworks for problem identification and problem-solving or other analytical methods, people will not be able to seize the opportunities they might see. Without sufficient time, the demands and distractions of everyday work can crowd out opportunities to take initiative. By carving out time for employees to work on improvement and equipping them with tools, organizations not only make such work possible, but they also provide an additional signal that improvement work is important to the organization and that the organization expects everyone to do it.

We have seen examples of systematic education and training in the leadership process and in other tools for improvement at Barry-Wehmiller and the Cleveland Clinic. There are many other examples of organizations creating time for people to improve and innovate:

- 3M and Google allocate a percentage of employee work time to improvement work.

- Atlassian, the Australian company that makes team collaboration software, sets aside one day each quarter (ShipIt Day) for employees to identify opportunities to make things better ("Find what inspires you. Develop that dream feature. Smash your nemesis bug. Or, maybe just upgrade racks in the bike room") and assemble a team to work on it ("This is your chance to combine ideas and skill sets from different teams").[46]

- Lantech, a Kentucky-based developer and manufacturer of stretch wrapping machines, sets aside time in every shift at its plants for "daily huddles" to give frontline workers and managers time to assess and review quality issues and seek out the resources and support needed to solve them.[47]

- In 2015, University of Iowa Health Care Internal Medicine began giving resident physicians dedicated time to identify, organize, and lead quality improvement projects.

- At WL Gore this kind of dedicated time is dubbed "Dabble Time," half a day every week to work on innovation. Dabble Time isn't just a benefit, available if employees choose to use it. It's an expectation that at least 10 percent of each employee's time will be dedicated to new ideas and initiatives that benefit the organization.

From Gore-Tex to Elixir guitar strings, many of the company's breakthrough products can be traced to Dabble Time.[48]

In summary, in the Leading Through paradigm organizations infuse their people with responsibility for improvement and innovation in four ways: they make improvement something that is expected of everyone; they nurture a culture of collective progress; they recognize and celebrate improvement; and they give people tools and dedicated time to make things better.

This is the modular framework for action in the Leading Through paradigm. By design, we have ended up where we began—with commitment and initiative that drives innovation. That is the design principle that governs the work of leadership everywhere in the organization. Everyone has personal agency and responsibility for improvement and innovation. Everyone is part of a team supported by the right kind of decentralized structure. Leaders and their teams do not have to grapple with bureaucratic rules. They use principles to guide their work and to connect with other work in the organization.

The work of leadership in this framework depends on people having the critical information they need to take initiative effectively. In Leading Through that means information about how to get things done, the standards and objectives that have to be met, and the organization's strategy. Making that information visible is the key to initiative with freedom of action and unity. We turn now to the issue of visibility in chapter 8.

Chapter Summary

- In Leading Through, the design of the organization is governed by the pursuit of *innovation through initiative*, achieved by empowering and preserving *personal agency* through:

  - *Teams* rather than hierarchical authority to create the structures needed to organize work and preserve agency.

- *Decentralized* rather than consolidated decision-making, pushing decisions as close to the action as possible.

- *Principles* and clear guidelines rather than rules to guide the work of the organization.

- A system of accountability that places *responsibility for innovation* in everyone's hands, making the necessary action, learning, and change a part of everyone's work.

CHAPTER 8

Visible Information

Making Freedom and Unity a Reality

Google was born first in a computer science lab at Stanford University and then in the proverbial garage (literally) in Menlo Park, California with a mission to "organize the world's information and make it universally accessible and useful." From the very beginning, Google made transparency of information a cornerstone of its culture.[1]

The founders, Sergey Brin and Larry Page, were relentless in making sure leaders at Google would never hoard information and would always be transparent. The phrase they made the watchword of the organization was "default to open." Their intent was that everyone at Google would start with the assumption that everything said or done was open and available to everyone else. There might be some things that were not open for legal or regulatory reasons, but the default for everything else was always to be open.[2]

It was pretty simple to make that a reality when Google was small. The founders gave all employees access to all of Google's internal code on day one of their employment, conducted a town hall meeting every Friday for all employees, and made sure everyone could see Google's priorities and its allocation of resources emerge in real time. It was informal and effective.

However, as Google grew (and Google grew very fast), information became more complex, and the number of people grew into the thousands.

The commitment to transparency did not falter, nor did the commitment to code access and the Friday meetings. But Google had to introduce new channels, new media, and new processes to make the information flow truly open and transparent in a large and growing organization.[3]

Google created an internal network accessible to every employee and posted information about new products, upcoming products, launch plans, and team goals. All of that was updated regularly and made available to everyone. Further, memos and presentations used in meetings of the board of directors were shared with everyone following the board meeting. Everything the board saw (except for some information that could not legally be shared), every employee could see.[4]

Transparency extended to individual information. Using the same internal network, each quarter employees posted their personal objectives and key results they had achieved (Google called this the OKR process.)[5]. That included all the senior people too. In fact, the senior people—founders, CEO—hosted an organization-wide meeting to discuss their results using a variety of technologies to connect with all employees. Employees also played a key role in creating questions for Friday meetings, voting on the best questions and posting key information to the network.[6]

Transparency and "default to open" were essential at Google because Google gave its people significant freedom of action to pursue ideas for new products or services. Those people needed information to effectively exercise their agency and to do whatever was best for the organization. Here is an example (one that is famous within Google).

One day Larry Page was searching for some things on the internet using Google search. The results kept turning up crazy ads completely unrelated to his search. He printed off the offending ads, highlighted them, and wrote a few scathing words on the top of the page and pasted it on the refrigerator in a break room. A search engineer (not on the ad team) saw the paper, got his team together, and began working the problem (i.e., initiated a leadership process). They came up with an idea, developed it, and tested it over that weekend and posted it on the system for anyone to see. They did this even though they were not part of the team in charge of the advertising system. It turned out that their idea solved the problem and was instrumental in the growth of Google's ad business.[7]

Visible Information

The Google story illustrates the power of visible information in unlocking the potential in leaders and the leadership process. The search team had real freedom of action because they had access to the ad system code and license to work on the issue even though they were not part of that team. What they knew about Google's moral and strategic context—its values, mission, and strategy—gave them clear direction and motivation. They could initiate the project, put the team together, and execute the solution. They knew what to do and how to do it all without any intervention by supervisors or a bureaucratic hierarchy.

In the Leading Through paradigm leaders and their teams have visible information that connects them to the moral and strategic context of the organization, including other work and other projects, and provides them with insights and freedom of action to accomplish the specific work of the project.[8] Information that is visible cannot be hidden or obscure. It must flow freely and be transparent (i.e., be open and accessible). But visible information goes much further. *Information becomes truly visible when it is known, understood, valued, and used.* In this chapter we focus on the types of visible information leaders and teams need and how that information becomes truly visible so that the full power of visible information in the modular leadership system becomes a reality.

Each of the types of visible information we introduced in chapter 6—objectives, standards, strategy, and context—play distinctive roles in equipping leaders and their teams with the ability to achieve their individual objectives while at the same time advancing the larger purposes and objectives of the organization.

- *Objectives* define what the organization seeks to accomplish in strengthening people, pursuing purpose, and improving productivity. They provide an overarching framework of aspirations and animate the moral context of the organization. Objectives inspire the work of leadership, infuse that work with meaning, and motivate initiative and innovation.[9] A vision brings those objectives to life, expressing ultimate purpose in vivid, concrete language that makes objectives memorable and promotes shared understanding and commitment.

- *Standards* capture the idea of a rallying point, a marker that establishes a pattern for guiding teams.[10] Standards include both values and principles and define a level of moral excellence that is both aspirational and operational. Aspirational because values clearly communicate what is important to the organization and the beliefs that underlie its objectives. Operational because clearly articulated principles emphasize those values in ways that make them actionable, providing guardrails to guide behavior and a gauge against which to evaluate day-to-day decisions. When a focused set of values and clearly articulated principles are anchored in an organization's objectives, they in turn strengthen shared understanding and commitment.[11]

- *Strategy* involves both strategic intent (the unique value the organization intends to create in solving a particular problem for a particular customer or beneficiary) and strategic capabilities (the resource-based building blocks of competitive advantage). Strategy defines both where the organization will focus its efforts in pursuit of its purpose and how it will do so through capabilities that create unique value. The details around intent and capabilities inform the pursuit of opportunities and the realization of leadership objectives by every leader and team. Further, the work of leadership often uncovers new strategic opportunities and new threats that lead to adjustments and even pivots in strategy. Thus, it is crucial that leaders and their teams know the organization's strategic intent, and where the strategic resources and capabilities are and how to get access to them.

- *Context* captures the who (key people, knowledge, and expertise), what (resources, teams, and projects), where (the location of
  people and information), and how (key processes to guide communication and the exchange of resources and information) of the
  organization. This kind of information helps teams get things done
  effectively, but in ways that connect with—contribute to, benefit
  from—other work going on in the organization. This is especially
  true of information that uncovers potential opportunities to collaborate, potential conflicts, and potential sources of ideas, solutions,
  and capabilities. That kind of information is especially valuable
  in leadership action that potentially could cut across the existing
  boundaries of the organization.

Although the different types of visible information play different roles,
they are closely connected. The power of visible information derives from
the fact that it provides everyone in the organization with a coherent,
unified set of objectives, standards and strategies, and clarity with respect
to the moral and strategic context of the organization. When that information is visible, it guides the work done all throughout the organization
with both freedom and unity. It is precisely the connections among these
elements of visible information that require and preserve that unity and
secure the freedom of action so essential to initiative and innovation.

We can see the role of visible information in action in the story of an
ongoing strategic pivot at Cemex, a global producer of cement and related
construction materials and services.[12]

A Strategic Pivot at Cemex

Cemex, a global corporation headquartered in Monterrey, Mexico, com-
petes in three businesses—Cement, Concrete (including aggregates), and
Urban Solutions. Operating on 4 continents with 64 cement plants, 1,348
ready-mix concrete operations, 246 quarries, 269 distribution centers, 68
marine terminals, and over 200 Urban Solutions projects, Cemex employs
43,000 people that generate over $15 billion in annual revenue.[13]

Cemex's strategy has two pillars: innovation and sustainability. It has a longstanding commitment to operational excellence; low costs are important in all the businesses. But it also has developed a deep commitment to the communities where it operates, and that commitment has brought sustainability to the forefront of its strategic intent. Achieving sustainability in the context of meeting customer needs means innovation. That kind of innovation looms large in every business, and it hinges on new ideas, new technologies, and the cultivation of innovative people and teams. As Cemex's leaders stated in the spring of 2023, "We are entering a new era, ready to take on new challenges, to make a difference driven by innovation, sustainability, passion, and agility. Inspiring a new generation, we are pushing boundaries toward a more digital and sustainable industry with a clear goal of building a better future together."[14]

Making that future a reality necessitates increasing freedom, pushing greater decision-making and creativity to local leaders. Though very much a work in progress, the organization understands that visible information is central to making that happen in a way that preserves the kind of unity that has helped the organization succeed in the past. To that end, the organization is working to clarify and sharpen its moral context, purpose, strategic objectives, and values and communicate them widely in the organization. It is working to make more information, including about context, available and visible locally.

What we see happening at Cemex in 2023 is the result of a profound strategic and cultural pivot driven by its geographic expansion, its investment in new businesses, and the growing importance of sustainability. With its pivot, Cemex forged a new path in which innovation across the whole organization—focused on customers and their needs and integrating sustainability into everything the organization does—has become a strategic and cultural imperative.

Sustainability and innovation have posed significant challenges for the large, well-entrenched Power Over version of Cemex. From its beginning in 1906, Cemex had an intense, driven focus on lowering the cost of producing cement. The core of its culture was captured by a phrase heard often at Cemex, "ruthless operating efficiency." Cement production is capital- and energy-intensive. Driven from the top through its hierarchy of managers and supervisors, the Cemex approach to increasing productivity in all its plants was disciplined, sophisticated, data driven, and highly systematic. Ruthless operating efficiency was not a slogan on the wall; it was a way of life. It yielded a system of rules, procedures, and practices that were enforced, then updated, improved, and enforced again.[15] Pressure was intense, and supervision was controlling and even coercive. It was control through compliance to achieve highly productive operations. Cemex was a quintessential Power Over organization.

Imagine what it would be like for Cemex people to pivot to an emphasis on taking initiative to innovate, listening to customers, responding with agility to their needs, and giving people much more freedom of action—and still pursue operating efficiency with energy and passion. Lorenzo Zambrano, Cemex's legendary CEO from 1985–2014 captured the need to pivot best when he said that Cemex needed to go from being an elephant to being a greyhound. Like the same work at the Cleveland Clinic, or at Barry-Wehmiller, making such a strategic pivot cannot be done in a matter of weeks or months; it will be a multiyear journey to a Leading Through future that is ongoing.

Visible information plays a significant role in that ongoing pivot. In the first place, information about leadership objectives and standards has created an overarching framework for leaders and their teams in all of Cemex's businesses. They have established and clarified overall direction and the values and principles that guide the work of leadership.

Objectives

In table 8-1 we summarize the key objectives related to people, purpose, and productivity that Cemex has communicated organization-wide and made publicly available on its website.[16]

All of this is brought to life by a vision of a future in which "Cemex drives innovation further to solve the world's construction challenges sustainably."[17]

The imperatives of innovation, customer focus, and sustainability are clear in the objectives, and so are the moral and strategic contexts. Cemex

TABLE 8-1

Cemex leadership objectives

Objectives category	Cemex leadership objectives
People	Provide a great workplace that helps employees grow, builds skills and expertise, and enables a strong sense of purpose
Purpose	Help the world reach the next frontier of sustainable living
	Customers: Tailor our offerings to solve our clients' construction needs, make it easy to work with us, and provide enhanced performance and reliability
	Neighbors: Be a relevant engine of economic growth; build more capable, inclusive, and resilient communities; reduce our impact on local air, water, and waste; and conserve biodiversity
Productivity	Overall: Grow revenue, reduce costs, optimize assets, and keep a tight rein on risks
	Supply chain: Encourage creation of innovative solutions to reduce costs while promoting sustainable goods and services

Source: Adapted from Cemex, "How We Create Value," accessed December 20, 2023, https://www.cemex.com/about-us/how-we-create-value.

seeks to engage and develop its forty-three thousand people with a compelling moral purpose, give them scope for initiative to drive innovation, and achieve demanding objectives for the productivity of all its resources. Sustainability is central to the organization's vision, and is an explicit objective both for innovative products and for reducing the organization's impact on local communities. Its overall goal for sustainability is to be a carbon-net-zero organization by 2050.

Standards

Table 8-2 summarizes the leadership standards—values and principles—at Cemex.

The standards sharpen the focus on the moral context. Words like *safety, integrity, innovation, diversity, respect, well-being, honesty,* and *duty* underscore the commitment to generating light. These standards are made

TABLE 8-2

Cemex leadership standards

Standards categories	Cemex leadership standards
Values[a]	Ensure safety; focus on customers; act with integrity; work as One Cemex; foster innovation; embrace diversity
Principles[b]	**Always remember:**
	We all have the right to work in an environment of respect that enables us to feel confident and succeed.
	We must support our communities by making them sustainable and fostering their quality of life and well-being, thus contributing to building a better future.
	We do what we can to avoid any risk that could impact Cemex's reputation, our sustainability, or our enterprise value.
	Our code:
	We do the right thing . . . even when no one is watching.
	Nothing comes before the health and safety of our people and the community.
	We should always carry out our business with honesty, respect, and integrity.
	We should follow all antitrust and competition laws and regulations.
	We should never put our own interest above our duty to each other and to Cemex.
	Protecting the confidentiality of personal data is a critical responsibility.

a. Listed under "Values" in Cemex, "How We Create Value," accessed December 20, 2023, https://www.cemex.com/about-us/how-we-create-value.

b. Cemex, "Integrity in Action: Our Code," accessed January 5, 2024, https://www.cemex.com/documents/d/cemex/code-of-ethics.

easily accessible on the company's website, and all board members, executives, and employees are expected to sign a letter of commitment indicating that they understand the values and principles and commit to following them day-to-day while employed at Cemex. Together with the objectives, the standards create a framework for leaders and their teams to initiate projects, mobilize people and partners, and empower teams with clarity about the organization's overarching direction and expectations. These two kinds of visible information create a strong foundation for the work of leadership.

Strategy

Visible information about strategy and the capabilities that make it real provides more specific direction for the action that drives the strategic dimension of the Cemex pivot. Two of its businesses, Concrete and Urban Solutions are dynamic, requiring significant innovation, speed, and responsiveness. Sustainability is a major issue in all three businesses, and therefore, innovation is crucial in all three. As the third-largest cement producer in the world, Cemex uses an enormous amount of energy and has a major carbon footprint. Efforts to reduce that footprint and make cement production much less dependent on carbon-based energy sources is a critical strategic priority.

Table 8-3 presents our interpretation of the strategic intent and critical capabilities in Cemex's strategy based on public filings.

Context

Information about context—the who, what, where and how in Cemex—comes through significant investments that Cemex has made in hardware and software to support global information systems. Context information about operations, distribution, sales, marketing, research, product and process development, and knowledge and expertise is available in these systems.[18] For example, information about new products, marketing strategies, and pricing is available in significant detail in a system that is available to marketers across the organization. In operations, local improvement teams have access to a system that supports sharing of insights and ideas from Cemex operations across the world. The French ready-mix operations, for example, recovered freight charges from customers very differently than operations elsewhere. Their approach was documented and shared in the system. Such sharing is especially important in efforts to work with local governments and energy suppliers to find innovative alternative sources of energy in things like household waste that German operations have pioneered.

Context information is crucial in the ready-mix concrete business, where people from managers to truck drivers get accurate information

TABLE 8-3

Strategic intent and capabilities at Cemex[a]

Business	Strategic intent	Capabilities
Cement	Market leader in bagged and bulk cement produced efficiently and sustainably, but at the highest quality possible and delivered with solutions that enhance customer success	Innovate and improve consistently and continually in internal processes that drive efficiency, quality, and sustainability Excellence in marketing and logistics enabling identification and delivery of innovative complementary services to customers
Concrete and aggregates	Market leader in ready-mix concrete and aggregates, produced sustainably, tailored to meet the unique construction challenges of each customer, and delivered rapidly and accurately	Build and maintain expertise in construction materials, methods, and innovative uses of concrete Excellence in product development processes that result in innovative products and systems that use them Operational excellence in customization, order fulfillment, and logistics to deliver tailored products with speed and reliability
Urbanization solutions	Market leader in smarter, sustainable urban construction, leveraging Cemex's worldwide experience and knowledge to integrate the urban construction value chain through expertise in performance materials (enhance building materials and construction systems), circularity (sustainable construction waste streams), value-chain management, and industrialized solutions (panels, modules, and complete structures)[b]	Build and maintain exceptional products, technologies, and expertise in sustainable urbanization, especially in urban construction systems and value chains Excellence in working collaboratively across organizations and stakeholders in the urban construction value chain Project management excellence to enable integrated solutions through complementary products and services that solve urbanization problems

a. These are summaries based on our interpretation of the information found on Cemex's corporate website (https://www.cemex.com/home) and in their annual reports and other filings (website and filings accessed between January 5 and January 8, 2024).

b. For information on these segments, see https://www.cemex.com/products-solutions/urbanization -solutions.

about inventories, loads, locations, and speeds constantly updated by the minute. On most days in most places, it is a dynamic, intricate ballet of people, software, hardware, and processes moving in synch to meet the needs of customers. (And it works; many of Cemex's ready-mix operations can deliver an order in twenty minutes!) We see the same pattern in Urban Solutions, where success turns on knowledge-sharing and collaboration across all of the businesses and all of the operations in Cemex.[19]

Context information sustained by global information systems is crucial in creating innovative capabilities at Cemex. For example, in 2020 during the Covid-19 pandemic, Cemex engineers used the global system to design a stand-alone hospital with forty beds that could be built in fifteen days. Existing hospitals were swamped and needed much more capacity quickly.

The idea did not come from senior executives; it started with a few engineers in the Cemex group that develops prefab concrete walls. They decided to take action and found key people in the Construhub group (a Cemex business that works with clients to design houses) who brought computer-based design and modeling expertise. They found the right antibacterial cement produced by another Cemex group. They brought in experts in hospital design, medical experts, and government officials as partners in the project. The upshot was that Cemex designed and built a dozen of these hospitals in Mexico, each of which was constructed in about fifteen days. This was exactly the greyhound that Lorenzo Zambrano envisioned.[20]

Making Information Visible

The Cemex story illustrates the potential influence of visible information on critical decisions and actions in the leadership process. It also underscores the power that flows from a unified system of visible information that is well adapted to the strategy of the organization and applied consistently over time. Even with all of that essential work, however, the organization needs to make sure that the information is truly visible.

What does it mean for information about objectives, standards, strategy, and context to be visible? Further, how does visibility happen? As a starting point, we know the information cannot be hidden, obscure, or hard to decipher. It must be accurate, flow freely in the organization, and be totally transparent and easily accessible to everyone. This is the foundation of visible information. Since leadership, and the work it cultivates, may come from anywhere in the organization, that information must be visible to everyone. This means that the frontline workforce will know as much about the organization and its objectives, standards, and strategy as the CEO.

In the Leading Through paradigm, that foundation is created and sustained in an organic, self-managed, and self-correcting way. We saw a glimpse of that in the Cemex story. The visibility of information was much easier to pursue in an environment of information transparency and availability. Information that was created as part of the normal flow of work in Cemex's global operations—e.g., project updates, test results, marketing strategies for new products—was made available through an internal searchable network. This is very different than the world of the Power Over paradigm, where information is carefully guarded and controlled and flows up and down a strict and bureaucratic hierarchy with departments and people to harbor it and direct it to limited users.

However, there is more to visibility than a good foundation, as essential as that is. Just like in the physical world, visibility in the realm of organizational information requires two things: (1) light that illuminates and (2) eyes to see clearly. With a good foundation of transparency and availability, light and eyes to see ensure that information is visible in ways that preserve freedom and promote unity.

Light

We introduced the concept of organizational light in chapter 3. The power of the metaphor is due, in part, to the role of information in the process of illumination. In the physical world, light creates the conditions for visibility by carrying information about the objects and space around us. For example, as electromagnetic waves of light move through space, reflecting and refracting along the way, their wavelengths (key information) can be interpreted to reveal the color of objects. The direction and distance they have traveled (more key information) can be interpreted to reveal an object's shape and location.

Light can be used to produce this effect in a general sense, illuminating the environment around us, and transmitting specific information across distances, as when its electromagnetic waves carry information over laser beams (as in satellite transmissions) or through conduits (as in fiber optics). In all cases, light is a powerful tool for illuminating the context around us and transmitting information from place to place. Light makes knowing and making sense of the world possible. Without it, there is only darkness, and the information we need remains beyond our reach.

The same thing is true in the relational world of organizations, where organizational light comes from a set of beliefs and attitudes that support actions, behaviors, and practices that illuminate the organization. It does so by filling the spaces and conduits of the organization with information-carrying capacity. Just like the physical world, this happens in both a general sense, illuminating the context immediately around us, and in a more specific, focused sense, enabling information to pass easily from any one place in the organization to another.

Consider, for example, the information-carrying impact of values and behaviors that strengthen relationships, including love and care, honesty, integrity, candor, trust, respect, shared purpose, and a vibrant community (see table 3-1 for a more comprehensive list). A commitment to these values produces actions that facilitate more openness, more sharing, and more communication. As these behaviors flow more freely, they function much like the movement of light particles in the physical world—they carry information, placing it within reach and creating and strengthening the conditions for visibility. These conditions are a product of the moral work of leadership—the soul of leadership—which illuminates the organization through the cycle of virtue as it generates light.

In contrast, actions that breed darkness—for example, arrogance, bully-ing, distrust, dishonesty, disrespect, and selfishness, among many others—diminish openness, sharing, and communication, dimming the context around us and reducing the flow of information, keeping it out of reach. Darkness—the absence of organizational light—closes people off, engen-ders confusion, and leads to disengagement. Darkness inhibits the modular leadership system by keeping information, even that which is intended to be clearly visible, in the shadows. Where darkness is present, everything about the organization is much less visible, and much less effective.

Light does just the opposite. That is why generating light—and driving out darkness—is one of the most important responsibilities of a leader. But although light is essential to visibility, it isn't sufficient. Just like the physical world, the process of illumination in organizations cannot pro-duce visibility without eyes to see.

Eyes to See

Physical eyes are a miraculous instrument. Lenses focus and direct light to the retinas, which are like sensors that convert the information in light into signals that travel through the optic nerve to the parts of the brain ca-pable of interpreting those signals. Our eyes give us the capacity to know, understand, and sense what is happening in the world around us. Without this marvelous capacity, the billions of information-carrying light parti-cles traveling in the space around us would be virtually useless.

People need a similar capacity when it comes to organizational light. While the presence and movement of light ensure that information flows and reaches the places it needs to be, organizational *eyes to see* serve as the instrument of interpretation, giving people the capacity to do four things: (1) *know* what the information is, (2) *understand* what the information means, (3) *value* its importance, and (4) know how it can be *used*.

Consider a thought experiment: imagine taking a walk in a park with a botanist. You may enjoy a pleasant walk, but unless you are a botanist, you will not see what she sees. She sees different species of flowers, grasses, shrubs, bushes, and trees, knows about them, can gauge whether they have been planted and cared for correctly. She may spot potential danger like disease or infestations of pests. While you are enjoying the walk, it is for her a much richer experience. She sees the wealth of information available because she has *eyes to see.*

People with eyes to see have learned deeply, developing a base of knowledge, experience, capabilities, and tools that enable them to decode and process information, what it is, what it means, and why it is important. When that happens, information is visible to them—it is not only available and accessible, but it is known, understood, valued, and used.[21] What they "see" has meaning to them and is useful because they have learned deeply: they have a perspective formed by experience, and they have ideas and concepts they connect to the information and to their own work.

Having eyes to see depends to some extent on the person themselves and their orientation toward learning. But when it comes to the kind of visible information we are talking about in this chapter—objectives, standards, strategy, and context—it also depends heavily on the organization, and the leaders of the organization, deliberately helping people have eyes to see.

Helping people have eyes to see has at least two components. The first involves capturing, storing, and communicating information in clear, concrete, unambiguous ways that people are capable of discerning, decoding, and interpreting. In the physical world of light, only certain wavelengths are discernible to the human eye. If the light and the information it carries are not in the visible spectrum, it won't produce visibility, no matter how hard we try. The same is true of objectives, standards, strategy, and context. If the information isn't communicated in discernible, meaningful ways, it simply won't become known, understood, valued, or used.

Second, organizations help people have eyes to see by creating a learning environment, including learning resources (e.g., information systems) and experiences (e.g., training) that build the knowledge and capabilities necessary to process and make sense of information about objectives, standards, strategy, and context. These resources and experiences help to develop the metaphorical eyes—the lenses, retinas, optical nerves, and brain power—that help people decode, make sense of, and use visible information. The best leaders are also teachers who ensure that people have access to the learning resources and experiences they need to have eyes to see.

Here is a simple example: when people in an organization first read or hear the vision of the organization, if it is communicated in vivid and concrete terms, images will come to mind. Those images will inspire them. The images will create implications for their work that they will begin to understand. If there also are learning experiences designed around the organization's purpose—opportunities for them to discuss the vision and how it connects to strategy and to hear others share ideas about what it means for them—additional connections will form. Furthermore, when they put what they have discovered into practice, those experiences will help them learn even more about how purpose and vision connect to their work. Some of those connections will be cognitive, but some will be in their hearts.

The visible information in Leading Through is not just technical. It is fundamentally aspirational and inspirational. If people know, understand, and value the purpose of the organization, for example, and then observe organizational actions that reinforce that purpose (because information about those actions and the associated outcomes is visible) and begin to achieve it to some degree, the purpose will become more real and more meaningful to them. We could say the same thing about the standards, about context, and about strategy. Over time, these learning processes truly will create "visible information" because people have eyes to see.

Some people may be born with eyes to see, but for most of us, that capacity is something we develop. And, therefore, it is something the Leading Through paradigm needs to help people develop. Thus, the visible information cannot just be published or posted in a context of organizational light. That is important, but making the information visible means communicating it in ways that are meaningful and discernable and helping people to learn deeply, to develop the capacity to know it, understand it, value it, use it, and therefore, see it.

An Example of Eyes to See: Helping People See Strategy

The two aspects of strategy—strategic intent and strategic capabilities—pose different challenges in helping everyone have eyes to see. When it comes to intent, it is clear that handing everyone a three-ring binder with a hundred PowerPoint slides is not going to work. The very first require-ment is that strategic intent be expressed in a way that is accurate, but simple, and easy to communicate, understand, value, and use. However, statements of intent also have to capture what is essential. It is crucial, therefore, to articulate the essence of intent succinctly and memorably with words that connect to purpose and vision, and thus inspire. Key questions that guide a search for such a conception of strategic intent are:

- *Know and understand it.* Can people describe it? Can they explain it?

- *Value it.* Do people feel connected to it, do they recognize its im-portance, its connection to a larger purpose? Does it inspire them?

- *Use it.* Can people apply it as a guide for action, learning, and change in a specific project?

One of the reasons the strategic pivot at Cleveland Clinic described in chapter 6 was so successful was the focus on *empathy* as the driving concept in the Clinic's adjusted strategy. That focus was reinforced by giv-ing everyone the title of caregiver. Those two choices were connected and important in helping people have eyes to see. Using empathy—seeing the hospital experience through the eyes of the patient—as the driving con-cept clarified the new definition of care, for everyone. For example, Cos-grove, Merlino, and their teams found that small innovations from many different departments (e.g., changes to visiting hours, better food quality, improved cleanliness, and the design of less-exposed hospital gowns) had a significant influence on the patient experience.[22] Moreover, the focus on empathy encouraged the use of language that established a different rela-tionship with patients and elevated everyone's work. Here is an example of how language can be used to relate to patients in a different way. Imagine a caregiver saying to a patient: "We will be kind and friendly, but we will do more. We will treat you with empathy—we will do our best to walk in your shoes, feel what you feel, treat you like family, alleviate suffering, create joy and care for you."[23]

The Clinic communicated these ideas using many videos that cap-tured the meaning of empathy and its implications for every caregiver in emotionally powerful ways.[24] These are powerful media, but the most powerful thing leaders do to help people have eyes to see is to create learning experiences that put the words and concepts into action. Leaders are teachers. They create learning experiences grounded in the words that define strategic intent and actions that make intent real. The words are essential, but without consistent actions, they are just words.

Taken together, words backed up by actions create far more powerful learning experiences when people have the opportunity to discuss them and ask questions about them. The Clinic followed this path precisely. With extensive communication of the new definition of care, and with living examples of its meaning all around, the Clinic's training for every employee made the new strategy and its implications come alive. For example, the training used a powerful example from an initiative in the emergency room (ER) that encouraged all employees to communicate with the patient during their time in the ER. As Merlino described it, even "the janitor sweeping the hallway near the patient might say, 'I know you've probably been here a long time. Is there anything I can get you?'"[25]

Simplicity, vivid communication, and meaningful learning experiences; these were the keys to helping people have eyes to see strategic intent at the Cleveland Clinic. The empathy and patient experience initiative, and the adjustments in strategy Cosgrove and his team made, had a remarkable impact on patients. From 2007 to 2011 patient satisfaction with the Clinic increased by 15 percentage points, an increase more than three times the national average. Patient perceptions of their interactions with caregivers improved even more dramatically: the data for nurses increased at five times the national average, while the data for doctors exceeded the national average by a remarkable eleven times.[26]

In addition to strategic intent, strategic capabilities pose unique challenges to helping everyone have eyes to see, and this shows up especially in the allocation of the strategic resources that serve as the building blocks of those capabilities.

In Leading Through, leadership that mobilizes action, learning, and change will occur all across the organization. But highly centralized resource allocation processes will impede investment in widespread leadership projects. Not only must the resources be placed much closer to the front lines, but people must also know where they are and how to access them. Yet senior executives have stewardship over the organization's resources and naturally want to maintain some level of control over how they are allocated and used. How can these apparently conflicting objectives be resolved?

At Google, part of that resolution happened very early in the organization's history. Given Google's mission-driven focus on innovation, the founders believed very strongly in hiring creative people and giving them lots of autonomy and freedom of action.[27] Of course, Page and Brin had influence, but they did not seek detailed control over what project teams worked on, nor how resources were allocated. Larry Page posting on a breakroom refrigerator a marked-up printout of misguided ads on Google search with penetrating, critical comments is a good example of his approach to influence but not control.

Google's focus on transparency of information reinforced the founders' commitment to influence without control and laid the foundation for helping people have eyes to see strategic resources. In fact, the actions Google took to make information transparent and to flow easily in the organization had two other important effects: first, they made information about strategic resources discernible and meaningful, and second, they helped people have learning experiences about how to use strategic resources effectively.

This got started in the early days with Friday meetings for everybody and with Larry Page's top 100 projects list on an Excel spreadsheet made available to everyone. That has evolved into a large, robust information system available to all that contains up-to-date information on new products, upcoming products, launch plans, and team goals for the whole organization. In addition, the system contains OKRs—objectives and key results—for everyone in the organization. This means people can see exactly what projects others are pursuing, what their priorities are, and what they have experienced. OKRs are published every quarter.[28] This not only helps people discern who is working with whom on what kinds of projects—key strategic resources—but also creates an environment for learning. People can see how those resources are deployed and what progress is being made over time. Further, their own OKRs become a useful part of this process, for themselves and others.

As Google has grown, significant effort has been made to help people learn where the key resources are, how to access them, and how to use them effectively. For example, in their first week with the organization, Google gives new employees training on the information system, Google culture, key activities like OKRs, and programs like the 20 percent rule (each employee can use 20 percent of their compensated time on projects of their choice). Moreover, each new employee is given a buddy, someone with experience to show them around, answer questions, explain how things really work, and be an ongoing resource. After new employees have been at Google for a few days, they are given a project to work on, often with other people. It's called a "starter project"; its intent is to get new people started on learning how to use strategic resources like their own time, the time of others, and key resources like software and information.[29]

Knowing that new people need to learn about how ideas emerge and are developed, and need to get to know people in the organization, different parts of Google have conducted activities to make that happen. One example is in the Google Search team, where Demo Days have played that role. During a Demo Days week everyone clears their calendar for those days and works on teams with at least two people to create something valuable for Google Search. This means that new people will have to work with at least one person and perhaps more with experience. New people can get training on systems or tools that they do not know. At the end of the week teams present their projects in a science fair style setup.[30]

The objectives of discern and learn are clear here: new people and others may see more clearly who is working on what with whom, what resources they are using, and what progress they have made in a few days. Demo Days and other activities like them have the effect of helping people discern strategic resources in a meaningful way and learn how to access and use them. However, all of that would fall very flat if those resources were not close to the people.

Google's solution to getting resources close to the people grew out of Page's 100 projects list. After Google grew significantly, it became clear that allocating resources based on the top 100 list would not scale. The list, however, showed that about 70 percent of projects were in current operating businesses, 20 percent were in emerging new areas, and 10 percent were in new initiatives. After a lot of discussion, that became the fundamental resource allocation rule. Thus, Google put 70 percent of strategic resources (e.g., budget and people) into the operating core. This meant that operating team leaders had innovation resources in their operating budgets. Coupled with giving people 20 percent of their time for their own projects, this put strategic resources close to the people.[31]

Together with the other kinds of things Google did to help people see, putting resources close to the people—especially their own time—activates discerning and learning when there is organizational light. Consider the experience of a new Google engineer working on a small project:

> In my first month at Google, I complained to a friend on the Gmail team about a couple of small things that I disliked about Gmail. I expected him to point me to the bug database. But he told me to fix it myself, pointing me to a document on how to bring up the Gmail development environment on my workstation. The next day my code was reviewed by Gmail engineers, and then I submitted it. A week later, my change was live. I was amazed by the freedom to work across teams, the ability to check in code [submit workable programs] to another project, the trust [placed] in engineers to work on the right thing, and the excitement and speed of getting things done for our users. . . . I didn't have to ask for anyone's permission to work on this.[32]

We see here a friend who counsels the new engineer to use the 20 percent time, knows how to access a critical document that has been placed on the information system, directs the new engineer to use the development environment, and has knowledge of how to get code tested and submitted to a group in which the engineer does not work. Clearly, the light of initiative, personal agency, freedom, and trust has illuminated the context and opened the way to improvement and innovation. And think of what the new engineer has learned—boundaries are permeable, you are trusted, there are strategic resources all around you, network to find them, the information system is powerful (use it!), use your agency to take initiative, and good ideas get implemented.

Senior Leaders and the Power of Freedom with Unity

In the Leading Through paradigm senior executives in the organization exercise their stewardship over resources and every other kind of visible information largely indirectly, based on the trust they have in people. We say largely because senior leaders do have direct responsibility for projects that affect the entire organization. But they exercise significant influence through the visible information itself.

They play a central role in the development of leadership objectives, and leadership standards, and they have stewardship over the strategy of the organization. They do not determine the strategy or the standards or objectives unilaterally, but they have strong influence. Further, they nurture the culture that supports making information visible, generating organizational light and helping people have eyes to see.

Their influence also is felt in decisions about hiring, developing, and promoting people, and in the decisions they make about delegating resources. In effect, senior leaders give up a large measure of direct control they might find in a more hierarchical system. Their influence, however, is significant and important. It plays an important role in setting the context and a framework that supports unity of purpose and effort, while at the same time people everywhere in the organization have freedom of action. While senior leaders give up control (and the kind of power that comes with it), they gain a far more vibrant, innovative, flourishing organization filled with engaged people initiating, innovating, and thriving. This is the power in Leading Through.

Chapter Summary

- In Leading Through, unity is achieved (and freedom preserved) through visible information that enables teams working independently to integrate their work with each other, and with the moral, strategic, and operational context of the organization.

- The key information that must be visible and is necessary for effective integration includes:

  - *Objectives* that define how the organization will strengthen people, realize purpose, and improve productivity, and a vision that ties them all together.

  - *Standards* that capture the values and principles that define moral excellence.

  - *Strategy* that defines both the organization's strategic intent—where it will focus its efforts—and the strategic capabilities that will ensure success.

  - *Context* that captures the who, what, where, and how of the organization's resources, processes, and people.

- Information becomes visible when it is *known, understood, valued,* and *used.*

- This standard can only be met when the organization is filled with *light* and people have *eyes to see.*

CHAPTER 9

Power in the Leading Through Paradigm

The Nucor Corporation is the largest steel producer in the United States, with 29.5 million tons of capacity in 26 steel mills. It is the country's largest recycler of steel scrap and produces a wide range of steel products. Over the last decade Nucor also has moved aggressively into fabricated steel products like insulated metal panels and steel warehouse systems. The company employs over 34,000 people who helped create $41.5 billion in annual revenue in fiscal 2022. Nucor has established a long track record of innovation in processes and products that has driven the company's remarkable growth and profitability.[1]

Nucor's roots go back to a decision that Ken Iverson and Sam Siegel made in the 1960s to resurrect the bankrupt Nuclear Corporation of America by divesting most of the company's businesses and focusing its operations entirely on steel. Eventually, they moved into the scrap-based mini-mill business and renamed the company Nucor Corporation.

Iverson and Siegel built the resurrected company around a set of practices aimed at empowering everyone, from frontline workers to executives, to build the most capable and innovative steel company in the world. Iverson described this transformation in vivid terms: "Two of the most fascinating sights to behold are hot metal in motion and a group of people in headlong pursuit of a shared purpose. Those images are the essence of Nucor. They convey how we turned a confused, tired old company on the brink of bankruptcy into a star player in the resurgence of American steel."[2]

That star player became a multi-billion-dollar *Fortune* 500 company and made Iverson well known among business reporters, consultants, executives, and academics. Yet Iverson is quick to set the record straight: "As children we learned that 'Andrew Carnegie built the steel industry' and 'Henry Ford built the automotive industry'. Carnegie and Ford were, without question, giants. But to suggest that any individual—even a giant—built an industry is hogwash. The most any manager can do is shape an environment that allows employees to fulfill the goals of the business. . . . Employees, not managers, are the engines of progress. If you keep them stuck in second gear, your business will perform below its true potential."[3]

The Nucor that Iverson and Siegel shaped is a vivid example of an organization that abandoned the paradigm of Power Over. Instead of relying on power to control people, Nucor made power much less concentrated and exclusive. The whole idea was to empower people throughout the organization.

As a result, Nucor had only four layers of management and a very decentralized structure for making decisions. Even at the height of Iverson's service as CEO, the central office of the multi-billion-dollar *Fortune* 500 company employed only twenty-two people. In Iverson's words, "The fewer [layers] you have, the more effective it is to communicate with employees and the better it is to make rapid and effective decisions. . . . We don't do much here at Charlotte. That's not a joke."[4]

Nucor's thrust to push decision-making and power out into the organization led to a thorough elimination of executive "perks" and other status symbols (e.g., think special parking place, dining rooms, and luxury hotels). This played a key role in reducing the social and psychological distance between executives and people on the front lines and made knowledge and information flow more easily in the operations. Moreover, as Iverson made clear in his blunt, direct way, Nucor's commitment to visible information was fundamental: "We prefer to tell employees everything. We hold back nothing."[5]

The Leading Through Paradigm and Power: From Power Over to Power Through

The Leading Through paradigm is a paradigm of power, but of a kind very different than Power Over. In Leading Through, power flows freely, becoming a means of lifting people, of achieving purpose, of improving viability and vitality. It is a source of strength and energy that fills the organization, amplifying the soul, heart, and mind of leadership. Power is essential to Leading Through; it is at the very heart of everything we have described so far in the book. From increasing organizational light to making decentralized teams the fundamental unit of the organization, from the LIVE framework to visible information, each of the features of Leading Through contribute to, and depend on, disrupting the power dynamics that prevail in the Power Over paradigm. Paradoxically, although Power Over dynamics make executives feel powerful, they actually limit the capacity of the organization and its people. Indeed, where Power Over prevails, feelings of powerlessness and futility are a common denominator.

The key to power in Leading Through is a fundamental shift from seeking *power over people*, to activating *power through people*. That distinction rests on a commonsense view of power in organizations.

Power in Organizations

There is a lot of confusion about power in organizations, confusion that enables and supports the Power Over paradigm. The confusion is rooted in the idea that power in an organization is about control over key resources and thus over people.[6] Control over others is one expression of power, but it is not the only one, and it is not what power *is*. Power is simply the capacity or potential for action.[7]

Given Power Over's emphasis on control, the idea of power as control readily took hold in the minds of managers and executives and those studying and observing them in the early decades of the twentieth century. It has continued ever since. Unfortunately, the widespread and deep-seated nature of the Power Over paradigm has infused our world with a very narrow concept of power that shows up almost everywhere: in organizations, in public discourse, and among students of leadership.

Here is an example. There is a framework for understanding power that divides its expressions into four "faces": coercion, manipulation, domination, and subjectification.[8] Each of these faces of power positions the concept as a means of control; they represent the ways that executives and organizations exercise dominion *over* people. When understood in this narrow sense, power becomes antagonistic and competitive; a political device; a means of regulating people and their behavior.

This version of power is decidedly negative and gets in the way of efforts to allow the soul, heart and mind of leadership to flourish.[9] To be clear, we believe that power is everywhere; it is all around us and it is crucial to leadership. Power can be a tremendous force for good, but the power dynamics that do this are not those we find in the Power Over paradigm. To see why, we need to consider the consequences of Power Over more carefully.

Negative Power Dynamics in the Power Over Paradigm

Consider one of Jonathan's colleagues, a faculty member who was invited to cochair a search committee aimed at filling two key joint appointments for new faculty in two of the largest colleges in the university. The appointments were critical to new initiatives in the university, and Jonathan's colleague accepted the invitation and threw himself into the assignment, building an outstanding search committee and executing a well-organized search process.

His efforts bore significant fruit. The pool of candidates was outstanding, filled with individuals with tremendous experience leading exactly the kinds of initiatives the university was planning to pursue. The committee voted unanimously to support two of the most promising in the pool and submitted its recommendation to the college deans. Jonathan's colleague expressed a sense of excitement and accomplishment at having led such a successful search.

Unfortunately, the very next day the search committee received an unexpected message from the deans: after conferring with university administrators, it was determined that the search process would be canceled because some stakeholder was not satisfied with the outcome, although who and why was not clearly articulated. The search would be reopened the following year with a search committee composed only of the most senior people involved.

This conclusion was surprising given the unanimous support of the committee (which included all key stakeholders) and the fact that the search had attracted exactly the kinds of candidates the university would need to successfully achieve its objectives. One stakeholder remarked, referring to the quality of the candidates, that "punting on this search is a little like letting Tom Brady fall to the sixth round of the NFL draft!" Jonathan's colleague was deflated, believing that the work he had done was futile and the real work was going on behind closed doors at higher levels of the organization. He felt powerless, disconnected, and diminished.

This is a common experience of people working under the Power Over paradigm. Simply stated, power in that paradigm is concentrated in a relatively few people at the apex of the hierarchy. That opens the door to destructive tendencies and behaviors on the part of high-power individuals, particularly those who are narcissistic and self-oriented.[10] These behaviors include exploitation of others and corruption that lead to the denigration of low-status individuals, and the increased feelings of powerlessness and barriers to personal progress of the people doing the work.[11]

The concentration of power creates a separation—in some cases a vast gulf—between those in control and those doing the work. That gap is magnified by the exclusive nature of power in Power Over organizations.[12] Exclusivity confers a special status on the powerful (e.g., through executive "perks" of all kinds) that further alienates the powerless. The powerful feel superior and grossly underestimate the value of the powerless, who are marginalized and alienated. The dynamics of exclusivity and alienation get in the way of alignment on goals and purpose and often lead the powerless to withhold knowledge, information, and other resources that could benefit the organization.[13] The impact on the organization and its long-term productivity is decidedly negative.

These dynamics of concentration, separation, and exclusivity create a fundamental inconsistency in the Power Over paradigm: power is coveted by senior executives because it gives them control. But control rooted in power over people is fundamentally self-limiting. It cannot mobilize people to achieve leadership objectives effectively. Where Power Over prevails, *people* feel more powerless and experience less progress; the organization limits its capacity to pursue its *purpose*; and *productivity* eventually suffers.[14] The net effect is actually to weaken long-run viability and vitality, even if, in the short run, it may seem to deliver "results."

Power Dynamics in the Leading Through Paradigm: The Positive Consequences of Power Through

The definition of power as the *capacity or potential for action* is relatively simple and has a long history, dating back to the fourteenth century. This definition means *there is power anywhere there is potential for action.*[15] Such potential derives from a variety of sources, including physical and mental health, experience, information, knowledge, skill, position, status, and relationships, among other things.[16] Power is cultivated from these underlying resources as people develop the ability to use them to take action; that is, to do something meaningful.

Our focus centers on the *positive* potential of power in leadership. That positive potential is expressed as *power through people*, and it is one of the critical elements of Leading Through. It allows the soul, heart, and mind of leadership to permeate the organization. Jonathan observed a vivid example of this in the fall of 2021.

When Hurricane Ida made landfall in Louisiana on August 29, 2021, the sixteenth anniversary of Hurricane Katrina, it caused more than $15 billion of insured damage to homes and communities and untold billions more in uninsured damage.[17] The Church of Jesus Christ of Latter-Day Saints has long provided aid in response to such disasters in the form of goods, services, and labor to help residents of the affected areas clean up and restore their homes and communities to working order. One of the most important ways it does so is through its "Helping Hands" initiative, an effort to organize ad hoc teams of volunteers to tackle specific projects in impacted areas (e.g., cleaning out homes, clearing out downed trees, tarping and covering damaged roofs).

When Hurricane Ida hit, Helping Hands volunteers from congregations in unaffected parts of Louisiana, Alabama, and East Texas were called into action. Four weeks after the storm there were still thousands of homes and neighborhoods that needed help, so the Church decided to expand its call for volunteers to congregations in Dallas, Fort Worth, Austin, and San Antonio, Texas. Those calls went out through the church's regional network of councils—a coordinating council of lay leaders of seven to ten "stakes" (local groups of congregations); a stake council of lay leaders with stewardship for individual "wards" (congregations), and a ward council of lay leaders that oversees the work of the Church in that congregation.

The call for Helping Hands teams went out to the coordinating councils on Saturday, September 25, 2021. The coordinating councils shared information and requests for teams of volunteers with stake and ward councils. As a member of the San Antonio Stake Council, what Jonathan observed over the next week was astonishing.

First, individuals and families made commitments of resources—time, money, vehicles, gas (most of the volunteers lived eight or more hours away from the epicenter of the storm), equipment, and food.

Second, leaders in the wards emerged to organize the volunteers into specific teams, combining resources, people, and expertise to work together on specific projects. Stake council leaders supported the teams with additional resources (e.g., cleanup sleds, N-95 masks) where necessary to ensure that all teams had what they needed.

Third, coordinating council leaders provided instructions for team leaders about the needs and processes being employed by all emergency response volunteers working in the affected area. This included an orientation to Crisis Cleanup, a networking website that matches teams of volunteers to disaster relief projects. Notably, Crisis Cleanup served as a key source of "visible information," enabling teams of volunteers to work relatively independently by connecting directly with homeowners and community leaders to arrange work on specific projects. Teams were then deployed to Louisiana.

By the following Sunday, October 3, 2021—in the span of a single week—the Helping Hands initiative among the Dallas, Fort Worth, Austin, and San Antonio coordinating councils had organized 923 volunteers into teams that provided a total of 30,187 volunteer hours and completed nearly 500 individual cleanup projects, providing much needed help to thousands of people affected by Hurricane Ida. This capacity for meaningful action reflects the kind of *power through people* that enables and facilitates the soul, heart, and mind of leadership—the kind of leadership in action in the councils and among the 923 volunteers.

The Helping Hands initiative illustrates how power lies in both the capacity of individuals and in the collective action of teams and organizations:

- *Power in people.* The potential and capacity of individuals for action. Power in people derives from resources like knowledge, experience, and skill that have a clearly defined technical application, but also from resources like mental health, self-awareness, confidence, empathy, and relationships that are primarily social or emotional in nature.[18] Power in people develops as individuals learn to turn these resources into capacity for action.[19]

- *Power in teams.* The capacity of an organized group of people to act effectively in concert. This is the type of power that makes organizations so valuable. Although we focus on power in teams, we observe this capacity for collective action in pairs of people (as in spouses building a family), in all kinds of groups, and in organizations as a whole. This manifestation of power results in collective abilities that go well beyond the sum of the abilities of the individual participants. In other words, the power expressed in teams is truly a property of the team; it is distinct from the power of each individual.

Harnessing Power in People and Power in Teams

Recall the automobile assembly plant workers we described earlier in the book: when we had a chance to meet and talk with union leaders and workers, we discovered something remarkable. Outside of work, the people on the line engaged in a wide range of creative and leadership activities. They built boats, restored old cars, coached the local baseball team, ran local civic organizations, ran the PTA at the local high school, served in local government, and a host of other things. What we had seen in that plant were a lot of very talented and capable people doing repetitive work that used none of their talents and skills to work together to make things better—a simple definition of leadership. It was as if people with proven talent for leadership walked into a workplace that did not engage that talent and, in fact, actively suppressed it. The people were like cogs in a machine. The loss of human potential was staggering.

In many ways, the inability of the automobile company to use the potential power within its employees mirrors the relative inefficiency of the internal combustion engine (ICE) vehicles they were directed to build. Today, the most efficient ICE vehicles only use about 40 percent of the potential energy stored in the fuel.[20] ICE vehicles fail to convert the other 60 percent of the *potential energy* into the *kinetic energy* that moves the vehicle forward. Most of that energy is lost through inefficiency, primarily through heat loss. The Power Over paradigm does something very similar to organizations. It leaves untapped much of the potential power in people and in the teams in which they work.

Remarkably, new companies with new ideas and new technologies have introduced electric vehicles (EVs) that are much more efficient than their ICE competitors. For example, electric vehicles like the Tesla Model S and the Lucid Air can convert 77 to 100 percent of the potential energy in their batteries into kinetic energy.[21] At the top end of that range, the Lucid Air uses innovative systems to capture heat and reduce heat loss all through the vehicle.[22] The upshot is that the Lucid and Tesla EVs take advantage of nearly all of the potential energy available to them. Leading Through does something very similar in organizations.

It activates the potential power in people and in the teams in which they work.

Erin has observed these dynamics in her experience helping clients implement a model of leadership development that is grounded in activating the power in individuals and the power in teams. The model draws leaders from across businesses, regions, and functions and positions them in teams to work on challenges facing the organization. The selection of the challenges has two requirements: (1) it must be of significant strategic importance but hasn't yet been addressed or is not currently being addressed effectively; (2) it has a clear executive sponsor who is willing to support the team. The model requires a significant commitment (and courage!) from the CEO and their senior team to put these challenges in the hands of people from across the organization. Said another way, it requires that they commit to the *power* in these individuals and teams, giving up control and activating the power in them to design and implement solutions. Over several years, Erin has seen this approach create significant value for some of her clients. For others, it has been much less successful. The difference is in senior teams that are willing to activate power through (even with some initial skepticism). Where senior executives were able to do so, letting go of Power Over tendencies, the results were above and beyond expectations, delivering millions of dollars of value to their organizations over time.

The essence of the Leading Through paradigm is in enabling the power dynamics Erin has observed with her successful clients filter through the entire organization. The paradigm shifts the dominant logic away from *power over people* to control them and instead relies on *power through people* to enable them to take meaningful action. This shift allows the soul, heart, and mind of leadership to permeate the whole organization. The work of that leadership unlocks the potential power that is in the people and in their teams to take action, learn, and change in extraordinary ways. Some of that extraordinary flourishing of power is inherent in the very nature of power through.

Giving power to, or sharing power with, another person (or team) activates potential power in the receiver. But the power of the giver does not diminish. In fact, it paradoxically increases.[23] This means that action under power through significantly increases the overall level of power available for action in the organization. This is the case in the willing C-suite leaders from Erin's example above. The reciprocal flow of power through others not only increases the capacity of those involved but amplifies the potential of the teams to which they belong. Summarizing years of research along these lines, Dacher Keltner put it this way: "The most direct path to enduring power is through generosity. Give resources, money, time, respect, and power to others. In these acts of giving we empower others in our social networks, enhancing our own ability to make a difference in the world. Such acts of generosity are critical to strong societies, and empowered individuals are happier. The more we empower others, the greater good is increased."[24]

Step by step, little by little, project by project, the dynamics of power through increase the power of individuals to use their own talents and resources to benefit the organization. That, in turn, increases the capacity of the teams in which they work. Leading Through recognizes that there is potential power all around us just waiting to be harnessed.

The Morning Star Company has created this kind of dynamic by recognizing that the power the company really needs can be found in the people and in its teams. As described by Gary Hamel, "the notion of empowerment assumes that authority trickles down—that power gets bestowed from above, as and when the powerful see fit . . . [at Morning Star] individuals aren't given power by the higher-ups; they simply have it."[25]

We do not mean to say that there never is a need in the Leading Through paradigm—a specific time and a place—for the exercise of authoritative power to direct others. But we do mean to say that such circumstances are the rare exception and not the rule. These circumstances may include situations in which the immediate health and safety of people are involved, or where there is intractable conflict in which there is no hope of finding common ground between competing perspectives. In Leading Through, *Power Over* is a rarely used, highly specialized tool that is kept locked away in the toolbox (not in the toolbelt).[26]

Making *Power Through* a Reality

A crucial aspect of the Leading Through paradigm is that power through is contagious. It is not concentrated, separate, or exclusive, but rather, is diffused, unified, and inclusive. It becomes woven into the work of leadership everywhere, part of the fabric of the organization. It is this feature of the paradigm that protects against the strong tendency in human nature for people who gain power to become less generous and seek dominion or control over others.[27]

Dacher Keltner describes this dynamic in the following terms: "We gain power and the capacity for influence through social practices that advance the interests of others, such as empathy, collaboration, open mindedness, fairness, and generosity. And yet, once we gain power, success, or wealth, those very practices vanish, leaving us vulnerable to impulsive, self-serving actions and empathy deficits that set in motion our fall."[28]

Simply stated, Leading Through is designed to diminish the emergence of self-serving quests for power over other people. Indeed, the modular leadership system is designed to facilitate power through by harnessing traditional sources of Power Over *to diffuse* power in the organization.

Here we highlight four sources of power that we think are particularly important and return to Nucor's experience to illustrate their application.

Authority

Decentralizing authority and decision-making to teams on the front lines serves as a direct diffusion of power. Coupled with a reliance on principles rather than rules, that diffusion enables greater expressions of power in people and in their teams through increased autonomy and freedom of action among the people doing the work.

The organizational structure at Nucor involved aggressively decentralizing decision-making authority. As Nitin Nohria and colleagues have noted, "Nucor confined its management structure to four layers—foreman, department head, plant manager, and CEO . . . managers at Nucor don't run meetings, write letters, and push paper. They answer questions from front-line teams and provide them with support and resources. . . . Managers at the steelmaker lead by staying out of the way."[29] The role of leaders at Nucor underscores the idea that hierarchy is most effective when it is geared toward supporting, facilitating, and enabling (rather than coercing) the success of frontline work.

Status

In the context of a more diffused structure, giving ownership and responsibility for improvement to everyone levels the playing field by elevating the status of frontline workers. The reduction of status differences in turn serves to confer power on the previously powerless. It adds to freedom and bestows a sense of ownership, matching it with increased responsibility for the viability and vitality of the organization.

Nucor was equally aggressive about demolishing status differences in the organization. This was especially evident in the lack of status symbols so common in organizations of all kinds: everyone on the factory floors wore the same jackets and hard hats; everyone (including executives) flew coach when they traveled; there were no executive dining rooms, no company cars, and no reserved parking spaces; and everyone got the same benefits, including the same insurance coverage and the same holidays.[30] Eliminating the separation between executives and employees was at the heart of Nucor's approach. Iverson explained, "The people at the top of the corporate hierarchy grant themselves privilege after privilege, flaunt those privileges before the men and women who do the real work, then wonder why employees are unmoved by management's invocations to cut costs and boost profitability."[31]

Knowledge and Expertise

Making interdisciplinary teams the fundamental unit of the organization, giving them authority to act, and elevating the status of frontline workers increases the flow of knowledge and expertise in the organization. There may not be a more important source of power in people and in teams than the knowledge and expertise each person in the organization brings to the work. In Leading Through, that knowledge flows because people and teams are empowered to share it and put it to productive use.

Nucor regarded its people as the "engines of progress" and knowledge as the fuel that drove them. The company supported knowledge development and sharing beginning at the front lines of the operations. Nucor ran its plants with 250–300 people, making it easier for plant leaders to build relationships of trust and ensure a free flow of information. Nucor encouraged people all through a given plant to visit other Nucor plants to share ideas and identify best practices. Plant leaders met often to compare performance and build understanding of what really worked and why.[32]

Nucor created an expectation that all employees would take responsibility to get training on the job and to seek new knowledge and new skills by getting cross-trained and taking on projects outside their areas of expertise. As Iverson described it, learning and personal growth hinged on "an unusually active and free exchange of ideas and solutions across divisional, geographical and functional boundaries."[33] He observed that when people "see an opportunity to improve their abilities . . . they fully expect their managers to help them make it happen."[34]

Information

A commitment to making information visible, including information in the modular leadership system—context, standards, objectives, strategy—gives power to the leadership process, enhances freedom of action, and makes initiative possible. The power that flows with authority, status, and knowledge is amplified by information that is also visible—that is known, understood, valued, and used. It fuels problem-solving, decision-making, and coordination and integration of work across the organization.

Ken Iverson looked at sharing information as an "all or nothing" proposition: "Sharing information is [a] . . . key to treating people as equals, building trust, and destroying the hierarchy. I think there are really only two ways to go on the question of information-sharing: tell employees everything or tell them nothing. Otherwise, each time you choose to withhold information, they have reason to think you're up to something."[35]

Nucor chose to share all information with the people, holding back nothing. Doing anything else would have undercut every other initiative Nucor launched to create an innovative, high-performance company in a very old and tired industry. In that sense, the visibility and free flow of information at Nucor acted like a source of energy and light, protecting against feelings of exclusion, alienation, and powerlessness and unifying decision-makers operating relatively independently of each other. Such protection and unity were essential to Iverson's vision of Nucor as "a group of people in headlong pursuit of a shared purpose."[36]

As these sources of power—authority, status, knowledge, and information—become more distributed, they become a unifying and inclusive force in the organization. They are crucial in shifting the dynamics toward power through—power to unlock the potential in people, and their teams. Putting these sources of power to work is central to getting the organization right, the kind of organization that infuses power through into the work of leadership, weaving it into the fabric of the organization.

We conclude this chapter with a vignette from Ken Iverson about one of those "engines of progress" enabled by power through people:

> Timothy Patterson is a 23-year-old engineer at Nucor-Yamato Steel in Blytheville, Arkansas. He worked summers at the mill while he was earning his degree, so he knows his way around, and when an idea pops into his head he's inclined to share it with somebody. "That's one reason I wanted to be an engineer here instead of someplace else," Tim says. "Some guys still treat me like I was their little brother. But they've always listened, even to a punk kid like me."
>
> Good thing. Last year, Tim calculated that we were spending about $1.5 million annually to lubricate and maintain a series of supporting screws under the Nucor-Yamato rolling line. He noted that shims (tapered pieces of metal) would require no lubrication, and that they might work even better than the screws designed into the equipment by the manufacturer. Turned out to be a pretty smart suggestion. It cut our downtime significantly and is saving us more than a million dollars a year in maintenance costs.[37]

That is the essence of power through: enable people to take meaningful action by shaping an environment in which power is a diffused, unifying, and inclusive force for good. It is power through that puts the framework of the leadership process and the modular leadership system into effective action. Such power dynamics ignite the power in individuals, increase the power in their teams and enable them to do remarkable work.

Chapter Summary

- The Power Over paradigm depends on power dynamics that concentrate control and influence in the hands of a few, generate separation between the powerful and the powerless, and confer exclusive status and benefits on those in authority.

- The Leading Through paradigm rejects these negative dynamics and recognizes that there is power anywhere there is potential for action in the organization—especially within individual people and within teams.

- By carefully attending to the organizational dimensions of leadership, Leading Through is designed to harness power as a unifying and inclusive force:

  - *Authority* is diffused through decentralized decision-making and a focus on principles over rules.

  - *Status* is diminished as the playing field is leveled through a flatter hierarchy and ownership of (and responsibility for) improvement that extends to everyone.

  - *Knowledge and expertise* become more diffuse as teams become the fundamental unit of the organization and the value of every contribution is recognized.

  - *Information* loses its function as a source of power over people as it is made visible to everyone in the organization.

PART FOUR

LEADING THROUGH CHANGE

Making the New Paradigm a Reality

CHAPTER 10

Leadership Touchpoints for Leading Through

Making Leading Through a reality is inherently a work of leadership. It will involve mobilizing people in a process of action, learning, and change whether the organization is a new startup or has been around for decades, is growing rapidly or not at all, is small or large, local or global, for-profit or nonprofit. The details and specific challenges may differ, but it will be a developmental journey—a leadership journey—no matter what.

In this chapter we introduce the idea of a leadership touchpoint as a way to provide critical leverage for senior executives in that work of leadership.[1] A leadership touchpoint is an outcome of the Leading Through paradigm that has important and productive connections to at least one of the paradigm's key elements. Touchpoints are powerful ways to focus and target the work and yet achieve productive development on a broad front. They can help leaders achieve significant progress in making the Leading Through paradigm a reality without requiring the whole paradigm to be implemented all at once. The touchpoints illuminate new and critical ways of thinking, feeling, and behaving that help leaders gauge how deeply the new paradigm is shaping and influencing the organization's culture.

Figure 10-1 illustrates the connection between key elements of Leading Through and leadership touchpoints. Starting on the left, there are six elements of the paradigm that connect to seven touchpoints. Those

FIGURE 10-1

Touchpoints of the new paradigm of leadership

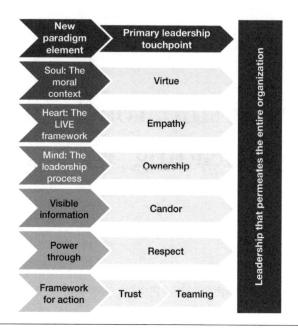

touchpoints drive a broad outcome of the paradigm—leadership that permeates the entire organization—that itself serves as an overarching touchpoint.

The diagram makes clear that the overarching touchpoint—leadership that permeates the entire organization—is the target to which the other touchpoints and paradigm elements lead. That is because we believe that when the elements of the paradigm are operative and working together, leadership will permeate the organization. Thus, the overarching touchpoint has deep connections to every element, and every element touches the organization as a whole.

That kind of abundant influence is a hallmark of each of the leadership touchpoints. Consider, as an example, the touchpoint of virtue—the strength and power of moral excellence. It is a leadership touchpoint in two senses. First, as a target of the soul of leadership, virtue is a key indicator of the extent to which work on that element of the paradigm is bearing fruit. It is a gauge of the extent to which the moral context is changing and the extent to which people are embracing the cycle of virtue—exercising moral discernment based on universal values and pursuing moral discipline. Second, pursuing virtue as a target touches the organization and the people in it in abundant ways. It requires teaching and learning, embracing new ways of thinking, working, and interacting. And it also requires supporting and encouraging people who need to act with energy and to learn and change throughout the process.

These connections mean that progress in making the soul of leadership a reality leads to progress in making virtue a reality in the organization. They also mean that virtue touches other elements like visible information and the mind of leadership and other touchpoints like candor and empathy. Thus, its influence is truly abundant. This is true of all the touchpoints in figure 10-1; they are the target of a specific element of the paradigm, but their influence is not siloed or limited. Their influence is abundant.

We now consider each of the leadership touchpoints with examples of their application. Senior executives do not have to pursue touchpoints in a fixed sequence, but we believe the work of making the Leading Through paradigm a reality will be far more successful if senior executives focus on the personal dimensions of leadership—soul, heart, and mind—before attempting to initiate work on the leadership system. Thus, we begin with the touchpoints of virtue, empathy, and ownership before turning to candor, respect, trust, and teaming.

Virtue

The organization cultivates *virtue—the power of moral excellence*—through the cycle of virtue, which frames and guides decisions and actions for everyone.

When Kim became dean of Harvard Business School (HBS) in 1995, the relationship between values and leadership had been the focus of course development and research for many years at the school. However, an episode of cheating discovered very early in his administration convinced him and his colleagues of the need for a foundation of moral values not just in what was taught in the classrooms, but in the whole HBS community.

The first step was to create a small team of faculty with staff support to define the core values of the HBS community. The charge given to the team was to search for values that are universal and central to the work of HBS, to keep the number of values small, and to consult widely with the faculty, staff, and students. After several months of work, the team proposed three values they felt were universal in their application and were fundamental to effective, responsible leadership:[2]

- Respect for the rights, differences, and dignity of others

- Honesty and integrity in dealing with all members of the community

- Accountability for personal behavior

The values had important implications for every aspect of the school:

- They were critical to the model of learning at the school that depended on active student preparation, engagement in small study groups, and participation in class. Creating a community of trust and mutual respect was essential.

- They were important for research since scholarship is a search for truth where honesty and integrity are vital.

- The values set the expectation for how members of the community should interact with one another, and they were important in leadership, and especially in developing leaders.

Once the values had been developed, Kim put together a team of faculty, staff, and students to review the system of accountability at the school, including standards for behavior and the disciplinary process, and make recommendations for a system based on the values. After careful review, the team proposed an entirely new system of accountability and discipline. Three themes characterized their proposal: clarity of expectations, simplicity of process, and transparency in outcomes. Both the community values and the new system were presented, debated, revised, and voted on by the faculty and the student body and approved in April of 1998.

After creating four teams of students, faculty, and staff to implement the values and standards in the school, Kim offered an optimistic view of the future:

> Laying down clear rules to guard against destructive behavior is basic to strengthening our community standards. But to create an exemplary environment for learning requires more. . . . What each of us does personally to make these changes work will bring them to life and give them power: personal integrity, respecting others, acting fairly and honorably, being courageous when circumstances demand it, and holding ourselves accountable for the consequences of our actions will make the difference.
>
> I look at the road ahead with great confidence. With the energy and excellence our students bring to this work, with the resolve and commitment of our faculty and staff, and with the strong support of our alumni, we will take the School forward and make it stronger and better.[3]

Kim and his colleagues believed that HBS should become a living model of the highest standards of the moral values the school established. It was crucial that students be immersed in those values in every aspect of their lives and work, and that they saw effective leadership in action, while they studied at HBS. He and his team believed that if the school did not live those values, what faculty taught the students would be hollow.

As experience with using the values and the accountability system developed, HBS launched a "Leadership and Values Initiative" (LVI) that led to a reevaluation of the MBA curriculum, a new first-year MBA course on leadership and corporate accountability, and the launch of new research.[4] LVI led to changes in many of the processes and systems across the campus, including the way the staff interacted with students, the processes in human resources, the way the school dealt with the media, and student government. Student leaders created and implemented educational activities and programs that promoted understanding of mutual respect, integrity, trust, and personal accountability.

Over the twenty-five years since it was launched, LVI has become deeply embedded in the life of the school. The engagement in the curriculum, in research, in programs, and with alumni has given LVI an aspirational dimension. As a statement on the HBS website in 2024 stated, "Our community values of mutual respect, honesty and integrity, and personal accountability support the HBS learning environment and are at the heart of a School-wide aspiration: to make HBS a model of the highest standards essential to responsible leadership."[5]

Where the soul of leadership abounds, virtue prevails, and there is light in the organization. Virtue is the primary touchpoint of the soul of leadership. The soul of leadership motivates and encourages people to learn about and then engage the cycle of virtue where action, learning, and change move people toward moral excellence. That process is driven and sustained by the moral context. As we see in the HBS story, senior leaders play a crucial role in that work. They intentionally help to shape and define the moral context by teaching, living, and reinforcing universal moral values.

Universal moral values like the virtues embraced in LVI at HBS are the foundation of the cycle of virtue. Moral discernment, a keen sense of what is right and just, is based on them, and learning to apply them, committing to live them, and helping others to do the same starts that cycle. But these commitments only yield virtue as people strive for the discipline to *do what is right, because it is right, even when it is hard.* That kind of moral discipline is more effectively developed and maintained when two things are true. The moral context—the culture of the organization—prizes and celebrates those values above all else, and executives communicate, encourage, and live those values in everything they do.

Empathy

Working within the LIVE framework, *empathy* is a common and consistent experience, strengthening love, inspiration, vitality, and expression everywhere in the organization.

Callous and unfeeling treatment of employees has shown up in the media (especially social media) at an increasing rate over the last decade. Such episodes may seem extraordinary, but unfortunately they are all too commonplace.[6] More than 60 percent of employees report being treated rudely at work on a regular basis.[7] These kinds of experiences are an artifact of the Power Over paradigm and its tendency to dehumanize people and treat them as appendages to machines and bureaucratic rules. In sharp contrast, empathy is the touchpoint of the heart of leadership in the new paradigm. Empathy begins with an understanding of the needs of others or the ability to feel what they feel. But empathy only has life when it triggers action to meet those needs and lift and strengthen others.

When senior executives make empathy a touchpoint, they focus on a quality that is central to leadership—understanding and responding to the deep needs of others. We capture those needs in the LIVE framework. People really do need love, inspiration, vitality, and expression. Within that framework a focus on empathy drives action to put LIVE into practice so that people feel valued, find direction and meaning, and experience well-being and voice.

Where the heart of leadership abounds, ruthless, callous, and selfish behaviors diminish, and empathy prevails. That is the power of the LIVE framework. Here is a personal example.

When Jonathan came down with Covid-19 in February of 2021, he disappeared from the University of Texas at San Antonio (UTSA). The severity of his case limited his ability to communicate with people on campus, but Jonathan's colleagues were paying attention.

First, Mary Kalicki, the department administrator, mobilized a group of faculty and teaching assistants to ensure that the immediate needs of the department and students were met. Mary had worked with Jonathan long enough to know that when he stopped communicating via text or email, something must be seriously wrong. She did not wait to find out the prognosis; she simply took the lead and acted to make sure Jonathan's responsibilities were covered.

Jonathan's colleagues responded. Mark Phillips, a retired military officer and seasoned executive, took over Jonathan's classes, and Vic Heller, an award-winning professor, university administrator, and Vietnam veteran, stepped in to take over Jonathan's department chair duties. Both colleagues already had very heavy loads, but they stepped in with empathic, selfless giving, something Jonathan had experienced from them many times in the past. Indeed, Vic Heller made supporting Jonathan almost ritual. When Jonathan had been named department chair three years before his illness, the two frequently found themselves the lone early morning occupants of the business building. Those early morning visits with a seasoned university leader had become a lifeline for Jonathan as he navigated his department through a series of difficult challenges.

Jonathan's illness turned out to be very serious, first because of severe Covid pneumonia and then because of multiple blood clots that developed in his lungs. Thankfully, Jonathan eventually recovered, but he was unable to return to work for two months and continued to struggle with long-Covid symptoms for months and years after that. In his absence, his colleagues made sure that the department (and his students) didn't miss a beat. When he did return, they made the process of getting back to work much easier, physically and emotionally.

Where people and organizations effectively embrace the heart of leadership, empathy flourishes. As Adam Grant has articulated, "Every day, employees make decisions about whether to act like *givers* or like *takers*. When they act like givers, they contribute to others without seeking anything in return. They might offer assistance, share knowledge, or make valuable introductions. When they act like takers, they try to get other people to serve their ends while carefully guarding their own expertise and time."[8] Power Over is a paradigm of takers. Leading Through is a paradigm of givers. The heart of leadership produces empathy, and empathy is contagious.[9]

Ownership

Employees feel a sense of *ownership* and responsibility to make things better; the organization deliberately gives people freedom and responsibility and teaches them how to take initiative to address problems and opportunities through the leadership process.

In the early 1980s the Fremont, California, assembly plant of General Motors was on life support. As one observer put it, "Productivity was among the lowest of any GM plant, quality was abysmal, and drug and alcohol abuse were rampant both on and off the job."[10] After shuttering the plant in 1982, GM entered a joint venture with Toyota. GM provided the plant; Toyota provided the expertise; and the United Auto Workers (UAW) union agreed to loosen some of its work rules to pave the way for rehiring. The result was *New United Motor Manufacturing, Inc. (NUMMI)*, which would eventually become the production home of the Chevrolet Nova and Toyota Corolla.

At NUMMI, Toyota's kaizen (i.e., "change for the better") approach to manufacturing loomed large. In this system, employees have primary responsibility for identifying problems/opportunities and making improvements. But the program was not just about extracting ideas from employees that were then considered by management in a back room. Instead, the process involved organizing frontline operators into teams with responsibility for improving a specific area of the production process. In other words, at NUMMI improvement was the purview of frontline workers, not back-office engineers. As one frontline team leader described it:

> I don't think industrial engineers are dumb. They're just ignorant. . . . it's [easy] to come up with the ideal procedure if you don't even bother to watch the worker at work, but just do it from your office, on paper. Almost anything can look good that way. Even when we do our own analysis in our teams, some of the silliest ideas can slip through before we actually try them out. There's a lot of things that enter into a good job design . . . the person actually doing the job is the only one who can see all factors. . . . engineers . . . don't know what they don't know. . . . Today we drive the process, and if we need help, the engineer is there the next day to work on it with us.[11]

By 1991, frontline teams were implementing more than eight thousand improvements to the production process in a single year. Not surprisingly,

NUMMI became the most productive plant among GM facilities, doubling the productivity of GM-Fremont, minimizing absenteeism, and virtually eliminating the substance abuse issues that plagued the previous workforce.[12]

The success of NUMMI was in no small way due to the ability of the plant to translate important elements of the Toyota production system to a US manufacturing facility. That system depends not only on pushing responsibility for improvement to frontline teams, but more importantly, equipping and enabling them to take ownership, with every frontline operator capable of leading improvement efforts. This means extensive training that is delivered directly in the flow of work.[13] It means supervisors serving as coaches, teaching and enabling frontline workers to develop the skills necessary to lead—initiate, mobilize, and empower—improvement efforts. It is a continuous effort to help everyone in the organization develop the mind of leadership.

Ownership is the touchpoint of the mind of leadership. Where the mind of leadership abounds, apathy, indifference, and disengagement fade, and ownership and initiative prevail. Ownership means that people feel a sense of responsibility and accountability for the excellence implied by the leadership objectives of people, purpose, and productivity. Ownership is to think and act like an owner. It is to understand and feel a personal stewardship for important aspects of the organization. Helping people to think and act like an owner involves more than giving people responsibility. Responsibility and authority are crucial elements, but so too are one's knowledge and understanding.[14]

That is why teaching the leadership process and helping people learn how to engage in the work of leadership is so crucial in the Leading Through paradigm. Doing so in the flow of work is especially important since, as the NUMMI and Toyota examples illustrate, that approach strengthens knowledge through direct observation. It enables learning by giving people the opportunity to receive instruction as they put that knowledge into practice.[15] Where people have the responsibility, opportunity, and knowledge required for the work of leadership, the mind of leadership will permeate the organization, and people will think and act like owners.

Candor

The organization develops a culture of *candor*; communication and information flow freely throughout the organization.

The animated film *Inside Out* tells the story of the emotional struggles of eleven-year-old Riley as she moves with her family from Minnesota to California. The story is told, in part, from the perspective of the "emotions" that live inside of Riley's mind. In one early scene, as Riley is confronted with her new surroundings, "Joy" (a character inside Riley's mind) goes to great lengths to suppress the thoughts, ideas, and memories associated with "Sadness." At one point, Joy draws a chalk circle on the floor around Sadness's feet:

> "And . . . there. Perfect. This is the circle of sadness. Your job is to make sure that all the sadness stays inside of it."
>
> "So . . . you want me to just stand here?" Sadness says in response.
>
> Joy counters, "Hey, it's not my place to tell you how to do your job. Just make sure ALL the sadness stays in the circle."[16]

Later, Joy's efforts to suppress Sadness backfire, and they both get lost in Riley's mind far from where Riley can feel or express them. Similar emotional dynamics play out in the minds of Riley's parents, and conflicts emerge. The "elephant in the room"—Riley's struggle to adapt to her new circumstances—remains unrecognized, and everyone's negative emotions boil over.

One of the ideas embedded in the film is that a lack of communication and the hesitancy of Riley and her parents to express how they really feel and what they really think get in the way of their ability to work together and solve problems.

It turns out that this idea reflects an important aspect of the culture at Pixar, the company that produced the film. Pixar's founders built its organization to support creativity and problem-solving that depend critically on the free flow of ideas, information, and communication. As Ed Catmull, one of the founders explained:

200 Leading Through Change

> A movie contains literally tens of thousands of ideas. They're
> in the form of every sentence; in the performance of each line; in
> the design of characters, sets, and backgrounds; in the locations
> of the camera; in the colors, the lighting, the pacing. The direc-
> tor and the other creative leaders of a production do not come up
> with all the ideas on their own, rather, every single member of the
> 200-to-250-person production group makes suggestions. Creativity
> must be present at every level of every artistic and technical part
> of the organization. . . . It's like an archeological dig where you
> don't know what you're looking for or whether you will even find
> anything.[17]

Catmull and his colleagues learned through success and failure that
making great films was essentially about "creating an environment that supports great people and encourages them to support one another so the
whole is far greater than the sum of its parts."[18] That environment was
built on the foundation of Pixar's operating principles:[19]

- Everyone must have the freedom to communicate with anyone.

- It must be safe for everyone to offer ideas.

- We must stay close to innovations happening in the academic
  community.

Catmull and his colleagues took those principles and turned them into
what James O'Toole and Warren Bennis have called "a culture of candor."[20]
A culture of candor fuses the way people share information—openly and
honestly—with psychological safety—a shared feeling of permission to
be candid without fear of negative consequences.[21] The effect is the free
flow of insight, information, and knowledge so crucial to creativity and
problem-solving.

It's hard to argue with the results. Pixar has had great success producing
digitally animated films that were both technological and artistic break-
throughs. *Inside Out*, for example, earned nearly $1 billion in box office
worldwide and won the Academy Award for Best Animated Feature. Overall, Pixar has produced 26 films with a total of $14.9 billion at the box office,[22]

1,021 nominations for major industry awards, and 485 award wins (including 18 Academy Awards, 10 Golden Globes, and 11 Grammy Awards).[23]

Candor is the touchpoint of visible information. When information becomes visible in a context of virtue and empathy, withholding and hoarding ideas and intelligence become much more difficult, allowing a culture of candor to prevail. A culture of candor makes it possible for people in the organization to observe, interpret, and make sense of what is happening around them. Making that possible begins with ensuring that the strategic, operational, and contextual details of the organization are transparent and visible, flowing all throughout the organization, top to bottom.

But visible information—and thus candor—also depends on productive interpersonal relationships, facilitating communication and the free flow of information, not only top-down, but, perhaps especially, bottom-up and side-to-side. That kind of information flow is only possible when there is psychological safety in the minds and behavior of everyone in the organization, including frontline employees. People need to feel safe sharing data and ideas and raising concerns openly and honestly. That can't happen where callousness and other forms of darkness impede communication, unleashing fear and clouding people's ability to know, understand, feel, and use information.

The kind of bottom-up, side-to-side communication and information flow we have in mind is crucial, not only to visible information, but also to producing the kind of initiative that is the kindling of leadership. That is because a culture of candor dispels fear, fosters open and honest communication, and stimulates problem-solving and innovation.[24] It has been an important ingredient in the success of Pixar, and it is a crucial touchpoint on the path to the new paradigm of leadership.

Respect

Respect for the value and potential in each person supersedes status in the fabric of the organization; employees on the front lines feel valued for their contributions, and senior executives proactively seek to reduce status-based differences in the organization.

In the early days of the airline, Jonathan flew on a JetBlue flight from New York to Salt Lake City. As he was settling into his seat before the cabin doors were closed, a tall, gray-haired man bounded onto the plane, grabbed the intercom handset and introduced himself to the passengers, "Hi everyone, I'm David Neeleman, CEO of JetBlue, and I'm excited to be joining you for this flight to Salt Lake City!" But Neeleman wasn't just joining the passengers for the flight, he was there to work. During the flight, he made announcements, served drinks and snacks to the passengers, and chatted up anyone who was willing to listen. More interesting was the way the other JetBlue employees on the flight interacted with him, treating him like he was just another member of the crew.

In the intervening years, we have learned that this episode is characteristic of the way Neeleman led JetBlue (Kim served on JetBlue's board during Neeleman's tenure as CEO). He described his approach in his own words:

> The way I live my life and run this company are colored by a couple of realizations I had more than 20 years ago. . . . I decided to go on a mission for my church and ended up living and working in the favela, or slums, of Brazil. . . . Living in the favelas, a few things struck me. The first was that most wealthy people had a huge sense of entitlement. They thought they were better than the people in the slums—and this rubbed me the wrong way. The second was that the poor people I met seemed happier than the rich, and they were also incredibly generous in sharing what little they had. And the third—and most striking—thing was that I was actually much happier, too.
>
> Two insights from that experience drive how I manage JetBlue: For myself and for the people I work with, I try to eliminate obvious differences in wealth and status, and I try to provide opportunities to serve others.[25]

This kind of deliberate effort to reduce status differences reflects an uncommon level of respect for people—especially those that might otherwise be considered the least among us. Respect is the touchpoint of power through and a hallmark in making the shift away from Power Over. As organizations successfully navigate that shift, status and position become less important, and respect for all prevails.

The whole idea of "power in people" and "power in teams" is that each person and each team has potential energy in them. Putting power through into action necessarily increases respect—regard and esteem— for the abilities, qualities, and contributions of everyone. Power through unlocks potential and thus highlights the capabilities and critical contributions made by everyone. That is where authority, knowledge, and information must flow to bring power through to life.

But that also means that status differences must fade. Nothing is more detrimental to power through, and thus respect for all, than the exclusivity and separation that occur when organizations unnecessarily accentuate the status of managers and executives over others.

The kind of respect we have in mind has prevailed at Lincoln Electric over its more than 125 years of business. George Willis, long-time president of the company once said, "We try to avoid barriers between management and workers. We're treated equally as much as possible. When I got to work this morning at 7:50, the parking lot was three-quarters full. I parked way out there like anyone else would. I don't have a special reserved spot. The same principle holds true in our cafeteria. There's no executive dining room. We eat with everyone else."[26]

At Barry-Wehmiller, everyone is given the same respect whether they work in accounting, marketing, or on the manufacturing floor. That means BW has eliminated time clocks and break bells; employees don't need a supervisor's sign off to attend a doctor's appointment; there are no assigned breaks for coffee and snacks; there is no micromanaging of employees, regardless of whether they work in traditional blue- or white-collar jobs. In fact, there are no collar colors at Barry-Wehmiller.

As the JetBlue, Lincoln Electric, and Barry-Wehmiller examples illustrate, respect that becomes a part of the culture of the organization requires the careful removal of the artifacts that unnecessarily emphasize status differences. As Jeff Pfeffer has noted, "This is accomplished in two principal ways—symbolically, through the use of language and labels, physical space, and dress, and substantively, in the reduction of the organization's degree of wage inequality, particularly across levels."[27] These kinds of symbolic and substantive efforts are simple but pay big dividends. They help to bring power through to life and embed respect—for everyone—in the fabric of the organization.

Trust and Teaming

Trust is cultivated throughout the organization; executives set the example by making and keeping meaningful commitments to their people.

Teaming becomes the organization's primary way of working; people collaborate, adapt, and learn to make things better, together.

The Ritz-Carlton Hotel Company has long cultivated a reputation for outstanding customer service. The company prides itself on producing unrivaled experiences for the "ladies and gentlemen" who visit the hotel as guests. It has built its business on a set of customer-focused governing principles including a "credo," a "motto," and a set of "service values." Here is an example of the principles in action:

> Two employees of the company's Dove Mountain Resort in Arizona went to great lengths to replace a lost Thomas the Tank Engine toy for a family who had visited Dove Mountain. They sent the replacement along with an elaborate set of pictures and stories chronicling the toys "extended stay" at the resort.[28]

This world-class level of service is reflected in at least two related characteristics of the organization that are visible, even to outside observers. First, there is a significant degree of trust in the organization—between coworkers and between employer and employee. Service value #3 is "I am empowered to create unique, memorable and personal experiences for our guests." Employees can spend up to $2,500 on the spot without seeking authorization to solve a problem or pursue an opportunity that enhances the experience of a particular guest. That kind of confidence and trust is significant in the minds of employees. As one long-time employee said,

"I know I could take what I have learned here to just about any company. However, I feel so supported and valuable that it would be difficult imagining being anywhere else."[29]

Second, teaming is commonplace, with executives, supervisors, and frontline employees working cooperatively to live the guiding principles and pursue the purpose of the organization with excellence. Teaming not only means working in teams, but it also means teamwork across teams to meet the needs of customers.[30] Service value #7 is "I create a work environment of teamwork and lateral service so that the needs of our guests and each other are met." Here is how one observer described the kind of teaming that emerges from the "lateral service" approach:

> This type of service occurs daily in the hotels and can be observed in the actions of individuals such as Ed Mady, general manager, and Christoph Moje, hotel manager, of The Ritz-Carlton, San Francisco. . . . These senior hotel leaders along with housekeepers, desk clerks, and other staff members from throughout the hotel rush to the aid of the culinary staff and banquet servers to plate up (that is, to place items on plates in an assembly-line process overseen with final approval from the chef) and turn a conference room into a dining room.[31]

Trust and teaming are the related touchpoints of the framework for action. Trust is nurtured by an organization that lives its values and makes and keeps commitments. In turn, that kind of trust makes the cooperative, collaborative work required for teaming possible. The framework for action reflects a set of values and commitments organizations make to their people. It embeds empowerment of frontline people into the formal structures of the organization, requiring executives to formally let go of authority and control with a high level of confidence in their people. Such commitments are central to the framework of action and thus to trust and teaming.

We recognize that keeping commitments is not easy. In a complex and dynamic world, extenuating circumstances happen. Pandemics, recessions, abrupt policy changes, natural disasters, wars, rapid shifts in customer demands, snarls in the supply chain, and much more can strike without much warning. But too many senior executives quickly take what they feel is necessary action without regard for the commitments they have made to the values and the people in their organizations. They fail to exercise leadership—and use the leadership process—to find a better way; a way that is consistent with the organization's values and as true as possible to the commitments they have made to their people.

Even in good times organizations large and small fail to keep commitments. They take action that contradicts stated values and fail to fulfill promises of promotion or professional development, or more and better information, or more autonomy and participation in decision-making. Many organizations engage in chronic, perpetual hypocrisy by espousing values that they often ignore. Failure to keep promises eats away at the trust and commitment of employees.

Such actions stand in stark contrast to the commitments companies like Ritz-Carlton make—and keep—to their employees. At its root, the failure to keep commitments, and the evident disregard of trust and teaming, lies in the paradigm of Power Over. When organizations keep their commitments to make the framework of action a reality—to value initiative over compliance; rely on principles, not rules; structure around teams, not coercive hierarchies; and decentralize authority and decision making to people on the front lines—Leading Through takes hold, and fear and self-interest give way to trust and teaming.

The trust and teaming that are so critical to long-term viability and vitality emerge from the modular framework for action with the powerful support of the other elements and touchpoints in the new paradigm. This is why we have addressed trust and teaming, and the framework of action, last in this chapter. That framework and its touchpoints depend on the elements that drive virtue, empathy, ownership, candor, and respect. With the soul, heart, and mind of leadership engaged, and with visible information and power through established, the framework for action has the moral context and the institutional support it needs to formalize trusting relationships and institutionalize the role of teaming as a driving force in the organization.

That work puts the last element of the new paradigm in place. As the whole paradigm takes hold, the organization will experience the remarkable impact of the overarching touchpoint: leadership—Leading Through—will permeate the entire organization.

Chapter Summary

- A leadership touchpoint is an outcome of Leading Through; it is a powerful way to achieve progress in making Leading Through a reality without requiring the whole paradigm to be implemented all at once.

- Touchpoints align with each of the elements of the Leading Through paradigm:

    - *Virtue* is the touchpoint of the soul of leadership.

    - *Empathy* is the touchpoint of the heart of leadership.

    - *Ownership* is the touchpoint of the mind of leadership.

    - *Candor* is the touchpoint of visible information.

    - *Respect* is the touchpoint of power through.

    - *Trust and teaming* are the touchpoints of the framework for action.

- When the elements and touchpoints of Leading Through are operative and working together, leadership permeates the entire organization; this represents the eighth and overarching touchpoint of the Leading Through paradigm.

CHAPTER 11

Making Leading
Through a Reality

With the touchpoints of Leading Through firmly in mind, we turn in this chapter to the challenge of implementation. Our focus on leadership permeating the whole organization springs from our hope that Leading Through will in time become so broadly influential that it will root out the legacy paradigm of Power Over. That kind of broad influence depends critically on the creation of a community of people with a strong commitment to the Leading Through paradigm, including senior executives with experience in making it work in many kinds of organizations. Such people will lead other organizations, create new ones, advise other executives, and serve on boards. They will play an important role in spreading the ideas and practice of Leading Through with energy and credibility. We address the chapter specifically, but not exclusively, to those senior executives. Indeed, while senior executives have organization-wide responsibility, everyone in the organization has the work of leadership to do in their sphere of responsibility and influence. No matter what your responsibilities may be, this chapter is for you. The more people there are who experience the power of Leading Through, the more people there will be who hear about it and want to experience that power themselves.

And so, we turn first to senior executives who seek to implement Leading Through in their organizations. Senior executives include people with titles like CEO, others with the word *chief* in their title, presidents or perhaps managing partners, or other such titles depending on the kind of organization they lead. These are individuals with responsibilities that span the entire organization. We assume that the number of such executives in an organization is relatively small (five to ten) and that these executives make up the "senior team."

We know that in reality you may be like Bob Chapman at the very beginning of his journey toward what he called the "general principles of leadership." Chapman was a quintessential Power Over executive, and Barry-Wehmiller was a Power Over organization. You may be like Toby Cosgrove and his team at the Cleveland Clinic, with some of the Leading Through ideas firmly in place but a need to change fundamental aspects of the organization. Or you may be like Kathy Giusti, with the opportunity to create a brand-new organization when she started the Multiple Myeloma Research Foundation. Wherever you are along that spectrum, whatever the situation you and your team face, our goal is to help you implement the Leading Through paradigm effectively.

It Begins with You

The starting point for implementing Leading Through is you, your personal leadership and the leadership of the senior team. Before we dive into the specific steps we recommend that you take, we feel it is important that you have a broad perspective on the work that lies ahead for you personally, as well as for the organization. Here are the first three principles we think will be helpful in gaining that perspective:

- *Leadership is a dynamic asset of the organization.* The Leading Through paradigm is not fixed; it is not an event or plan to be attained or achieved. It is always changing and evolving. It must be embraced, nurtured, and improved over time. It is natural to think of leadership as personal, because it is! But it is also an asset of the organization with a very long life. It is a living, dynamic asset. And, like other assets of the organization, it has both a current and future economic value. When was the last time you considered the return on your leadership assets? Perhaps it's time to consider it. After all, these are the assets that will secure both the present and the future for your organization, which means they are among the most important and precious assets you have.

- *Leadership must be intentionally designed.* Leading Through is flexible and must be adapted to fit *your* organization's context and circumstances. This means that the elements of the new paradigm must be designed, tested, and refined not only at the beginning, but also whenever the relevant circumstances of the organization change. This is precisely what is intended in the elements of the modular leadership system summarized in chapter 6.

- *Senior executives are responsible for the leadership assets in their organization.* The initiative to design and implement Leading Through is your responsibility. This is not an effort that can be assigned to others. It is not the responsibility of HR. This goes beyond execution. It includes any action taken by the organization and the impact those actions have—on people, customers, partners, communities, and society. Unless you and the senior team, indeed the organization and its people, remain intentional and deliberate about designing, testing, and refining Leading Through into the fabric of the organization, the Power Over paradigm will easily seep back into the organization and bring with it the damage of darkness.

- *Leaders who walk the talk of personal leadership have greater success.* Senior executives who embrace the personal dimensions of leadership—striving to live them in their own lives and leadership—before they attempt to implement the elements of the leadership system will be far more successful in implementing Leading Through.

- *The leadership process is a framework for the work of leadership, including implementation of the Leading Through paradigm.* The leadership

process with its three phases—Initiate, Mobilize, and Empower—
is a learnable, teachable, repeatable model for approaching the work
of transformation and change. It provides a template that can be
applied to each paradigm element as it is implemented.

Implementing the New Paradigm

The energizing power of the new paradigm is in the personal dimensions
of leadership—the soul, heart, and mind. Considering them together is
important. The integration of soul, heart, and mind is critical because
the implementation of the modular leadership system is most effectively
set in motion by *the integrated application* of these personal dimensions by
the leaders doing the work. That is true for at least two reasons.

First, each of the elements of the modular leadership system benefit
from one or more of the touchpoints of the personal dimensions of leadership. The culture of candor that is the target of visible information is enabled and amplified by virtue and empathy. The respect that comes from
power through flourishes in a context of empathy and ownership. And
the trust and teaming that are unleashed by the framework for action
thrive in a context where virtue, empathy, and ownership prevail. Thus,
an organization that is progressing toward virtue, empathy, and ownership (i.e., engaging the soul, heart, and mind of leadership) is in a stronger
position to effectively implement the elements of the leadership system.

Second, the rethinking and redesign of what goes on inside the
organization—the kind of work required to implement the modular leadership system—depend on what's going on inside of the leaders initiating,
mobilizing, and empowering that work. You know that leadership is a
personal process. And you may also know it is most effective when the
soul, heart, and mind of leadership become part of the identity and character of the leader.

Which brings us back to you. *The very first thing we recommend you do is
to work on your own leadership, both personally and as a senior team.* The soul,
heart, and mind of leadership come first. We recommend that you launch
your personal effort with the soul of leadership. The moral foundation of

leaders cannot be overemphasized. This is not only because leadership is inherently a moral work, but also because the power and effectiveness of the heart and mind of leadership depend on the soul. As we articulated in chapter 3, the connections, meaning, and purpose that come from attending to moral and spiritual needs—the soul of leadership—are an essential source of strength that feeds and amplifies the other personal dimensions of leadership.

That kind of moral strength comes from the motivation and commitment to make the cycle of virtue a pattern for your life and your leadership. Every opportunity to love a colleague puts your values as a leader to the test. The same is true of opportunities to give someone voice or to attend to the well-being of an overwhelmed employee. Any time you experience a moment of influence, the cycle of virtue is relevant. These opportunities materialize in the leadership process and represent a test of your moral discipline as a leader. In those moments, you always hold some part of the life of another person in your hands. The question is, what will you do with it? And what guides the choices you are making about what to do with it?

When you have developed a keen sense for the moral context of the decisions you are making and have the integrity and discipline to do what is right, even when it is hard, there will be more love, more inspiration, more vitality, and more expression (that is, more heart) in the leadership processes necessary to make Leading Through a living reality. Such personal development doesn't happen superficially or unintentionally. It only becomes a reality when you sincerely and deliberately seek to shape the moral context of your own life and leadership. It becomes a reality as you strive to distinguish right from wrong, light from darkness, and adopt a framework of beliefs and values to guide you in putting the cycle of virtue into practice.

So, we recommend that you start with the soul of leadership. But how do you start? The leadership process is a sure and valuable guide. The leadership process suggests that the starting point is to seek clarity around the problems and opportunities in front of you—in this case around the soul of *your* leadership. It suggests that you need to connect with the people in the organization to gain a broader, more complete perspective of your leadership. You and the senior team are familiar with Leading Through, but the people in the organization may not be. You have strong feelings about the need to strengthen leadership and some ideas about how to do it. The people may have strong feelings too, but their ideas about what to do may be different than yours. You need to be open, vulnerable, ask questions, share ideas, and (perhaps most importantly) listen.

The late Clayton Christensen—a dear friend and colleague of all three of us—once framed the importance of questions in this way: "Questions are places in your mind where answers fit. If you haven't asked the question, the answer has nowhere to go. It hits your mind and bounces right off. You have to ask the question—you have to want to know—in order to open up the space for the answer to fit."[1]

Questions are essential to your work. They help to frame and focus your search for understanding, insight, and answers. They create the space to consider many possible solutions and keep your focus on what you are really trying to accomplish. Table 11-1 lays out a set of questions to guide your work in implementing Leading Through using the leadership process. They will be useful in all the steps we lay out to help you get started, and in all the subsequent work you will do.

The questions in the Initiate row are a powerful tool for getting started. They can help to focus your efforts to identify the opportunity and connect the work to people and the ongoing work of the organization. They serve as a framework for communication. And communication—interactive, open—is crucial. And so, our first recommendation as you get started is to talk with and listen to the people who make up your organization.

Getting Started: Step 1—Talk with and Listen to the People

In order to effectively listen and communicate, we recommend that you use as many interactive channels of communication as you can. There are many tools available to you. Do not rely only on one, like email. Email can

TABLE 11-1

Questions for the senior team to guide realization of the new paradigm of leadership

Phase	Animating questions
Initiate	1. What behaviors—individual and collective—are we looking for to strengthen leadership? What learning and change will result if this work is successful?
	2. To whom do we need to listen—which perspectives, relationships, and priorities do we need to understand—to ensure that we have a more complete picture of the context and the work ahead?
Mobilize	1. What is our vision for this work—how can we communicate that reality with vivid clarity to ensure shared understanding?
	2. How will we know if the vision is becoming reality?
	3. Which people—potential team members—have the necessary perspectives, relationships, and priorities to contribute meaningfully to the work?
	4. How can we ensure that the team and the work have the resources and credibility they need to make progress?
Empower	1. What is necessary to ensure that the team remains on its established trajectory?
	2. How can we help the team—and the people on it—learn and grow in ways that benefit them and the work?
	3. What can we do to better support the team and ensure that it has both freedom of action and unity?

be useful, but there are many others. Use multiple channels that will give you and the senior team the opportunity to share ideas, ask questions, and, very importantly, listen to other people, whether virtually or in person.

Because you are focused on the soul of leadership, your efforts to listen and communicate will need to center on the values of the organization and of the people—what they believe—and how well you and the senior team reflect and live those values. The discussions you hold and the listening you do will need to extend broadly and deeply into the organization, ensuring that you and the senior team gain a broad and accurate perspective on the moral context of the organization.

As you lay the foundation for that work, there are three messages that are important for the people to hear and understand, and for you to use as the basis for discussion and listening. How to craft them and how to deliver them deserve careful reflection on your part and input from people in the organization.

The first message is about the need and desire to strengthen leadership in the organization. That need is manifest in the power of the Leading Through paradigm and in your desire to see people thrive and the organization grow and prosper. Expressing the need of the organization is important here but not nearly as important as expressing *your desire*—for stronger leadership, for the people in the organization to thrive, and for all of you, together, to grow and prosper.

The second message is that this process of action, learning, and change will begin with you and the senior team. You are step 1. This is a message about your desire and willingness to begin by strengthening your leadership in the spirit of Leading Through. It is a message that you and the senior team are serious about changing what needs to be changed in the soul of *your* leadership (and in the heart and mind as well).

The third is a message that you cannot take step 1 alone. You need their help, their engagement, and their involvement in this first step. They will be essential in helping you and the senior team in understanding Leading Through, identifying and validating the organization's values and in assessing progress in the soul of leadership.

This last message will animate people—get them talking and sharing—if you create the space for people to give voice to their ideas, perspectives, and experiences. That involves ensuring that individuals feel psychologically safe, especially when their perspective involves something about you—perhaps something negative. If they don't feel safe, it will be much more difficult—perhaps impossible—to develop a realistic picture of yourself and the moral context of the organization as they really are. Amy Edmondson's work on the fearless organization is a good place to start in thinking about creating the kind of psychological safety you will need.[2]

Getting Started: Step 2—Establish a Baseline

Step 2 is to establish a baseline—yours and the senior team's—for the soul of leadership. At this stage of the process, you are preparing to mobilize.

You have gained important insights from the listening you did as part of step 1, and that information provides you with some clues as to where you stand on leading with virtue. It helps you to answer important questions around how well you are doing on leading according to the organization's values. Is there a gap? How big is it?

Establishing a baseline for the soul of leadership requires decisions around two design choices critical to Leading Through. What are the moral values—the beliefs—that will guide the cycle of virtue for your organization? And how will you assess progress in putting the cycle of virtue into action (moral excellence)? The answers to these questions will provide you with a more vivid vision of the work ahead (ensuring a shared understanding of what you are aiming for) and help you determine how you will know if you are successful in that work.

The organization may already have a set of moral values. But the kinds of moral values that drive the cycle of virtue have universal application. They are not limited in scope but, rather, are values that resonate across people, countries, and cultures. If the organization already has such a set of values, your task is to validate them. Are these the values we believe are important for leadership in our organization now? Are they universal and do they resonate with our people? Similar questions can be used to identify a set of values if the organization doesn't have them (or hasn't embraced values that have universal application). Once it is clear what your values are (or should be), assessing moral excellence is simply a matter of determining how well your behavior consistently matches those values— that is, the extent to which your behavior reflects virtue. That is why the cycle of virtue is the framework and virtue is the touchpoint for putting the soul of leadership into action.

To ensure that your baseline assessment reflects reality, we recommend undertaking an effort to "ask the people" in a more focused and systematic way. As depicted in figure 11-1, we recommend that the process begin with you and the senior team. Assess yourselves, each other, and the group (some of this self-assessment will have already occurred naturally, if you approached step 1 with openness and vulnerability). From there, we recommend that your efforts move to people who interact with you often and see you in action as a leader. Finally, your assessment would not be

FIGURE 11-1

Asking the people

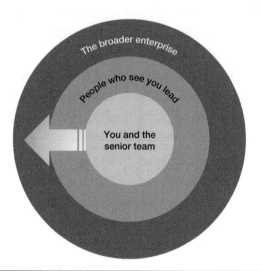

complete without asking people in the enterprise more broadly—people who may not interact with you regularly but are nonetheless affected by your work and your leadership.

At this point you are moving full steam ahead into the Mobilize phase of the leadership process. You have developed a shared vision of the work ahead (the values you aspire to and the kind of moral excellence you desire), and you have determined how you will know you are successful (how you will monitor the touchpoint of virtue). There is still a lot of discovery that needs to occur, but you are also doing the work necessary to ensure that the core team (in this case, the senior team, perhaps with the addition of one or two of people with special experience or expertise relevant to your work) is established on the right trajectory. Further, you are beginning to form a network of partners—people who can help and support what you are doing. This may be especially important as you move toward a systematic assessment of your moral excellence by those beyond the senior team.

That systematic assessment may be most valuable when carried out using several different methods. The methods should be tailored to your organization and might include a simple survey, interviews with individuals and small groups, town hall meetings, and digital tools that give the people the option of anonymity. You may find it useful to have help in crafting these instruments from the HR organization or others with relevant expertise, especially if your efforts in step 1 revealed an organization with a climate of fear. The same kind of psychological safety so essential to step 1 is critical to step 2. At this point in the process, it is essential that you communicate with the organization about what you are doing and the progress you are making.

Getting Started: Step 3—Make Progress in the Flow of Work

Once you have established a baseline—and thus a sense of where to focus your personal efforts—you are ready for step 3: make progress in the flow of work. Your regular work is the perfect place for you to experiment, learn, and make changes. Every day, all day long, you and the senior team are in meetings, interacting with people, dealing with issues, making decisions, and talking to customers, investors, members of the Board, and many others. This is the flow of work, and it presents you with opportunities to make progress on the soul of leadership.

This stage of the work also represents the transition in the leadership process from Mobilize to Empower. This is the time when you and the senior team develop a plan of action, learning, and change and work on that plan personally and together. You work together to ensure the necessary resources and support—including ongoing feedback and accountability—to empower your personal and collective efforts to shape the moral context of your work, embrace the cycle of virtue, and put the soul of leadership into practice.

Suppose your baseline shows that you need to work on trust—a universal value you and the senior team have decided to embrace. On a scale of one to ten, where ten means you inspire complete trust in people, and one means you are not to be trusted at all, your baseline puts you somewhere between five and six. Suppose further that the discussions you had in step 2 convinced you that two issues were important for you to address—keeping commitments and being open in communicating with people.

Addressing those issues in the flow of work is a matter of paying attention to the commitments you make—small and large—and following through on them without fail. A commitment like "I will get back to you this afternoon" is just as important in establishing trust as a commitment to buy a business. It also is a matter of paying attention to what open communication means to the people with whom you interact. It might mean, for example, that you need to follow up with someone who did some work for you to explain why a transaction developed in a slightly different way than you (and they) had expected. Or it might mean that you stop being quite so abrupt in your explanations, as though communicating with people is a burden.

The other people on the senior team and others around you can help you in this work if you will let them. They also can pay attention and give you feedback on how you are doing. You *empower* them; they *empower* you. And, of course, you will need to do periodic reassessments using the tools that allow you to get broad-based information about how you are doing in closing the trust gap and growing in the soul of leadership. Our counsel is to share what you are learning and what the reassessments are showing with the organization. That is true for you and for the whole senior team.

Beyond Getting Started

Getting started with the soul of leadership is a very big commitment. When you interact with the whole organization about the new paradigm, and when you commit to taking these steps, you are officially—publicly—signing up to be the stewards of the Leading Through paradigm and the process of implementing it. Importantly, you should not take the necessary steps without making sure that you and everyone on the senior team understand fully what that means.

You also are making a commitment about the kind of leader you will be. For example, getting started means letting go of the idea of the heroic, charismatic executive who has all the answers and can consistently make the right decisions, and whose charisma and presence are enough to motivate the masses to act, learn, and change. This is a Power Over construct of a leader, and it comes with unrealistic expectations, celebrity culture, and social norms that influence how many people perceive senior executives. Ideally, this is not you, and you won't have a hard time getting rid of that idea. But we also know that Power Over is so deeply embedded that this caricature of senior executive leaders may manifest in more subtle ways. It may be more difficult to let go of than you might think. That is why starting with the soul, being explicit about the kind of leader you will be, is so critical.

When your efforts around the soul of leadership begin to bear fruit, you will sense that you are learning and changing, and so is your team. You and they are starting to become the kind of leaders you want to be, but that process won't be whole until you add the heart of leadership to the work you've done on the soul. As the cycle of virtue takes hold, you will begin to feel more deeply the moral imperative for leaders—for you and your team—to help people thrive. That is the very essence of the heart of leadership. At that point, you should initiate a new effort focused on the LIVE framework, with empathy as the key touchpoint.

Fortunately, you will not have to reinvent the wheel. You already have some practice using the leadership process (that is what you were doing in executing steps 1, 2, and 3), and much of the work you did to lay the groundwork for the soul of leadership will be relevant to the heart of leadership too. The content will be different; you will have to communicate with the organization, teaching them about LIVE. Your discussions and data collection will focus on how your leadership reflects love and care, inspiration and meaning, and helping people achieve vitality and expression. There is a lot to be done, but the essential process is the same.

Working on the soul and heart of leadership this way also gives you experience with the mind of leadership. By the time you make progress with the heart of leadership, you will have a good idea of what the leadership process requires and how you might make progress in using it more broadly in your own work. There will also be benefits for the organization. You have taught them quite a bit about the soul and heart of leadership and about the new paradigm because you engaged them in your efforts. And you have taught them about the mind of leadership; your work on the leadership process has produced protocols, methods, and patterns of working that anyone in the organization can apply to any element of the new paradigm of leadership. You have made progress in establishing trust and credibility with the people in the organization. You have made good on commitments to them, and they have first-hand evidence that what you have said and taught about Leading Through is real.

Bringing Soul, Heart, and Mind to the Entire Organization

As stewards of the new paradigm and of the process to make it a reality in your organization, you and the senior team are responsible for leading the work necessary to bring the soul, heart, and mind of leadership to the entire organization. In many ways, the work you have done on yourselves—engaging the entire organization in that effort—has already initiated that process. Some people and groups in the organization may have observed what you have done and taught and will initiate similar work in their own units and groups. You may also find it necessary to initiate some of that work yourself by inviting a division or a department to be involved where you feel you have the people and the situation ready for the action, learning, and change the work requires. As you do so, you will need to let go of any tendency to control the process. This means inviting, persuading, and supporting rather than mandating and directing. This kind of shift may necessitate more action, learning, and change on your part—developing new habits and new ways of working and nurturing greater confidence in the people in your organization.

No matter how you decide to launch and support getting the organization engaged, our counsel is to invest in teaching people about the soul, heart, and mind of leadership. There are many ways to do that, but our advice is to follow the pattern established in your own work. Start with the soul of leadership, teach them what you have learned, enough to get started themselves, and then let the bulk of the teaching and learning happen in the flow of the work. The sequencing might look something like this:

- *Begin with the soul of leadership.* Initiate a leadership process to shape the moral context all throughout the organization, laying the groundwork for generating light and driving out darkness by embracing, teaching, and living the cycle of virtue.

  - Animate the soul of leadership in the organization through purpose.

- *Train and educate people* on the soul of leadership in the flow of their work.

- *Bring the heart of leadership to life.* As the moral context takes shape, initiate work on the LIVE framework, with a goal of making it the basis of leadership and relationships all throughout the organization.

- *Solidify the leadership process.* Progress on the soul and heart of leadership have given people experience with the leadership process; they are beginning to understand the mind of leadership. Now, teach people to take initiative and use the leadership process to solve problems and pursue opportunities in the flow of their everyday work.

- *Monitor the touchpoints.* Use the touchpoints of virtue, empathy, and ownership to gauge the organization's readiness for formal implementation of the modular leadership system.

The last point is crucial. The touchpoints are targets to aim for as your organization teaches, practices, and makes changes around the personal dimensions of leadership. We urge you to monitor these touchpoints—virtue for the soul, empathy for the heart, and ownership for the mind.

The touchpoints provide a useful lens through which to evaluate the status of your efforts to embrace the new paradigm. Everyone in the organization can use the same approach you used to assess virtue, and they can use that very same approach to assess empathy and ownership. The ownership touchpoint provides an especially important benchmark at this stage. It indicates the extent to which people embrace opportunities to lead and do the work of leadership using the leadership process in ways that are clear and consistent across the organization. You and the senior team play a crucial role in achieving that clarity and consistency. You embrace, teach, and use the leadership process to frame and guide your work in making the new paradigm a reality in your organization.

Lay the Foundation for the Modular Leadership System

As the personal dimensions of leadership—and the touchpoints that characterize them—begin to take shape in the organization, senior executives will need to be cognizant of their own attitudes and behaviors. This is an opportunity for senior executives to put new patterns into practice, let go of control, and let initiative and leadership begin to take hold in the organization. The spirit of Leading Through—leadership facilitated by freedom and unity—ought to play a significant role in guiding you and the senior team in this effort. If you fall back on Power Over methods—directives, rules, unilateral decision-making—the effort will fail. It is crucial that you lead the effort using the principles of the Leading Through paradigm. That is why this chapter started with you: you need to teach, communicate, encourage, support, and guide using Leading Through in your own work.

As people all throughout the organization begin to practice the cycle of virtue, make LIVE a part of their relationships, and take initiative in their stewardship, you and the senior team will need to help enable the natural progression of these new patterns of working. People will come to see that the work they've been doing leads naturally and directly toward an environment of increased freedom and unity. The modular leadership system is the mechanism by which such freedom and unity can be more fully activated, institutionalized and sustained.

While all the good work on the soul, heart, and mind of leadership is going on, you can lay the foundation for the leadership system. We propose that you teach and practice a sequence of actions that will prepare the whole organization for the leadership system, and that can be used by any group to implement elements of the system. This sequence has a natural, organic flow, as one action sets the stage for the next.

- *Make information visible.* Build on the work done to shape the moral context and generate light by developing the processes and practices that make information visible: increase transparency and availability, dispel darkness, and give people "eyes to see" (understand, value, and use the information available).

- *Let go of Power Over.* Building on the work of distributing and making information more visible in the organization, do the same thing with status, knowledge, and authority, unleashing power through.

- *Make freedom of action with unity the new reality through the framework for action.* Power through turns the gears that formalize and institutionalize the framework for action, yielding greater trust and supporting teams as the principal unit of organization.

- *Monitor the touchpoints.* Use the touchpoints of candor, respect, trust, and teaming to gauge the organization's success with visible information, power through, and the framework for action. Use the overall touchpoint of leadership permeating the entire organization to gauge the organization's overall success with Leading Through.

The process begins with visible information because your work on the soul of leadership made it clear that for the cycle of virtue to permeate the organization, both the moral context and its animating purpose need to be visible (known, understood, valued, and used). That can only happen as you work on the processes and actions necessary to make information visible. There is much you can do to make information about objectives, standards, strategy, and context more transparent, accessible, understood, valued and used. Such visibility will be strengthened by the light generated as people and teams embrace and practice the cycle of virtue.

As information becomes more visible, power through will flow naturally. That is because information is a key source of power, and making it more visible facilitates broader distribution of power throughout the organization. And there is much more you can do to build on that foundation, including uplifting people by addressing status differences in the organization and making knowledge (e.g., opportunities for learning and growth) more widely available.

The need to distribute authority makes work on the framework for action a necessary and natural outgrowth of your efforts to distribute the sources of power more broadly. Indeed, the structural elements of the framework for action reinforce and sustain the kind of distributed authority necessary to make power through a reality. In this way, the beginning of your work on the framework for action flows naturally from your efforts to empower the organization. And, again, the sequence continues with much work for you and other leaders in the organization to do to embed freedom and unity in the structures and processes of the organization.

Along the way, assessing the touchpoints of the modular leadership system—a culture of candor, respect, trust, and teaming—is critically important. As before, you can get that started by initiating work on methods and instruments to be tried, tested, and improved as the organization works on the leadership system. In all of this, your commitment and engagement are crucial, both because of what you need to do (initiate and guide organization-wide leadership processes) and for what you need to avoid (attempt to control the process).

At the heart of that ongoing work are the soul, heart, and mind of leadership. And the key process in all of that is the leadership process. Early in this chapter we emphasized the importance of questions that you might use to engage people in the organization. Questions are always crucial, regardless of what you're working on. That is true at the beginning; it is also true when Leading Through is well established and needs to evolve.

The kinds of questions that are most valuable are animating questions whose answers lead to action, learning, and change. In asking and answering the questions necessary to guide your journey toward the new paradigm, we encourage you to view them from the vantage point of two perspectives we introduced in chapter 5:

- What does this question suggest about what we *are doing* that we should *stop doing*—or do differently?

- What does this question suggest about what we *are not doing* that we should *start doing*?

Viewing things from these two perspectives can help you and the senior team frame and focus your work of leadership—the action, learning, and change necessary to embrace, launch, and sustain the Leading Through paradigm in your organization.

This is a work with no end. The Leading Through paradigm is a living asset. While the fundamental principles do not change, the specific applications and the way the paradigm works in your organization will change and evolve over time. All of that ongoing work is the work of leadership. It is your work and the work of everyone in the organization. And it is great work! It is the work of lifting and strengthening people, helping them to grow, take initiative, innovate, and thrive. It is the work of building a flourishing organization with vitality and viability for the long term. It is the work of Leading Through.

Chapter Summary

- Making Leading Through a reality in your organization begins with senior executives embracing five key principles:

  - Leadership is a dynamic asset of the organization.

  - Leadership must be intentionally designed.

  - Senior executives are responsible for leadership assets.

- – Leaders must walk the talk of personal leadership.

- – The leadership process is the framework for implementing Leading Through.

- Implementation of Leading Through begins with the soul of leadership. Its success will depend on what's inside the leaders doing the work and the extent to which they embrace the soul of leadership as the foundation of their work on Leading Through. Their work thus becomes the pattern for implementing the paradigm throughout the organization.

- The work of Leading Through has no end; it is an ongoing work to activate the soul, heart, and mind, enabling leadership to permeate the entire organization—helping people to thrive, enabling the organization to pursue purpose more effectively, and strengthening productivity.

Acknowledgments

We are especially grateful to Jeff Kehoe at Harvard Business Review Press for the kindness, firmness, and encouraging spirit he brought to the editing of *Leading Through*. We are also grateful to David Moss for his insights, wisdom, and encouragement, and for believing enough in the ideas to invest in helping us learn how to teach Leading Through to others.

KIM

I am grateful for the love, example, and support of Sue, my wife and best friend for fifty-three years, and for the inspiration and love of my family.

I want to thank Harvard Business School colleagues and coauthors Steve Wheelwright, Carliss Baldwin, and Taka Fujimoto; their influence is evident in this book. My Brigham Young University colleagues Paul Godfrey, Ben Galvin, and Jeff Bednar read early drafts of this book and gave me valuable insights and guidance. Spenser Clark and Kena Anderson provided superb research assistance. Four colleagues—Dallin Oaks, Henry B. Eyring, Jeffrey Holland, and David Bednar—were my predecessors in university leadership and my leaders during my service as a general authority in the Church of Jesus Christ of Latter-day Saints. Their examples, encouragement, and wise counsel have had a profound effect on me and my understanding of the work of leadership.

JONATHAN

I would like to acknowledge the love and support of my wife, Deborah, and my sons Isaac, Owen, and Jasper. None of this would have any meaning without them. They have played important roles in leading me through the joys, triumphs, and challenges of life.

In addition, I would like to thank Giovanni Araujo and Ruben Molina for their tireless efforts to assist me with much of the research I did in connection with this book. I couldn't have done it without them. I also want to thank Sara Singer and Gordon Bloom for asking pointed questions and offering meaningful feedback. Their inquiries, ideas, and suggestions had a material impact on important aspects of Leading Through. I am also grateful to my colleagues and co-authors Drew Carton and Chad Murphy for helping me to see the importance of studying leaders and leadership. Finally, I want to thank my many colleagues and friends at The University of Texas at San Antonio. The support and encouragement played an important role in this project.

ERIN

I am grateful, first and foremost, to my children Kira, Kat, Mason, Matthew, and Charlotte. They inspire me to be a better person, a better mother—a better leader. They have supported and encouraged me in my work and have each demonstrated great patience and love in this process. I am blessed to call them mine.

I also want to thank the many clients who have trusted and continue to trust me as their coach and adviser. While I am unable to name all of them, each had a meaningful impact on me and my work and helped to shape the ideas in this book. I have also been privileged to work with incredible colleagues and want to specifically acknowledge Michael Griffiths, Kristen Chester, Marly Siegal, Jessie Reese, and Therese Russell, whose partnership and assistance have been especially important in support of this book. It is a privilege to work with inspiring leaders in the work I do every single day.

Notes

Chapter 1

1. For the definition of a paradigm, see the entry for "paradigm" in https://www.merriam-webster.com/dictionary/paradigm; for additional insight into paradigm as worldview, see the chapter on "Paradigms and Worldviews" in Alex Mackinnon and Barnaby Powell, *China Calling* (London: Palgrave Macmillan, 2008), https://doi.org/10.1057/9780230594203_5.

2. The organizations cover most of the industries listed under the US two-digit Standard Industrial Classification (SIC) codes.

3. The roots of the Power Over paradigm and its framework for action lie in the history of the modern industrial enterprise. See Alfred D. Chandler, *Scale and Scope: The Dynamics of Industrial Capitalism* (Cambridge, MA: Harvard University Press, 1990); A. D. Chandler, *The Visible Hand: The Managerial Revolution in American Business* (Cambridge, MA: Harvard University Press, 1977).

4. These ideas were popularized by Frederick Taylor. See F. W. Taylor, *The Principles of Scientific Management* (New York: Harper & Brothers, 1911).

5. T. P. Hughes, *American Genesis* (New York: Penguin, 1989), 187, 191; Taylor, *Principles of Scientific Management*, 128.

6. Regarding power, see C. Perrow, *Organizing America: Wealth, Power, and the Origins of Corporate Capitalism* (Princeton, NJ: Princeton University Press, 2002), 162–163, 217. This is true even in a multidivisional structure where bureaucratic tools allow senior executives to retain significant control over the organization; see J. Yates, *Control through Communication: The Rise of System in American Management* (Baltimore: John Hopkins University Press, 1993), 72.

7. For the classic statement of this idea, see James Macgregor Burns, *Leadership* (New York: Harper and Row, 1978). See also Ronald A. Heifetz, *Leadership without Easy Answers* (Cambridge, MA: Belknap, 1994), 23–24. For the view that leadership is morally neutral, see Manfred Kets De Vries, "Organizations on the Couch: A Clinical Perspective on Organization Dynamics," *European Management Journal* 22, no. 2 (2004): 183–200.

8. See: J. M. LeBreton, L. K. Shiverdecker, and E. M. Grimaldi, "The Dark Triad and Workplace Behavior," *Annual Review of Organizational Psychology and Organizational Behavior* 5 (2018): 387–414.

9. For background on narcissism, see Michael Maccoby, "Narcissistic Leaders: The Incredible Pros, the Inevitable Cons," *Harvard Business Review*, January 2004, 92–101.

10. For evidence along these lines, see Benjamin M. Galvin et al., "Narcissistic Organizational Identification: Seeing Oneself as Central to the Organization's Identity," *Academy of Management Review* 40, no. 2 (2015): 163–181; Suzanne J. Peterson, Benjamin M. Galvin,

and Donald Lange, "CEO Servant Leadership: Exploring Executive Characteristics and Firm Performance," *Personnel Psychology* 65, no. 3 (2012): 565–596.

11. See Dacher Keltner, *The Power Paradox: How We Gain and Use Influence* (New York: Penguin, 2016), 98–114.

12. In just a few weeks in the fall of 2023 we witnessed the conviction of Sam Bankman-Fried for a massive fraud he perpetrated at FTX, a crypto currency exchange, and revelations of widespread bullying, discrimination, and sexual harassment and misconduct at the Federal Deposit Insurance Corporation. See also Kristin Rivera and Per-Ola Karlsson, "CEOs Are Getting Fired for Ethical Lapses More Than They Used To," *Harvard Business Review*, June 6, 2017, https://hbr.org/2017/06/ceos-are-getting-fired-for-ethical-lapses-more-than-they-used-to?autocomplete=true; Michael Hobbes, "The Golden Age of White-Collar Crime," Huffington Post, 2020, https://www.huffpost.com/highline/article/white-collar-crime/; M. S. Salter, "Innovation Corrupted: The Rise and Fall of Enron," Cases 905-048 and 905-049 (Boston: Harvard Business School, 2004).

13. See Keltner, *The Power Paradox*, 101–103.

14. See Gallup, "State of the Global Workplace: 2023 Report," accessed January 10, 2024, https://www.gallup.com/workplace/349484/state-of-the-global-workplace.aspx.

15. See P. F. Drucker, *Concept of the Corporation* (Piscataway, NJ: Transaction, 1993), 37–38.

16. K. B. Clark and T. Fujimoto, *Product Development Performance: Strategy, Organization, and Management in the World Auto Industry* (Boston: Harvard Business School Press, 1991).

17. S. J. Spear and H. K. Bowen, "Decoding the DNA of the Toyota Production System," *Harvard Business Review*, September–October 1999, 96–106.

18. See Chandler, *The Visible Hand*, 345.

19. For background on Jeff Bezos and Amazon, see Jeff Bezos, "We Are What We Choose," Princeton University 2010 Graduation Remarks, https://www.princeton.edu/news/2010/05/30/2010-baccalaureate-remarks; Jodi Kantor and David Streitfeld, "Inside Amazon: Wrestling Big Ideas in a Bruising Workplace," *New York Times*, August 15, 2015, https://archive.nytimes.com/www.nytimes.com/2015/08/16/technology/inside-amazon-wrestling-big-ideas-in-a-bruising-workplace.html; Jodi Kantor, Karen Weise, and Grace Ashford, "The Amazon Customers Don't See," *New York Times*, June 15, 2021, https://www.nytimes.com/interactive/2021/06/15/us/amazon-workers.html; John Rossman, *The Amazon Way: Amazon's 14 Leadership Principles*, 3rd ed. (Seattle: Clyde Hill, 2021).

20. For a description of each principle, see https://www.amazon.jobs/content/en/our-workplace/leadership-principles.

21. For anecdotal evidence on these challenges, see Brad Stone, "Burnt Out Amazon Engineers Are Embracing the Great Resignation," *Bloomberg*, January 24, 2022, https://www.bloomberg.com/news/newsletters/2022-01-24/amazon-employees-are-burned-out-and-leaving-their-jobs?embedded-checkout=true.

22. For a review of these findings, see Brian Resnick, "How Power Corrupts the Mind," *The Atlantic*, July 9, 2013, https://www.theatlantic.com/health/archive/2013/07/how-power-corrupts-the-mind/277638/.

23. See, for example, Mary Parker Follett, *Freedom and Coordination: Lectures in Business Organization* (New York: Routledge, 2015); Mary Parker Follett, *Dynamic Administration: The Collected Papers of Mary Parker Follett* (New York: Routledge, 2003); Fritz J. Roethlisberger and William Dickson, *Management and the Worker* (Cambridge, MA: Harvard University Press, 1939).

Chapter 2

1. See BW's published data on revenue, employment, and the number of countries in which they have operations at https://www.barrywehmiller.com/news/company-news /release/surpassing-100-acquisitions-barry-wehmiller-looks-to-the-future.

2. Bob Chapman and Raj Sisodia, *Everybody Matters: The Extraordinary Power of Caring for Your People Like Family* (New York: Portfolio/Penguin, 2015), 51–53.

3. This paragraph summarizes the principles of THL. For a complete account, see Dylan Minor and Jan Rivkin, "Truly Human Leadership at Barry-Wehmiller," Case 717-420 (Boston: Harvard Business School, 2016), 4–5, exhibit 2.

4. Chapman and Sisodia, *Everybody Matters*, 59.

5. See Minor and Rivkin, "Truly Human Leadership," 6–7.

6. L3 stands for Living Legacy of Leadership. For more information about Barry-Wehmiller University, see the Barry-Wehmiller website: https://www.barrywehmiller.com.

7. See Minor and Rivkin, "Truly Human Leadership," 2–3.

8. See Chapman and Sisodia, *Everybody Matters*, 41–42.

9. See Minor and Rivkin, "Truly Human Leadership," 4.

10. J. Richard Hackman, "What Is This Thing Called Leadership?" in *Handbook of Leadership Theory and Practice* (Boston: Harvard Business Press, 2010), chapter 4; Ronald A. Heifetz, *Leadership without Easy Answers* (Cambridge, MA: Belknap, 1994); Ronald A. Heifetz and Donald L. Laurie, "The Work of Leadership," *Harvard Business Review*, December 2001, 131–141.

11. In developing this definition and the Leading Through paradigm, we have drawn on several streams of research and writing about practice. These streams include (1) transformational leadership: see B. M. Bass and R. E. Riggio, *Transformational Leadership* (New York: Psychology Press, 2006); Daan van Knippenberg and Sim B. Sitkin, "A Critical Assessment of Charismatic–Transformational Leadership Research: Back to the Drawing Board?" *Academy of Management Annals* 7, no. 1 (2013): 1–60; (2) servant leadership: see Robert K. Greenleaf, *Servant Leadership: A Journey into the Nature of Legitimate Power and Greatness* (Mahwah, NJ: Paulist Press, 2012); N. Eva et al., "Servant Leadership: A Systematic Review and Call for Future Research," *Leadership Quarterly* 30, no. 1 (2019): 111–132; (3) authentic leadership: see Bill George, *Authentic Leadership: Rediscovering the Secrets of Creating Lasting Value* (San Francisco: Jossey-Bass, 2003); Bill George, *Discover Your True North: Becoming an Authentic Leader* (San Francisco: Jossey-Bass, 2015); (4) adaptive leadership: Ronald Heifetz, Alexander Grashow, and Marty Linsky, *The Practice of Adaptive Leadership: Tools and Tactics for Changing Your Organization and the World* (Boston: Harvard Business Press, 2009). These more recent ideas about leadership have important antecedents in classic works on leadership. See, for example, Chester Barnard, *The Functions of the Executive* (Cambridge, MA: Harvard University Press, 1968); Philip Selznick, *Leadership in Administration: A Sociological Interpretation* (Berkeley: University of California Press, 1984); James MacGregor Burns, *Leadership* (New York: HarperCollins, 1978); and Warren Bennis, *On Becoming a Leader* (New York: Basic Books, 1989).

12. There are other words we might have used to capture the sense of moving forward to take action—*marshal, assemble, organize, adapt*. We follow Heifetz and use the word *mobilize* because it conveys a sense of moving forward to take vigorous action in the face of challenges. Mobilize is an important part of the framework of adaptive leadership developed by Ronald Heifetz. See Heifetz, *Leadership without Easy Answers*.

13. We have not attached adjectives to the process of leadership. We take the position that leadership is leadership. It is our view that the many adjectives in the literature (e.g.,

transformational, authentic, servant, adaptive) represent different dimensions of the work of leadership.

14. Martin Luther King Jr., *Strength to Love* (New York: Harper and Row, 1963), chapter 5, "Love Your Enemies."

15. The metaphor of organizational light has been developed by Kim Cameron and his colleagues in the Center for Positive Organizations at the University of Michigan. An important focus of that work has been the effect of light in the form of positive relational energy on human beings and its specific application to leadership. See Kim Cameron, *Positively Energizing Leadership: Virtuous Actions and Relationships That Create High Performance* (Oakland, CA: Berrett-Koehler, 2021).

16. Hubert Joly has used this metaphor in his book about his experiences at Best Buy. See Hubert Joly, *The Heart of Business* (Boston: Harvard Business Review Press, 2021).

17. This is not a new idea. For example, the work on transformational leadership has treated leadership as a change process. However, apart from setting up that perspective, few researchers have delved into the operational nature of the process or the actual work of leadership.

18. This implication—that everyone has the work of leadership to do—is profound. Leading Through takes a view of people that is positive and uplifting. It asserts that every person in the organization not only can execute their current work, but also can learn. They can recognize opportunities and challenges within their sphere of responsibility and influence, and they can create projects to solve problems and seize opportunities.

19. For more on the collective motivating impact of purpose, mastery, and autonomy, see D. H. Pink, *Drive: The Surprising Truth about What Motivates Us* (New York: Penguin, 2011). The theory underlying Pink's arguments is similar to the underpinnings of the job characteristics model. For more on this model, see J. R. Hackman and G. R. Oldham, *Work Redesign* (Reading, MA: Addison-Wesley, 1980).

Chapter 3

1. This account is based on Ryan W. Buell, Joshua D. Margolis, and Margot Eiran, "Babcom: Opening Doors," Case 418-026 (Boston: Harvard Business School, 2018). See also the company's website: https://babcomcenters.com/he/.

2. The debate about whether there are universal moral values is centuries old. However, recent research in anthropology has established quite clearly that universal moral values exist. See Oliver Scott Curry, Daniel Austin Mullins, and Harvey Whitehouse, "Is It Good to Cooperate? Testing the Theory of Morality as Cooperation in 60 Societies," *Current Anthropology* 60, no. 1 (2019), https://www.journals.uchicago.edu/doi/full/10.1086/701478.

3. Kim Cameron and colleagues at the Center for Positive Organizations (University of Michigan) have studied extensively the positive influence of organizational light in leadership and on performance. For a review of their work and additional evidence, see Kim Cameron, *Positively Energizing Leadership: Virtuous Actions and Relationships That Create High Performance* (Oakland, CA: Berrett-Koehler, 2021).

4. For evidence of the influence of actions of organizational light on people in the organization, see Cameron, *Positively Energizing Leadership*, 37–42.

5. It is true that such an organization may have economic success, at least in the short run. Enron, for example, racked up several years of apparent growth and profitability while the darkness that engulfed that company, its auditors, and many of its partners and suppliers grew and grew. In the end, when the truth was known, Enron and its audit firm, Arthur Anderson, ceased to exist.

6. Buell, Margolis, and Eiran, "Babcom: Opening Doors," 9.

7. See Eagle Hill Consulting's National Survey on Attrition at http://www.eaglehill consulting.com/insights/retaining-top-employees-low-performers-destroying-culture/.

8. In related work on virtue, Cameron and colleagues at the Center for Positive Organizations have made virtuousness, and virtuous behaviors like gratitude, central to their leadership framework. See Cameron, *Positively Energizing Leadership*, 67–69.

9. See the entry for "virtue" in *Merriam-Webster Dictionary*, https://www.merriam -webster.com/dictionary/virtue?src=search-dict-hed.

10. For background on Hamdi Ulakaya, see https://www.forbes.com/profile/hamdi -ulukaya/?sh=7baf25114052.

11. This story is based on the company's website and Arvinna Lee, "How Chobani Dominated the Yogurt Market in Just 8 Years," ReferralCandy, April 27, 2016, https://www .referralcandy.com/blog/chobani-marketing-strategy.

12. Chobani, "The Chobani Way," https://www.chobani.com/about/.

13. The legal and regulatory actions of local and national governments have established the concept that the organization is a citizen of the communities in which it operates, with responsibilities to its neighbors.

14. This example is drawn from Robert E. Quinn and Anjan V. Thakor, "Creating a Purpose-Driven Organization," *Harvard Business Review*, July–August 2018, 78–85.

15. Quinn and Thakor, "Creating a Purpose-Driven Organization," 4.

16. Rebecca Henderson has called this concept "shared value" and linked it to architectural innovation—innovation that primarily changes the relationships between the components of a system. See Rebecca Henderson, *Reimagining Capitalism in a World on Fire* (New York: Public Affairs, 2020), 71–83.

17. See the DTE website for information about these initiatives: https://empowering michigan.com/dte-impact/.

18. In an important sense, making its neighbors' needs a part of its purpose was essential to DTE's desired identity. Without making neighbors and their communities part of its purpose, DTE's stated purpose would ring hollow; it would be seen as hypocritical, even by its own people. By pursuing that purpose in ways that connect with its work, DTE seized an opportunity that is its true purpose—to lift and strengthen people and communities. For additional information, see Robert Quinn and Andrea Meyer, "DTE Energy (A-C)," Case W69C35 (Ann Arbor, MI: WDI Publishing, 2018) (available through Harvard Business Publishing).

Chapter 4

1. In 2022 Best Buy was named among the World's Most Admired Companies by *Fortune* for the seventh year in a row. See Nadvia Davis, "Best Buy Named to Fortune's 2022 List of World's Most Admired Companies," Best Buy Partner Portal, February 2, 2022, https://partners.bestbuy.com/-/bby-named-fortunes-2022-list-worlds-most-admired -companies-newsupdate.

2. This account is based on Hubert Joly, *The Heart of Business* (Boston: Harvard Business Review Press, 2021).

3. Joly, *The Heart of Business*, 29.

4. Joly, *The Heart of Business*, 81.

5. Joly, *The Heart of Business*, 141.

6. R. Carucci, "Behind the Scenes of Best Buy's Record-Setting Turnaround with Hubert Joly," *Forbes*, April 4, 2021, https://www.forbes.com/sites/roncarucci/2021/04 /04/behind-the-scenes-of-best-buys-record-setting-turnaround-with-hubert-joly/?sh =18ea1dc53f0a.

7. Barsade and O'Neill have called this "companionate love." S. G. Barsade and O. A. O'Neill, "What's Love Got to Do with It? A Longitudinal Study of the Culture of Companionate Love and Employee and Client Outcomes in a Long-Term Care Setting," *Administrative Science Quarterly* 59, no. 4 (2014): 551–598.

8. See E. V. George, *Triumphs of Experience: The Men of the Harvard Grant Study* (Cambridge, MA: Belknap, 2015).

9. Vivek H. Murthy, "Our Epidemic of Loneliness and Isolation," Office of the Surgeon General, May 2023, https://www.hhs.gov/sites/default/files/surgeon-general-social-connection-advisory.pdf.

10. D. Richo, *How to Be an Adult in Relationships: The Five Keys to Mindful Loving* (Boulder, CO: Shambhala, 2002).

11. Names and other details have been disguised or omitted to protect the privacy of the organization and individuals involved in the story.

12. See the entry for inspire at https://www.merriam-webster.com/dictionary/inspire?src=search-dict-hed#note-1.

13. T. M. Thrash et al., "The Psychology of Inspiration," *Social and Personality Psychology Compass* 8, no. 9 (2014): 495–510.

14. T. Hart, "Inspiration: Exploring the Experience and Its Meaning," *Journal of Humanistic Psychology* 38, no. 3 (1998): 7–35; T. M. Thrash et al., "Inspiration and the Promotion of Well-being: Tests of Causality and Mediation," *Journal of Personality and Social Psychology* 98, no. 3 (2010): 488.

15. A. Lewis and J. Clark, "Dreams within a Dream: Multiple Visions and Organizational Structure," *Journal of Organizational Behavior* 41, no. 1 (2020): 50–76; J. R. Clark, V. Kuppuswamy, and B. R. Staats, "Goal Relatedness and Learning: Evidence from Hospitals," *Organization Science* 29, no. 1 (2018): 100–117.

16. A. M. Carton, "'I'm Not Mopping the Floors; I'm Putting a Man on the Moon': How NASA Leaders Enhanced the Meaningfulness of Work by Changing the Meaning of Work," *Administrative Science Quarterly* 63, no. 2 (2018): 323–369.

17. RC Willey has opened onsite care clinics in its Utah stores. See: https://www.rcwilley.com/Jobs.

18. McKinsey Health Institute, "Addressing Employee Burnout: Are You Solving the Right Problem," McKinsey Insights, May 2022, https://www.mckinsey.com/mhi/our-insights/addressing-employee-burnout-are-you-solving-the-right-problem.

19. Lyra Health and the National Alliance of Healthcare Purchaser Coalitions, "American Worker in Crisis: Understanding Employee Health in Unprecedented Times, July 2020, https://www.lyrahealth.com/wp-content/uploads/2020/07/LYRA-NA-Employee-Mental-Health-Report.pdf.

20. McKinsey Health Institute, "Addressing Employee Burnout."

21. For additional information on burnout from the World Health Organization, see https://icd.who.int/browse11/l-m/en#/http://id.who.int/icd/entity/129180281 (accessed July 22, 2022).

22. Deloitte, "Workplace Burnout Survey: Burnout without Borders," accessed July 22, 2022, https://www2.deloitte.com/us/en/pages/about-deloitte/articles/burnout-survey.html.

23. S. Mo and J. Shi, "Linking Ethical Leadership to Employee Burnout, Workplace Deviance and Performance: Testing the Mediating Roles of Trust in Leader and Surface Acting," *Journal of Business Ethics* 144, no. 2 (2017): 293–303; L. M. Cortina et al., "Incivility in the Workplace: Incidence and Impact," *Journal of Occupational Health Psychology* 6, no. 1 (2001): 64; R. Cross, R. Rebele, and A. Grant, "Collaborative Overload," *Harvard Business Review*, January–February 2016, 16.

24. E. W. Morrison, "Employee Voice Behavior: Integration and Directions for Future Research," *Academy of Management Annals* 5, no. 1 (2011): 373–412.

25. J. E. Hunton, T. W. Hall, and K. H. Price, "The Value of Voice in Participative Decision Making," *Journal of Applied Psychology* 83, no. 5 (1998): 788; M. R. Cooper and M. T. Wood, "Effects of Member Participation and Commitment in Group Decision Making on Influence, Satisfaction, and Decision Riskiness," *Journal of Applied Psychology* 59, no. 2 (1974): 127–134.

26. For additional work in the spirit of the new paradigm, see A. C. Edmondson, *The Fearless Organization: Creating Psychological Safety in the Workplace for Learning, Innovation, and Growth* (Hoboken, NJ: John Wiley & Sons, 2018).

27. T. M. Amabile, "How to Kill Creativity," *Harvard Business Review*, September–October 1998, 76–87; T. M. Amabile and M. G. Pratt, "The Dynamic Componential Model of Creativity and Innovation in Organizations: Making Progress, Making Meaning," *Research in Organizational Behavior* 36 (2016): 157–183.

28. Amabile, "How to Kill Creativity."

29. Joly, *The Heart of Business*, 106–108.

Chapter 5

1. This account of Kathy Giusti and the MMRF is based on R. G. Hammermesh, J. D. Margolis, and M. C. Preble, "Kathy Giusti and the Multiple Myeloma Foundation," Case 9-814-026 (Boston: Harvard Business School, 2017); the MMRF website, https://themmrf .org/about/; and Kathy Giusti's website, https://kathygiusti.com/kathys-story/.

2. For more on the idea of leadership as a process, see A. J. Murphy, "A Study of the Leadership Process," *American Sociological Review* 6, no. 5 (1941): 674–687; J. L. Pierce and J. W. Newstrom, *Leaders and the Leadership Process* (New York: McGraw-Hill/Irwin, 2003).

3. Giusti did not use the leadership process just once. She used it many, many times over the years as new opportunities emerged.

4. Students of leadership have explored and sketched leadership processes as they play out in a variety of contexts, including organization-wide change, groups and teams, and other social systems (e.g., families, communities, nations). Our research suggests that these frameworks bear many commonalities and, when synthesized and integrated, give life, shape, and structure to the generalizable leadership process we develop in this chapter. For examples of these frameworks, see J. Stouten et al., "Successful Organizational Change: Integrating the Management Practice and Scholarly Literatures," *Academy of Management Annals* 12, no. 2 (2018): 752–788; F. Rashid, A. C. Edmondson, and H. B. Leonard, "Leadership Lessons from the Chilean Mine Rescue," *Harvard Business Review*, July–August 2013, 113–119; R. A. Heifetz and M. Linsky, *Leadership on the Line* (Boston: Harvard Business School Press, 2002).

5. R. A. Heifetz and M. Linsky, "A Survival Guide for Leaders," *Harvard Business Review*, June 2022, 65–74.

6. For additional work on these issues, see B. Williams and R. Hummelbrunner, *Systems Concepts in Action: A Practitioner's Toolkit* (Stanford, CA: Stanford University Press, 2010).

7. Betsy Morris and Patricia Sellers, "What Really Happened at Coke," *Fortune*, January 10, 2000, https://money.cnn.com/magazines/fortune/fortune_archive/2000/01/10 /271736/index.htm. For more on Ivester's rise and fall as CEO of Coca-Cola, see Michael D.

Watkins, Carin-Isabel Knoop, and Cate Reavis, "The Coca-Cola Company (A): The Rise and Fall of M. Douglas Ivester (Abridged)," Case 808-074 (Boston: Harvard Business School, 2007).

8. R. J. Hackman, *Leading Teams: Setting the Stage for Great Performances* (Boston: Harvard Business Press, 2002).

9. For additional work on the language of vision, see A. M. Carton, C. Murphy, and J. R. Clark, "A (Blurry) Vision of the Future: How Leader Rhetoric about Ultimate Goals Influences Performance," *Academy of Management Journal* 57, no. 6 (2014): 1544–1570; C. Murphy and J. R. Clark, "Picture This," *Organizational Dynamics* 2, no. 45 (2016): 139–146.

10. For more on this experience, see Rashid, Edmondson, and Leonard, "Leadership Lessons," 113–119.

11. See S. G. Cohen and G. E. Ledford Jr., "The Effectiveness of Self-Managing Teams: A Quasi-Experiment," *Human Relations* 47, no. 1 (1994): 13–43; R. Wageman, "How Leaders Foster Self-Managing Team Effectiveness: Design Choices Versus Hands-on Coaching," *Organization Science* 12, no. 5 (2001): 559–577.

12. See S. A. Mohrman, R. V. Tenkasi, and A. J. Mohrman Jr., "The Role of Networks in Fundamental Organizational Change: A Grounded Analysis," *Journal of Applied Behavioral Science* 39, no. 3 (2003): 301–323.

13. See J. E. Dutton et al., "Moves that Matter: Issue Selling and Organizational Change," *Academy of Management Journal* 44, no. 4 (2001): 716–736.

14. There may be initiatives that propose pursuing an opportunity by doing things in a different way or doing completely new things. However, the principles are the same, and solid content and an effective wrapper remain vital.

15. For more on credibility and leadership, see J. M. Kouzes and B. Z. Posner, *Credibility* (San Francisco: Jossey-Bass, 1993).

16. See C. A. O'Reilly and K. H. Roberts, "Relationships among Components of Credibility and Communication Behaviors in Work Units," *Journal of Applied Psychology* 61, no. 1 (1976): 99.

17. For seminal work on engagement, see J. R. Hackman and G. R. Oldham, "Motivation through the Design of Work: Test of a Theory," *Organizational Behavior and Human Performance* 16 (1976): 250–279.

18. Hackman, *Leading Teams*.

19. See A. C. Edmondson, *The Fearless Organization: Creating Psychological Safety in the Workplace for Learning, Innovation, and Growth* (New York: John Wiley & Sons, 2018).

20. R. A. Heifetz and D. L. Laurie, "The Work of Leadership," *Harvard Business Review*, December 2001, 124–134.

21. The idea of common ground is an application of the notion of a "holding environment" as developed by Heifetz. See Ronald A. Heifetz, *Leadership without Easy Answers* (Cambridge, MA: Belknap, 1994), 104.

22. T. L. Ruble and K. W. Thomas, "Support for a Two-Dimensional Model of Conflict Behavior," *Organizational Behavior and Human Performance* 16, no. 1 (1976): 143–155; M. P. Follett, *Creative Experience* (New York: Longman, Green and Co., 1924), 156.

23. Some scholars have begun referring to this process as "creative abrasion." For example, see L. A. Hill et al., *Collective Genius: The Art and Practice of Leading Innovation* (Boston: Harvard Business Review Press, 2014).

24. Hill et al., *Collective Genius*.

25. For more detail on methods of "regulating distress" see Heifetz and Laurie, "The Work of Leadership"; Heifetz and Linsky, "A Survival Guide for Leaders."

Chapter 6

1. The clinic operates as a nonprofit physician-led group practice with a long-standing history of medical excellence. Doctors are signed to single-year contracts, renewed on the basis of metrics reflecting their quality of care, and receive salaried wages to encourage needs-based, rather than quota-based treatment. Its mission is "caring for life, researching for health, educating those who serve," "Mission, Vision & Values," https://my .clevelandclinic.org/about/overview/who-we-are/mission-vision-values. The original mission of the Cleveland Clinic, as determined by its founders in 1921, was "better care of the sick, investigation into their problems, and further education of those who serve."

2. According to *U.S. News*, Cleveland Clinic has been rated among the "The Best of the Best Hospitals" in the United States for twenty-four consecutive years as of 2023, and has been ranked number one in cardiology and heart surgery for twenty-eight consecutive years as of 2023. For more information concerning performance in other specialties, see "U.S. News Rankings," https://health.usnews.com/best-hospitals/area/oh/cleveland-clinic -6410670. For its 2022 international ranking, see https://my.clevelandclinic.org/-/scassets /files/org/about/who-we-are/cleveland-clinic-facts-and-figures-2022.pdf?la=en.

3. For more information concerning surgical outcomes, see Cleveland Clinic, "Treatment Outcomes," https://my.clevelandclinic.org/departments/patient-experience /depts/quality-patient-safety/treatment-outcomes/913-outcomes-summary; data on locations obtained from "2019 Year-End Facts and Figures," https://my.clevelandclinic.org/about /overview/who-we-are/facts-figures.

4. Ananth Raman and Anita L. Tucker, "Cleveland Clinic: Improving the Patient Experience," Case 612-031 (Boston: Harvard Business School, 2013).

5. Cosgrove emphasized Patients First from the beginning of his time as CEO. See https://newsroom.clevelandclinic.org/2017/05/01/toby-cosgrove-m-d-announces-decision -transition-president-ceo-role.

6. For additional background on the discussion, see Raman and Tucker, "Cleveland Clinic."

7. D. M. Cosgrove, "A Better Patient Experience: A Letter to Our Readers from Delos M. Cosgrove, M.D., CEO and President," *Cleveland Clinic Magazine*, Summer 2007, 3. http://www.clevelandclinic.org/clevelandclinicmagazine/pdf/summer_07.pdf.

8. See Toby Cosgrove, *The Cleveland Clinic Way: Lessons in Excellence from One of the World's Leading Health Care Organizations* (New York: McGraw Hill Education, 2014), 109–111.

9. Cleveland Clinic, "Mission, Vision & Values," https://my.clevelandclinic.org/about /overview/who-we-are/mission-vision-values.

10. The job demands–resources model provides insight into the impact of bureaucracy and compliance on employee satisfaction, well-being, and engagement. It casts bureaucracy, and specifically "red tape," as a "hindrance" to the fulfillment and satisfaction people gain from their work. For examples, see M. Tadić, A. B. Bakker, and W. G. Oerlemans, "Challenge Versus Hindrance Job Demands and Well-being: A Diary Study on the Moderating Role of Job Resources," *Journal of Occupational and Organizational Psychology* 88, no. 4 (2015): 702–725; A. B. Bakker and E. Demerouti, "Job Demands–Resources Theory: Taking Stock and Looking Forward," *Journal of Occupational Health Psychology* 22, no. 3 (2017): 273; Sanjay K. Pandey, "The Psychological Process View of Bureaucratic Red Tape," in *Research Handbook on HRM in the Public Sector*, ed. Bram Steijn and Eva Knies (Cheltenham, UK: Edward Elgar, 2021); B. Steijn and J. Van der Voet, "Relational Job Characteristics and Job Satisfaction of Public Sector Employees: When Prosocial Motivation and Red Tape Collide," *Public Administration* 97, no. 1 (2019): 64–80.

11. See P. Verme, "Happiness, Freedom and Control," *Journal of Economic Behavior & Organization* 71, no. 2 (2009): 146–161; G. Brulé and R. Veenhoven, "Freedom and Happiness in Nations: Why the Finns Are Happier Than the French," *Psychology of Well-being* 4, no. 1 (2014): 1–14.

12. R. Gulati, "Structure That's Not Stifling," *Harvard Business Review*, May–June 2018, 68–79.

13. For an in-depth look at modularity, see Carliss Y. Baldwin and Kim B. Clark, *Design Rules: The Power of Modularity* (Cambridge, MA: MIT Press, 2000).

14. Baldwin and Clark present an extensive discussion of modularity in digital devices. See Baldwin and Clark, *Design Rules*, 77–88, 90–154.

15. Clothing: see, for example, Ying Chen and Meng-Mi Li, "Modular Design in the Fashion Industry," *Journal of Arts and Humanities* 7, no. 8 (2018): 27–32; Chanjuan Chen and Kendra Lapalla, "The Exploration of the Modular System in Textile and Apparel Design," *Clothing and Textile Research Journal* 39 (2021): 39–54. For analysis of modularity in the early days of the auto industry, see R. N. Langlois and P. L. Robertson, "Explaining Vertical Integration: Lessons from the American Automobile Industry," *Journal of Economic History* 49, no. 2 (1989): 361–375; Nicholas Argyres and Lyda Bigelow, "Innovation, Modularity, and Vertical De-integration: Evidence from the Early U.S. Auto Industry," *Organization Science* 21, no. 4 (2010): 803–954. For an analysis of modularity in the twenty-first century automobile industry, see John Paul MacDuffie, "Modularity-as-Property, Modularity-as-Process, and Modularity-as-Frame: Lessons from Product Architecture Initiatives in the Global Automobile Industry," *Global Strategy Journal* 3 (2013): 8–40. Complex systems: H. A. Simon, "The Architecture of Complexity," *Proceedings of the American Philosophical Society*, 106, no. 6 (1962): 467–482. Biological systems: for example, see J. Clune, J. B. Mouret, and H. Lipson, "The Evolutionary Origins of Modularity," *Proceedings of the Royal Society B* 280 (2013): 2012–2863. Human systems: for example, see M. E. Newman, "Modularity and Community Structure in Networks," *Proceedings of the National Academy of Sciences* 103, no. 23 (2006): 8577–8582.

16. Modularity has important organizational consequences. For example, "the mirroring hypothesis" notes that the modular structure of a product is mirrored in the organizational patterns of the organization. See L. J. Colfer and C. Y. Baldwin, "The Mirroring Hypothesis: Theory, Evidence, and Exceptions," *Industrial and Corporate Change* 25, no. 5 (2016): 709–738.

17. See Baldwin and Clark, *Design Rules*, 77, for a discussion of the requirements of a modular system.

18. This example is based on the account in Eric Schmidt and Jonathan Rosenberg, *How Google Works* (New York: Grand Central, 2014), xxvii–xxix.

19. Regarding the system: In modularity terms these criteria are generally referred to as "criteria for testing," and they determine whether a module can function in the system and what value one module creates relative to another. The key idea is that with such criteria, a module may be tested independently from the other modules. Accurate and reliable module-level testing eliminates the need to put the whole system together before knowing if the module works well. Regarding other teams: In modularity terms fit and cohesion are ensured through clearly specified "interfaces," which specify the standards by which modules exchange resources, effort, and information when necessary. The idea is that as long as the work of the modules complies with the interface, it can be designed, produced, and executed in relative independence from the other modules. In other words, a given module does not have to be custom fitted to the specific modules it needs to join in the system.

20. The independence and autonomy of a team/module as described here pertains to its design and its production. The absence of interaction simply means that there are

no design parameters in the module that depend on the design parameters of any other module. However, all modules in a system must interact in operation according to the visible information. See Baldwin and Clark, *Design Rules*, 43–53, 64–70, for an extended discussion of interactions across modules.

21. The integrated practice unit (IPU) idea was first developed in Michael E. Porter and Elizabeth Olmstead Teisberg, *Redefining Health Care: Creating Value-Based Competition on Results* (Boston: Harvard Business Press, 2006); see also Cleveland Clinic, "Medicine Institute: 2016 Outcomes," https://my.clevelandclinic.org/-/scassets/files/org/outcomes /outcomes-medicine.ashx, p 34.

22. For more information, see https://my.clevelandclinic.org/departments/heart/depts /heart-failure-center (accessed January 10, 2023).

23. See Cleveland Clinic, "Mission, Vision & Values," accessed January 10, 2023, https://my.clevelandclinic.org/about/overview/who-we-are/mission-vision-values.

24. See Cleveland Clinic, "Empathy: The Human Connection to Patient Care," accessed January 10, 2023, https://youtu.be/cDDWvj_q-o8.

25. Our approach to strategy is based on the framework developed in A. G. Lafley and Roger Martin, *Playing to Win: How Strategy Really Works* (Boston: Harvard Business Review Press, 2013).

26. Toby Cosgrove, *The Cleveland Clinic Way: Lessons in Excellence from One of the World's Leading Health Care Organizations* (New York: McGraw Hill Education, 2014), 118–119.

27. A. M. Carton, C. Murphy, and J. R. Clark, "A (Blurry) Vision of the Future: How Leader Rhetoric about Ultimate Goals Influences Performance," *Academy of Management Journal* 57, no. 6 (2014): 1544–1570.

28. Authors' analysis of Hospital Consumer Assessment of Health Care Providers and Systems (HCAHPS) data, available from The Centers for Medicare & Medicaid Services at https://data.cms.gov/provider-data/.

29. The principles of modularity are found in many other organizations, including those that have embraced the "agile" approach to software development. When done well, the principles of modularity can be observed on a smaller scale in the many product development projects that rely on agile principles. Specifically, agile teams are composed of interdependent, cross-functional professionals (including both business- and technical-oriented team members). Agile principles ensure that these teams have the resources and freedom of action to take initiative and innovate in solving the problems and pursuing the opportunities that are the focus of their work. Moreover, agile teams are guided by a set of values, norms, and principles and operate in an environment of information transparency, providing the visible information necessary to ensure that the team's work is unified with the overall product development process and with the organization as a whole. When approached as a mindset applied to an entire organization, the agile approach envisions something similar to what we have outlined here: a network of decentralized, empowered teams, supported by a flat hierarchy and transparent, visible information. See Wouter Aghina et al., "The Five Trademarks of Agile Organizations," McKinsey & Company, January 22, 2018, https://www.mckinsey.com/capabilities/people-and-organizational -performance/our-insights/the-five-trademarks-of-agile-organizations.

Chapter 7

1. See: https://www.morningstarco.com/wp-content/uploads/2023/06/Statistics -Brochure-2023.pdf for 2023 data on Morning Star and its production facilities.

2. The Morning Star story is based on Francesca Gino et al., "The Morning Star Company: Self-Management at Work," Case 914-013 (Boston: Harvard Business School, 2016).

3. The academic and professional literatures have reinforced this idea with concepts of leadership like "shared," "collective," "collaborative," "distributed," "integrative," or "relational," or in observations of the need for "leadership at all levels" or "leaders at all levels." A summary of the research in these areas can be found in J. L. Denis, A. Langley, and V. Sergi, "Leadership in the Plural," *Academy of Management Annals* 6, no. 1 (2012): 211–283.

4. See, for example, B. M. Bass and B. J. Avolio, eds., *Improving Organizational Effectiveness through Transformational Leadership* (Thousand Oaks, CA: Sage, 1994). Similar elements of empowerment are part of concepts like "servant leadership" and "authentic leadership."

5. On initiative, see M. Frese and D. Fay, "Personal Initiative: An Active Performance Concept for Work in the 21st Century," *Research in Organizational Behavior* 23 (2001): 133–187.

6. D. G. Renlund, "Abound with Blessings," *Liahona,* November 2019, https://www.churchofjesuschrist.org/study/general-conference/2019/04/41renlund?lang=eng.

7. B. Chapman and R. Sisodia, *Everybody Matters: The Extraordinary Power of Caring for Your People Like Family* (New York: Penguin, 2015).

8. For examples of this research and experience, see K. W. Thomas, *"Intrinsic Motivation at Work: What Really Drives Employee Engagement* (Oakland, CA: Berrett-Koehler, 2009); D. H. Pink, *Drive: The Surprising Truth about What Motivates Us* (New York: Penguin, 2011).

9. Seth Godin, "It's Easier to Teach Compliance than Initiative," Seth's Blog, February 26, 2010, https://seths.blog/2010/02/its-easier-to-teach-compliance-than-initiative/.

10. The classic reference is P. R. Lawrence and J. W. Lorsch, "Differentiation and Integration in Complex Organizations," *Administrative Science Quarterly* 12, no. 1 (1967): 1–47. See also H. Mintzberg, "Structure in 5's: A Synthesis of the Research on Organization Design," *Management Science* 26, no. 3 (1980): 322–341.

11. J. Pfeffer, "Seven Practices of Successful Organizations," *California Management Review* 40, no. 2 (1998): 104.

12. J. Richard Hackman, *Leading Teams: Setting the Stage for Great Performances* (Boston: Harvard Business School Press, 2002).

13. J. Schwartz et al., "Organizational Performance: It's a Team Sport: 2019 Global Human Capital Trends," Deloitte Insights, https://www2.deloitte.com/us/en/insights/focus/human-capital-trends/2019/team-based-organization.html; in 2019, Deloitte consulting reported that only 8 percent of companies said that almost all work is done by cross-functional teams.

14. For more on the different types of teams, see S. C. Wheelwright and K. B. Clark, *Revolutionizing Product Development: Quantum Leaps in Speed, Efficiency, and Quality* (New York: Free Press, 1992), 190–217.

15. Schwartz et al., "Organizational Performance."

16. For more on how this structure works in practice, see "Squads, Sprints and Stand-ups," ING, November 23, 2017, https://www.ing.com/Newsroom/News/Squads-sprints-and-stand-ups.htm.

17. For more, see "ING's Agile Transformation," *McKinsey Quarterly,* January 10, 2017, https://www.mckinsey.com/industries/financial-services/our-insights/ings-agile-transformation.

18. For more, see "ING's Agile Transformation."

19. For a summary of the Spotify model, see J. Kamer, "How to Build Your Own 'Spotify Model,'" February 9, 2018, https://medium.com/the-ready/how-to-build-your-own-spotify-model-dce98025d32f.

20. Pfeffer, "Seven Practices," 106.

21. See P. S. Adler, "Building Better Bureaucracies," *Academy of Management Perspectives* 13, no. 4 (1999): 36–47.

22. See Donella H. Meadows, *Thinking in Systems: A Primer* (London: Earthscan, 2009), 10; Adler, "Building Better Bureaucracies," 36–47.

23. We are not part of the "bureaucracy busting" movement, nor are we aligned with the extreme positions of some in the self-organization movement who argue in favor of eradicating hierarchy and the need to "fire all the managers." We hold neither view.

24. Bob Sutton, "Hierarchy Is Good. Hierarchy Is Essential. And Less Isn't Always Better," LinkedIn Blog, https://www.linkedin.com/pulse/20140112221140-15893932 -hierarchy-is-good-hierarchy-is-essential-and-less-isn-t-always-better/.

25. See A. Bejan, *Freedom and Evolution: Hierarchy in Nature, Society and Science* (Cham, Switzerland: Springer Nature, 2019).

26. See M. L. Fein, *Human Hierarchies: A General Theory* (New Brunswick, NJ: Transaction, 2012).

27. From the WL Gore website, accessed February 9, 2022: https://www.gore.com/about /working-at-gore.

28. For more, see Gino et al., "The Morning Star Company."

29. H. A. Simon, "Applying Information Technology to Organization Design," *Public Administration Review* 33, no. 3 (1973): 268–278.

30. R. B. Shaw, *Extreme Teams: Why Pixar, Netflix, Airbnb, and Other Cutting-Edge Companies Succeed Where Most Fail* (New York: Amacom, 2017).

31. For more on integrated practice units, see M. E. Porter and E. O. Teisberg, *Redefining Health Care: Creating Value-Based Competition on Results* (Boston: Harvard Business Press, 2006).

32. "Our Program," Northwestern Medicine Women's Integrated Pelvic Health Program, 2024, https://iphp.nm.org/integrated-pelvic-health-program.html.

33. M. E. Porter and T. H. Lee, "Integrated Practice Units: A Playbook for Health Care Leaders," *NEJM Catalyst: Innovations in Care Delivery* 2, no. 1 (2021), https://catalyst.nejm .org/doi/full/10.1056/CAT.20.0237.

34. Chapman and Sisodia, *Everybody Matters*.

35. See Reed Hastings and Erin Meyer, *No Rules Rules: Netflix and the Culture of Reinvention* (New York: Penguin, 2020).

36. R. Gulati, A. O'Connell, and C. De Laclivier, "Alaska Airlines: Empowering Frontline Workers to Make It Right," Case 9-418-063 (Boston: Harvard Business School, 2020).

37. D. Fisher, *Character Driven: Life, Lessons, and Basketball* (New York: Simon & Schuster, 2009).

38. R. Gulati, "Structure That's Not Stifling," *Harvard Business Review*, May–June 2018, 68–79.

39. See A. M. Grant and S. J. Ashford, "The Dynamics of Proactivity at Work," *Research in Organizational Behavior* 28 (2008): 3–34.

40. For additional insight into the Morning Star Company's vision, see: https://www .morningstarco.com/exploring-morning-stars-mission-focused-self-management-model /#:~:text=Our%20vision%20is%20about%20uplifting,in%20driving%20innovation%20 and%20success.

41. Gino et al., "The Morning Star Company," 4.

42. Chapman and Sisodia, *Everybody Matters*, 177.

43. B. Walsh, S. Jamison, and C. Walsh, *The Score Takes Care of Itself: My Philosophy of Leadership* (New York: Portfolio Trade, 2009).

44. Chapman and Sisodia, *Everybody Matters*, 175.

45. See the story of Lance Johnson's machining group in Chapman and Sisodia, *Everybody Matters*, 194.

46. "ShipIt: When Teams Come Together to Turn Ideas into Reality," Atlassian, accessed February 9, 2022, https://www.atlassian.com/company/shipit.

47. J. Lancaster, *The Work of Management: A Daily Path to Sustainable Improvement* (Cambridge, MA: Lean Enterprise Institute, 2017).

48. G. Hamel and B. Breen, *The Future of Management* (Boston: Harvard Business Press, 2007), chapter 5.

Chapter 8

1. For background on the founding of Google, see "From the Garage to the Googleplex," Google, https://about.google/intl/ALL_us/our-story/. For an in-depth look at Google five to ten years after its founding, see Benjamin Edelman and Thomas R. Eisenman, "Google Inc.," Case 910-036 (Boston: Harvard Business School, revised 2011); Benjamin Edelman and Thomas R. Eisenman, "Google Inc. in 2014," Case 915-004 (Boston: Harvard Business School, revised 2017).

2. For more information on transparency at Google, see Laszlo Bock, *Work Rules! Insight from Inside Google That Will Transform How You Live and Work* (New York: Twelve, 2014), 41–42.

3. Eric Schmidt and J. Rosenberg, *How Google Works* (New York: Grand Central, 2017), 175–178.

4. Schmidt and Rosenberg, *How Google Works*, 175.

5. Bock, *Work Rules!* 151–152.

6. Schmidt and Rosenberg, *How Google Works*, 180.

7. For additional information about this episode, see Schmidt and Rosenberg, *How Google Works*, 27–29.

8. For a powerful example of what happens in a modular system when critical information is not visible, see J. P. MacDuffie, "Modularity-as-Property, Modularization-as-Process, and 'Modularity'-as-Frame: Lessons from Product Architecture Initiatives in the Global Automotive Industry," *Global Strategy Journal* 3, no. 1 (2013), 22–26.

9. This is precisely the work of leadership: to take action that increases the vitality and viability of the organization by making the three objectives complements to one another. Thus, in the short run, leadership action must improve at least one of the leadership objectives, with no impact on the others, or with an impact that is commensurate with the expected value the action will create in those objectives in the longer term.

10. See definitions 1 and 3 at https://www.merriam-webster.com/dictionary/standards?src=search-dict-hed.

11. A. M. Carton, C. Murphy, and J. R. Clark, "A (Blurry) Vision of the Future: How Leader Rhetoric about Ultimate Goals Influences Performance," *Academy of Management Journal* 57, no. 6 (2014): 1544–1570; Chad Murphy and Jonathan R. Clark, "Picture This: How the Language of Leaders Drives Performance," *Organizational Dynamics* 45 (2016): 139–146.

12. For additional background used in the Cemex story, see Thomas A. Stewart, "Cemex's Strategic Mix," *Strategy+Business*, Summer 2015, https://www.strategy-business.com/article/00325; Rosabeth M. Kanter, Pamela Yatsko, and Ryan Raffaelli, "Cemex (A): Building the Global Framework, 1985–2004," Case 308-022 (Boston: Harvard Business School, 2009); Pankaj Ghemawat and James L. Matthew, "Globalization of Cemex," Case 701-017 (Boston: Harvard Business School, 2000); Arthur I. Segal, Michael Chu, and Gustavo Herrero, "Patrimonio Hoy," Case 805-064 (Boston: Harvard Business School, 2006).

13. Data on Cemex is from Cemex, "Shaping the Future Together: Cemex Integrated Report 2022," https://www.cemex.com/documents/d/cemex/integratedreport2022, 4, 84.

14. Cemex, "Shaping the Future Together."

15. This was the pattern internally and with acquisitions. See Stewart, "Cemex's Strategic Mix," 6.

16. See Cemex, "How We Create Value," accessed December 20, 2023, https://www .cemex.com/about-us/how-we-create-value.

17. This vision is highlighted in the section "What We Do" in Cemex, "How We Create Value."

18. See Stewart, "Cemex's Strategic Mix" (see especially the section "A World of Shared Knowledge").

19. For background on the development of the ready-mix information system, see Kanter, Yatsko, and Raffaelli, "Cemex (A)," 10. For information on the Urban Solutions business, see Cemex, "Shaping the Future Together."

20. For background on this project, see Matt Alderton, "3 Examples of Modular and Prefab Hospitals Constructed to Fight COVID-19," Redshift EN, October 20, 2021, https://www.autodesk.com/design-make/articles/modular-hospitals; Cemex, "Shaping the Future Together," 74–75; Cemex, "Our Covid 19 Actions," https://web.archive.org/web /20220928145920/https://www.cemex.com/covid19.

21. Murphy and Clark, "Picture This," 139–146; Carton, Murphy, and Clark, "A (Blurry) Vision of the Future," 1544–1570. This research underscores the importance of expressing information like values and principles in vivid, clear, concrete language, so that people can know and understand that information, feel its importance, and use it well.

22. Toby Cosgrove, *The Cleveland Clinic Way: Lessons in Excellence from One of the World's Leading Health Care Organizations* (New York: McGraw Hill Education, 2014), 113–114, 121–122.

23. Adapted from Cleveland Clinic, "Mission, Vision, and Values," https://my .clevelandclinic.org/about/overview/who-we-are/mission-vision-values.

24. See, for example, this YouTube video produced by the Cleveland Clinic: https:// youtu.be/cDDWvj_q-o8.

25. James Merlino, "How Cleveland Clinic Improved Patient Satisfaction Scores with Data and Analytics," https://web.archive.org/web/20210302142743/https://www .healthcatalyst.com/insights/how-cleveland-clinic-improve-patient-satisfaction-scores-data -analytics.

26. See Murphy and Clark, "Picture This," 139.

27. Schmidt and Rosenberg, *How Google Works*, 98.

28. Bock, *Work Rules!* 151–152; Schmidt and Rosenberg, *How Google Works*, 176.

29. For background and further reading about the practices described in this paragraph see Zavvy, "How Google Onboards New Hires (And How You Can Easily Replicate It)," https://www.zavvy.io/hr-examples/employee-onboarding-at-google.

30. Schmidt and Rosenberg, *How Google Works*, 229.

31. Schmidt and Rosenberg, *How Google Works*, 223.

32. Bala Iyer and Thomas H. Davenport, "Reverse Engineering Google's Innovation Machine," *Harvard Business Review*, April 2008, 58–68.

Chapter 9

1. See "Nucor 2022 Annual Report," https://nucor.gcs-web.com/static-files/8b88e651 -db97-460a-803b-7df2f01b3451.

2. K. Iverson and T. Varian, *Plain Talk: Lessons from a Business Maverick* (New York: John Wiley & Sons, 1997), 3–4.

3. Iverson and Varian, *Plain Talk*, 84–85.

4. Pankaj Ghemawat and Hendricus J. Stander, "Nucor at a Crossroads," Case 793-039 (Boston: Harvard Business School, 1992), 7.

5. Iverson and Varian, *Plain Talk*.

6. From this perspective, power is a concept focused exclusively on relationships in which "A has power over B to the extent that [A] . . . can get B to do something that B would not otherwise do." See R. A. Dahl, "The Concept of Power," *Behavioral Science* 2, no. 3 (1957): 201–215.

7. This is definition 1 in *Merriam Webster*, https://www.merriam-webster.com/dictionary /power?src=search-dict-hed.

8. P. Fleming and A. Spicer, "Power in Management and Organization Science," *Academy of Management Annals* 8, no. 1 (2014): 237–298.

9. Bunderson and Reagans, drawing on the work of McClelland, refer to this flavor of power as "personalized power" and present a comprehensive review showing how this kind of power serves as an obstruction to meaningful learning in organizations. For more, see J. S. Bunderson and R. E. Reagans, "Power, Status, and Learning in Organizations," *Organization Science* 22, no. 5 (2011): 1182–1194; D. McClelland, *Power: The Inner Experience* (New York: Irvington, 1975).

10. S. Chen, A. Y. Lee-Chai, and J. A. Bargh, "Relationship Orientation as a Moderator of the Effects of Social Power," *Journal of Personality and Social Psychology* 80, no. 2 (2001): 173; D. Keltner, D. H. Gruenfeld, and C. Anderson, "Power, Approach, and Inhibition," *Psychological Review* 110, no. 2 (2003): 265.

11. See D. Kipnis, "Does Power Corrupt? *Journal of Personality and Social Psychology* 24 (1972): 33–41; D. Kipnis, *The Powerholders* (Chicago: University of Chicago Press, 1976).

12. D. Kipnis et al., "Metamorphic Effects of Power," *Journal of Applied Psychology* 61, no. 2 (1976): 127–135.

13. A. Lewis and J. Clark, "Dreams within a Dream: Multiple Visions and Organizational Structure," *Journal of Organizational Behavior* 41, no. 1 (2020): 50–76. See also I. M. Nembhard and A. C. Edmondson, "Making It Safe: The Effects of Leader Inclusiveness and Professional Status on Psychological Safety and Improvement Efforts in Health Care Teams," *Journal of Organizational Behavior* 27, no. 7 (2006): 941–966.

14. Keltner argues that these problems are resident inside of powerful people. See D. Keltner, *The Power Paradox: How We Gain and Lose Influence* (New York: Penguin, 2016), 99–102.

15. Others have claimed similar definitions of power, including Mary Parker Follett, in H. C. Metcalf and L. Urwick, *Dynamic Administration: The Collected Papers of Mary Parker Follett* (Abingdon, UK: Routledge, 2004); and Martin Luther King, in Martin Luther King Jr., "Where Do We Go from Here?" Annual Report Delivered at the 11th Convention of the Southern Christian Leadership Conference, August 16, 1967, Atlanta, GA. See also P. Pansardi, "Power To and Power Over: Two Distinct Concepts of Power?" *Journal of Political Power* 5, no. 1 (2012): 73–89; H. Pitkin, *Wittgenstein and Justice* (Berkeley: University of California Press, 1972); P. Morriss, *Power: A Philosophical Analysis* (Manchester, UK: Manchester University Press, 2002).

16. G. A. Klein, *Sources of Power: How People Make Decisions* (Cambridge, MA: MIT Press, 2017).

17. Katherine Chiglinsky, "Hurricane Ida Seen Costing Insurers at Least $15 Billion," Bloomberg, August 31, 2021, https://www.bloomberg.com/news/articles/2021-08-30 /hurricane-ida-seen-costing-insurers-at-least-15-billion.

18. Pansardi uses the label "power within" only to refer to the "soft" resources described here, while the "hard" resources are described using the label "power to." See Pansardi, "Power To and Power Over," 73–89.

19. For more on the classic categorization of power into six bases, see J. R. P. French and B. H. Raven, "The Bases of Social Power," in *Group Dynamics*, ed. D. Cartwright and A. Zander (New York: Harper & Row, 1959), 150–167; B. H. Raven, "Social Influence and Power," in *Current Studies in Social Psychology*, ed. I. D. Steiner and M. Fishbein (New York: Holt, Rinehart, Winston, 1965), 371–382.

20. For an in-depth analysis of ICE energy efficiency, see Felix Leach et al., "The Scope for Improving the Efficiency and Environmental Impact of Internal Combustion Engines," *Transportation Engineering* 1 (2020): https://www.sciencedirect.com/science/article/pii /S2666691X20300063?ref=pdf_download&fr=RR-2&rr=7d9ee928bda51f2.

21. US Department of Energy, "Where the Energy Goes: Electric Cars," June 15, 2021, https://www.fueleconomy.gov/feg/atv-ev.shtml.

22. For data on the Lucid Air, see Eric Adams, "How the 'Dead Zone' Could Help This Car Take on Tesla," *Wired*, https://www.wired.com/story/lucid-air-efficient -powertrain/.

23. J. Battilana and T. Casciaro, *Power, for All: How it Really Works and Why It's Every-one's Business* (New York: Simon & Schuster, 2021).

24. Dacher Keltner, "How to Find Your Power—And Avoid Abusing It," *Greater Good* (Greater Good Science Center, University of California, Berkeley), May 16, 2016, https:// greatergood.berkeley.edu/article/item/how_to_find_your_power_avoid_abusing_it.

25. Gary Hamel, "First, Let's Fire All the Managers," *Harvard Business Review*, December 2011, 48–60.

26. C. M. Christensen, M. Marx, and H. H. Stevenson, "The Tools of Cooperation and Change," *Harvard Business Review*, October 2006, 72–80; H. H. Stevenson, J. L. Cruikshank, and M. C. Moldoveanu, *Do Lunch or Be Lunch: The Power of Predictability in Creating Your Future* (Boston: Harvard Business School Press, 1998).

27. Bunderson and Reagans, "Power, Status, and Learning," 1182–1194.

28. D. Keltner, "Why Leaders Must Give Away Power in Order to Keep Influence," *Fortune*, May 2016, https://fortune.com/2016/05/18/power-paradox-influence/.

29. N. Nohria, W. Joyce, and B. Roberson, "What Really Works," *Harvard Business Review*, July 2003, 42–116.

30. Ghemawat and Stander, "Nucor at a Crossroads," 7.

31. Iverson and Varian, *Plain Talk*, 54–55.

32. Ghemawat and Stander, "Nucor at a Crossroads," 10.

33. Iverson and Varian, *Plain Talk*, 6.

34. Iverson and Varian, *Plain Talk*, 94–95.

35. Iverson and Varian, *Plain Talk*, 67.

36. Iverson and Varian, *Plain Talk*, 3–4.

37. Iverson and Varian, *Plain Talk*, 79–80.

Chapter 10

1. We apply the concept of a touchpoint based on work developed in the context of customer experience and child development. For more, see Karen Lellouche Tordjman and Marco Bertini, "High-Tech Touchpoints Are Changing Customer Experience," hbr.org, March 20, 2023, https://hbr.org/2023/03/high-tech-touchpoints-are-changing-customer

-experience; see T. Berry Brazelton and Joshua Sparrow, *Three to Six* (Boston: Da Capo, 2008) for a framework that treats touchpoints as critical phases in the child's developmental journey.

2. The values are stated here in the language of 2024, with modest adjustment to the original language adopted in 1998. See Harvard Business School, "Community Values," accessed January 17, 2024, https://www.hbs.edu/about/campus-and-culture/Pages /community-values.aspx.

3. Kim B. Clark, email to HBS students, faculty, and staff, May 18, 1998.

4. That research has led to many books and articles and more than five hundred teaching cases since the initiative was launched.

5. See Harvard Business School, "Community Values."

6. For more on incivility in the workplace, see C. Porath, *Mastering Civility: A Manifesto for the Workplace* (New York: Balance, 2016).

7. C. Porath, "The Hidden Toll of Workplace Incivility," *McKinsey Quarterly*, December 14, 2016, https://www.mckinsey.com/capabilities/people-and-organizational -performance/our-insights/the-hidden-toll-of-workplace-incivility.

8. Adam Grant, "In the Company of Givers and Takers," hbr.org, April 2013, https:// hbr.org/2013/04/in-the-company-of-givers-and-takers#:~:text=When%20they%20act%20 like%20givers,their%20own%20expertise%20and%20time.

9. For more on the contagion of empathy and compassion, see E. Seppälä, "Why Compassion in Business Makes Sense," *Greater Good Magazine*, April 15, 2013, https:// greatergood.berkeley.edu/article/item/why_compassion_in_business_makes_sense; J. H. Fowler and N. A. Christakis, "Cooperative Behavior Cascades in Human Social Networks," *Proceedings of the National Academy of Sciences* 107, no. 12 (2010): 5334–5338.

10. P. S. Adler, "Time-and-Motion Regained," *Harvard Business Review*, January– February 1993, 97–108.

11. Adler, "Time-and-Motion Regained," 100.

12. Adler, "Time-and-Motion Regained," 99.

13. S. J. Spear, "Learning to Lead at Toyota," *Harvard Business Review*, May 2004, 78–91.

14. See J. L. Pierce, T. Kostova, and K. T. Dirks, "Toward a Theory of Psychological Ownership in Organizations," *Academy of Management Review* 26, no. 2 (2001): 298–310.

15. Spear, "Learning to Lead," 78–91.

16. P. Doctor and R. Del Carmen, directors, *Inside Out*, Walt Disney Pictures/Pixar Animation Studios.

17. E. Catmull, "How Pixar Fosters Collective Creativity," *Harvard Business Review*, September 2008, 3.

18. Catmull, "How Pixar Fosters," 5.

19. Catmull, "How Pixar Fosters," 9.

20. J. O'Toole and W. Bennis, "A Culture of Candor," *Harvard Business Review*, June 2009, 54–61.

21. See Amy Edmondson, "Psychological Safety Is a Sense of Permission for Candor at Work," *Leadercast Podcast*, https://www.leadercast.com/podcast/amy-c-edmondson-on -building-a-psychologically-safe-workplace/; for additional work on this fusion, see Jeff Dyer et al., "Why Innovation Depends on Intellectual Honesty," *MIT Sloan Management Review*, January 2023.

22. For more details, see "Box Office History for Disney-Pixar Movies," The Numbers, accessed May 2023, https://www.the-numbers.com/movies/production-company/Pixar.

23. Wikipedia, "List of Pixar Awards and Nominations (Feature Films)," accessed May 17, 2023, https://en.wikipedia.org/w/index.php?title=List_of_Pixar_awards_and_nominations_(feature_films)&oldid=1154412084.

24. For additional insight into the power of overcoming fear, see A. C. Edmondson, *The Fearless Organization: Creating Psychological Safety in the Workplace for Learning, Innovation, and Growth* (New York: John Wiley & Sons, 2018).

25. Daisy Dowling, "Lessons from the Slums of Brazil: David Neeleman on the Origins of JetBlue's Culture," *Harvard Business Review*, March 2005, 24.

26. Norman Berg and Norman Fast, "The Lincoln Electric Company," Case 376-028 (Boston: Harvard Business School, 1983), 9.

27. J. Pfeffer, "Seven Practices of Successful Organizations," *California Management Review* 40, no. 2 (1998): 97.

28. M. Solomon, "Heroic Customer Service: When Ritz-Carlton Saved Thomas the Tank Engine," *Forbes*, 2015, https://www.forbes.com/sites/micahsolomon/2015/01/15/the-amazing-true-story-of-the-hotel-that-saved-thomas-the-tank-engine/?sh=5ac92e0e230e.

29. J. A. Michelli, *The New Gold Standard: 5 Leadership Principles for Creating a Legendary Customer Experience Courtesy of the Ritz-Carlton Hotel Company* (New York: McGraw Hill Professional, 2008).

30. For more on teaming, see A. C. Edmondson, *Teaming: How Organizations Learn, Innovate, and Compete in the Knowledge Economy* (New York: John Wiley & Sons, 2012).

31. Michelli, *The New Gold Standard*.

Chapter 11

1. Clay shared this insight with us personally in a variety of contexts—both personal and professional—but it can also be seen in various public sources, including a personal tweet from Clay (Christensen, C. [@claychristensen] "Questions are places in your mind where answers fit. If you haven't asked the question, the answer has nowhere to go." Twitter, August 3, 2012). The text we use here comes from a *Medium* blog post by Jason Fried: J. Fried, "What Are Questions? An Unexpected Answer from Clayton Christensen," *Medium*, August 1, 2016, https://medium.com/signal-v-noise/what-are-questions-51c20fde777d.

2. A. C. Edmondson, *The Fearless Organization: Creating Psychological Safety in the Workplace for Learning, Innovation, and Growth* (New York: John Wiley & Sons, 2018).

Index

Note: Page numbers followed by *f* or *t* indicate figures or tables, respectively.

About the Authors

KIM B. CLARK served as dean of the faculty at Harvard Business School from 1995 to 2005. He also served as the fifteenth president of Brigham Young University–Idaho from 2005 to 2015, Commissioner of Education for the Church of Jesus Christ of Latter-day Saints from 2015 to 2019, and is Distinguished Professor of Management at Brigham Young University.

JONATHAN R. CLARK is a professor of management at The University of Texas at San Antonio, where he has also served as department chair and associate dean. His work focuses on helping leaders create the conditions under which individuals, groups, and organizations do their best collective work.

ERIN E. CLARK is a managing director with Deloitte Consulting, Human Capital, where she works with clients to improve their performance, drive change, and create sustainable advantage through people.